BEHAVIOURAL FOUNDATIONS OF ECONOMICS

By the same author

SOCIAL AND PSYCHOLOGICAL FOUNDATIONS OF ECONOMIC ANALYSIS

Behavioural Foundations of Economics

J. L. Baxter
Senior Lecturer in Economics
Sheffield University Management School

150th YEAR
M
St. Martin's Press

First published in Great Britain 1993 by
THE MACMILLAN PRESS LTD
Houndmills, Basingstoke, Hampshire RG21 2XS
and London
Companies and representatives
throughout the world

A catalogue record for this book is available
from the British Library.

ISBN 0–333–55239–3

Printed in Great Britain by
Antony Rowe Ltd
Chippenham, Wiltshire

First published in the United States of America 1993 by
Scholarly and Reference Division,
ST. MARTIN'S PRESS, INC.,
175 Fifth Avenue,
New York, N.Y. 10010

ISBN 0–312–09148–6

Library of Congress Cataloging-in-Publication Data
Baxter, J. L., 1934–
Behavioural foundations of economics / J. L. Baxter.
p. cm.
Includes index.
ISBN 0–312–09148–6
1. Economics—Psychological aspects. 2. Economics—Sociological aspects. 3. Consumer behavior. I. Title.
HB74.P8B39 1993
330'.01'9—dc20 92–37142
CIP

To Margaret, Sue and Neil

Contents

List of Figures

List of Tables

Preface

The present work is a sequel to an earlier book by the author (Baxter, 1988) on the *Social and Psychological Foundations of Economic Analysis*. The aims remain the same: to develop much broader foundations for economic analysis, in order that economics can have something useful to say about a much wider range of issues, and to make economic analysis much more policy oriented than has been the practice in recent years. Happily, there are signs that an increasing number of the profession is beginning to recognise the sterility of a great deal of current economic analysis, which might aptly be described as 'Paganini variations', to use a musical metaphor. The variations exhibit much technical virtuosity, but they seldom result in significant advances in theoretical or applied research.

While the present work builds on the analysis of the previous book, it attempts to take it a good deal further. A much more comprehensive framework is now adopted, and there is a particular concern with decision-making, both by individuals and socioeconomic groups. No single work, however, can hope to deal adequately with all aspects of decision-making, and the title of the present book quite deliberately omits the definite article, to indicate that it makes no claim to comprehensiveness. The aim rather is to construct a basic, unified structure which can be amended and extended as necessary.

One difficulty for some readers may be that, whereas they see the need to end the present neo-classical dominance of standard economics, they tend to align themselves with a particular stream of critical thought, be it Post-Keynesian, institutionalist or whatever. Whereas difficulties may arise, however, between the latter apparently competing approaches, the differences often seem to be more of emphasis than substance. Furthermore, whenever individuals are involved in the analysis, as they invariably are in economics, there must be psychological and sociological bases for their actions. I prefer, therefore, to view the different approaches which are critical of neo-classical economics as, on the whole, complementary rather than competing. Indeed, it is hoped that the present work will have something to offer all economists, whatever their theoretical persuasion.

Students with a grounding in economics will also, it is hoped, find stimulation in the present study. Too many, it seems, find their present neo-classical diet wanting and often difficult to relate to the world around them. By and large, the profession does a very effective job in brainwashing its students to the conventional way of thinking, but economics courses are now taught in a great variety of institutions, such as management schools, and in conjunction with a great many other subjects, which makes it increasingly difficult for economics to retain its dominantly isolationist stance. This means, too, that the present book should appeal not only to economists and students of economics, but to a wide range of others who see the relevance of economics to their own areas of study and practice.

It remains, finally, to thank all those who have contributed in any way to the present study. Special mention should be made of Trevor Noble and Gerard Hodginkson, with whom I had a number of helpful discussions when still trying to decide upon a suitable framework for analysis. Yet again, I must also acknowledge the continued benefit I have derived from the advice and support of Jim Ford, a former colleague who has continued to take an interest in my work. As is usual on such occasions, however, the author must make it clear that he alone is responsible for what appears in print, and that those named may not be in total agreement with the contents of the book.

The typing of a book remains a major undertaking, even in these days of the word processor. In this task I have received unstinting help from Jane Roe, and I should also mention the contributions of Sue and Neil.

J.L. BAXTER

Acknowledgements

The author and publishers wish to thank the following for permission to use copyright material:

University of Chicago Press and H.L. Davis and B.P. Rigaux-Bricmont for Figure 4.1.

The Dryden Press for Figure 7.1.

The Organisation for Economic Cooperation and Development for Table 11.1.

Part I
The Basic Building Blocks

Part I
The Basic Building Blocks

1 Introduction

The present study builds on an earlier work (Baxter, 1988), which examined how psychological and sociological concepts contributed to a better understanding of economic behaviour, in particular in the fields of consumer behaviour and labour market behaviour. An interesting feature of the earlier analysis was the manner in which the common behavioural foundations helped to cement links between these disparate fields of study. In economics, the common links are provided by the basic assumption of 'rational' behaviour, as exemplified by utility maximisation and profit maximisation. It is increasingly being recognised, however, that these basic axioms have to be supplemented if economics is to extend its analysis into new fields. But the question arises that if we are continually having to supplement the basic axioms, would it not be preferable to take the matter to its logical conclusion and adopt much broader behavioural foundations? Such an alternative approach becomes increasingly attractive if it can be demonstrated that these broader foundations both encourage the development of meaningful hypotheses for empirical testing, and leave ample scope for the rigorous mathematical analysis which is now such a feature of economics.

A major difficulty with the broader approach – and indeed also with the conventional approach to economics – is in establishing how the basic micro foundations may be extended to the macro level. Economics at present generally only manages the transition by introducing simplementary hypotheses, to the effect that economic agents have uniform characteristics and can therefore conveniently be aggregated. The present study attempts to devise a more comprehensive analytical framework which enables the behavioural analysis to be extended beyond that in Baxter (1988). I shall, in essence, be posing a number of questions which I think economists ought to be asking themselves:

1. what are the key personal characteristics which help determine economic behaviour, and do these require a broader approach than that currently adopted in economics?
2. which features of the general environment surrounding the activities of individuals and organisations does economics currently neglect, to the detriment of its analysis?
3. how do 1 and 2 above impinge on individual decision-making, and do they even alter the nature of individual decision-making?

1 Introduction

The present study builds on an earlier work (Baxter, 1988) which examined how psychological and sociological concepts contributed to a better understanding of economic behaviour, in particular in the fields of consumer behaviour and labour market behaviour. An interesting feature of the earlier analysis was the manner in which the common behavioural foundations helped to cement links between the different fields of study. In economics, the common links are provided by the basic assumption of 'rational' behaviour, as exemplified by utility maximisation and profit maximisation. It is increasingly being recognised, however, that these basic axioms have to be supplemented if economics is to extend its analysis into new fields. But the question arises that, if we are continually having to supplement the basic axioms, would it not be preferable to take the matter to its logical conclusion and adopt much broader behavioural foundations? Such an alternative approach becomes increasingly attractive if it can be demonstrated that these broader foundations would still permit the development of meaningful hypotheses for empirical testing, and even offer scope for the rigorous mathematical analysis which is now such a feature of economics.

A major difficulty with the behavioural approach – as indeed it is with the conventional approach to economics – is in establishing how the basic micro foundations may be extended to the macro level. Economics at present generally only manages the transition by introducing supplementary hypotheses to the effect that economic agents have uniform characteristics, and can therefore conveniently be aggregated. The present study attempts to devise a more comprehensive analytical framework which enables the behavioural analysis to be extended beyond that in Baxter, 1988. I shall, in essence, be posing a number of questions which I think economists ought to be asking themselves:

1. what are the key personal characteristics which help determine economic behaviour, and do these require a broader approach than that currently adopted in economics?
2. which features of the general environment surrounding the activities of individuals and organisations does economics currently neglect, to the detriment of its analysis?
3. how do 1. and 2. above impinge on individual decision-making, and do they even alter the nature of much decision-making?

4. how far does individual decision-making provide a reliable guide to the nature of decision-making at a more aggregated level, such as the family, the firm, the trade union or government?
5. how might the various components of a more broadly based behavioural model fit together and interact with each other, and with the income and price variables on which conventional economic analysis places such strong emphasis?

At this stage, I offer only a brief indication of the answers I give to these and other questions. First, however, it is worth saying a word about the issue of rationality, since, in the opinion of many, it is this issue which lies at the heart of the debate about how the standard economic approach might usefully be modified and extended. My comments on rationality will only be brief, since the topic has been pursued at great length elsewhere – for a good discussion see Hogarth and Reder (1987), with some of the most cogent comments in the text being made by Arrow. The latter severely knocks on the head any idea that economic theory is only economic theory if it is based on the customary rationality hypothesis. He gives an example:

> In the case of consumer demand, the budget constraint must be satisfied, but many theories can easily be devised that are quite different from utility maximisation. For example, habit formation can be made into a theory; for a given price-income change, choose the bundle that satisfies the budget constraint and that requires the least change (in some suitably defined sense) from the previous consumption bundle . . . this theory is not only a logically complete explanation of behaviour but one that is more powerful than standard theory and at least as capable of being tested.

He goes on to extend the gist of his comments even further:

> Not only is it possible to devise complete models of the economy on hypotheses other than rationality, but in fact virtually every practical theory of macroeconomics is partly so based.

Arrow's claim is no less than that much economic analysis rests not on the rationality hypothesis alone, but also crucially on essential *supplementary* hypotheses:

> Rationality hypotheses are partial and frequently, if not always, supplemented by assumptions of a different character . . . Its [rationality's]

useful and powerful implications derive from the conjunction of individual rationality and the other basic concepts of neoclassical theory – equilibrium, competition and completeness of markets.

The introduction of supplementary hypotheses may be laudable in itself, since it greatly extends the range and relevance of economics, but if the development of economics is to rest solely on the ad hoc introduction of supplementary hypotheses, then the subject itself must surely increasingly degenerate into little more than a collection of 'ad hoceries'. It would be much better, it seems, to seek broader and surer foundations at the outset. This does not mean, it must be stressed, that neo-classical economics should be entirely abandoned. There is a great deal of value in it which ought to be retained, if only as a yardstick against which alternative behaviour can be assessed. Neo-classical economics would become, in effect, very largely a special case at one extreme of a spectrum of possible behaviour.

The foundations we need for a more broadly based economics can be found, I believe, in the other social sciences. At some point the social sciences must merge with each other – indeed we do not have to go back very far in history to find common origins and sources of inspiration. It is time, it seems, for economics to return closer to the mainstream. Much has happened there in recent years from which economics might draw. Noted below are some of the topics which I feel economists could with benefit study, and which feature prominently in the present book.

I begin with human motivation, since it is motivation which both activates the individual and gives him, or her, direction. The standard economic view of motivation says no more than that consumers aim to maximise their utility, within a budget constraint. This tells us nothing, however, about which factors determine utility, or how they might be expected to change over time. Most economists, it seems, are quite happy to allot a central role in their theories to a concept which they neither understand nor wish to understand – surely a very vulnerable intellectual stance to adopt. The basis of individual motivation in our study is personal needs, not only physical but psychological. Many of these needs, as we shall see, clearly vary over the life cycle, so that, despite the avowal by economists to the contrary, individuals have marked time preferences in their consumption of many goods and services. I will argue, also, that individuals are strongly motivated by considerations of equity, a topic with which a number of economists have grappled, but which most are again content to put to one side, since it raises many awkward questions.

The present study also attempts to place the individual fairly and squarely in his environment, not just the economic environment but also the physical, and especially the social, environments. Economists really cannot hope to sustain indefinitely the fiction that we can best analyse the behaviour of consumers (and for that matter firms) in what amounts to a social vacuum. We are all influenced in our behaviour by what goes on around us: the families we grow up in, the people with whom we mix, and so forth. The transformation of our needs into particular wants, or preferences, is very much the product of this complex of influences. The poet John Donne long ago summed up the situation in a nutshell in an oft-quoted sentiment:

> No man is an Island, entire of it self; yet every man is a piece of the continent, a part of the main. (1987 edn)

It is a matter of some wonder, too, that the representative consumer of standard economic theory has neither age, sex nor marital status, and therefore represents no known individual living on our planet – an asexual person is hardly an adequate representation of the male and female sexes, certainly not when it comes to the consumption of many types of product.

Yet another source of wonderment to commentators who have attempted a dispassionate view of economics is the way in which a number of what we call socioeconomic organisations, such as firms and trade unions, are assumed to make decisions. It is not the organisations as such which make the decisions, of course, but rather individuals belonging to such organisations, who make decisions on the organisations' behalf. Furthermore, these individuals do not somehow discard all their personal characteristics when engaged in socioeconomic decision-making. They retain their personal goals, which may conflict as between individuals, as well as with 'organisational goals', where such might be said to exist independently of the goals of members. I maintain that an analysis of decision-making units within socioeconomic organisations is a very useful aid in explaining the behaviour of these organisations.

Decision-making by individuals, both on their own behalf and on behalf of others, is central to the present study. Two contrasting features tend to emerge repeatedly. On the one hand, although the assumption in economics is generally that decision-making is complex by nature, in reality a good deal of it is of a simple, repetitive, habitual kind which can be undertaken with little or no thought or consideration. When making purchases, for example, individuals are often able to draw on their past experience, as they do when buying particular types, or brands, of goods. For such purchases, the best guide to individuals' future purchases is often their purchases in the recent past.

On the other hand, at the opposite extreme, an important element of decision-making is by nature very complex – just how important an element is a subject deserving of study. In standard economic theory, the assumption is usually that such complex decision-making can be reduced to probabilities. In reality, however, decisions are frequently too complex for individuals to cope with in the manner presumed. Frequently, too, full information is simply not available, and a true state of uncertainty therefore exists in which there is little or no guide to the future. In such circumstances – and there is a great deal of evidence to bear this out – individuals are obliged to resort to a variety of simplifying decision-making rules, or heuristics. Fortunately, this is not true of all complex decision-making, as actuarial and other work amply demonstrate, but trying to reduce all complex decision-making to probabilities is merely to assume away very real problems not conducive to such treatment.

So far I have highlighted what I believe to be a number of major deficiencies in the standard neo-classical economic models, and have suggested desirable elements of a more broadly based economics. This still leaves the problem of how to combine the various parts into a coherent whole. One of the principal strengths of economics is that, although based on narrow foundations, it has developed into an extensive, unified theoretical structure which enables the consequences of changes in the relevant variables to be traced and analysed. There is no comparable achievement in any of the other social sciences. In psychology, for example, there is a variety of schools of thought which, although they may in large measure be complementary rather than competing, are not bound together by any overarching theory. On the other hand, psychology has been the focus of a great deal of successful experimental work, mostly at the level of the individual, but also increasingly in the study of group and organisational behaviour. The same is true of areas of sociology. Ideally, what is needed is some means of linking together these different areas of study – and also those of other fields in the social sciences.

As a growing number of social scientists are coming to appreciate, economics may be able to provide just the sort of unifying structure which is needed – in certain areas of study, at least – although not in the shape of the neo-classical model which at present has such a stranglehold on the economics profession. The basic building block must be the individual. Not, however, the constrained optimising individual of neo-classical economics, but rather the individual 'in the round' who is to be found more adequately represented in psychology, and in those other fields, such as consumer behaviour (as taught on management courses) which base themselves on psychology.

Economics is not, however, just the study of individual behaviour: it also embraces socioeconomic organisations, and, perhaps most important of all, provides in addition a link with developments in society as a whole. It therefore touches on society at all levels of aggregation, even if not in what we would regard as a satisfactory manner. The need is for a more acceptable unifying structure which draws on the strengths of economics, psychology, sociology and the other social sciences. The present study aims to do just that, even if, in the space available, it must perforce be somewhat selective. It does, however, retain the cornerstones of the structure required: the individual, socioeconomic organisations, the environment and aggregate behaviour.

Although almost any model designed for general use in the social sciences must be a simplification of reality, even at the level of the individual, since all individuals are different, some psychologists and others may feel that we have gone too far in that direction. In particular, those concerned with *process*, for example in decision-making, may feel that too many steps have been omitted. A problem, however, is that, whereas some stages in the decision-making process may be reasonably well documented and understood, this certainly does not seem to be true of all stages. It might well be the case, nevertheless, that more stages in decision-making could be introduced into the sort of model proposed.

The author is also well aware that the institutional aspects of the model could be much more fully developed. Indeed, it must be stressed as a general comment that the author is not implying that anything omitted is of little interest or usefulness. This is certainly not the case. A major difficulty with the task attempted is that it touches on such a diverse range of subject areas that no individual – and certainly not the writer – is likely to be proficient in them all. It is very much to be hoped, therefore, that those with more specialised knowledge will be able to build on what is presented here.

The present study, it should also be stressed, is a sequel to Baxter (1988) and the reader will therefore come across numerous references to this source in the text. If the reader finds the present study of interest, he, or she, will also be likely to find its predecessor useful. I noted in the introduction to the earlier study that the methodological standpoint adopted differed sharply from Friedman's (1953) 'mature positivist view of economic science' (Caldwell, 1982), or 'instrumentalism' as many writers on methodology have described it. This stance applies with equal force to the present book. Prediction is, of course, important, but it cannot be the sole purpose of the social sciences, as Friedman maintained it was. Improved understanding is also a perfectly legitimate goal of the study of economics, and indeed it is difficult to believe that prediction and understanding can be divorced. The latter surely reinforces the former. In any case, the record of predictions in economics is not such that we can afford to rest on our laurels. The tendency is for association between variables to be reasonably close during certain periods, but to break down on occasions, sometimes dramatically. Or, the associations may not yield sufficient accuracy of prediction in the first place. Only improved understanding is then likely to yield the answers sought – after all, only a measure of understanding in the first instance is likely to have suggested reasons why certain variables might be associated.

The structure of the present book follows the lines indicated above. Part I is concerned principally with setting out the overall analytical structure. It also examines the personal characteristics of the individual which are deemed to be most relevant to our study. Part II examines at some length the environmental factors bearing on individuals, and on socioeconomic organisations, with special emphasis on the social environment. Part III brings together personal characteristics and social influences to show how together they affect individual decision-making. Part IV, again building on what has gone before, turns to decision-making in the key socioeconomic organisations: the family, trade unions, the firm and government. Finally, at the aggregate level of the total economy I shall examine the implications of my analysis for the sorts of behavioural equations we would expect to find in a macroeconomic model. The additional variables introduced are generally in the nature of 'intervening variables' (see Baxter, 1988), and as such would figure as supplementary explanatory variables in macro-economic models.

Our study can therefore be expected to make novel and important contributions at all levels of economic analysis, although it is probably at the individual and group levels that these contributions will be most noticeable. Inevitably, as aggregation increases, effects which might be important at the micro level will tend to be suppressed or simply ironed out. Nevertheless, sufficient remains to make the study of interest to economists concerned principally with macroeconomic analysis. After all, as economists have become increasingly aware, macroeconomics cannot be divorced from its microeconomic foundations.

2 The Basic Model in Outline

The starting point of my analysis, and central to all that follows, is individual behaviour. I am concerned to try and determine, so far as possible given our present state of knowledge, what factors determine the actions of individuals, and how they arrive at their decisions. Unlike standard economics, however, I do not envisage individuals as living very largely in a vacuum, with their actions determined by forces somehow detached from the very strong social influences which surround their daily lives. Moreover, individuals not only take decisions on their own, they also participate in institutions, where their actions and decisions are generally taken in consort with other individuals. Together, decisions taken by individuals on their own behalf, and those taken in conjunction with others, or on behalf of others, make up aggregate behaviour. All these decisions are taken within an environment which is part given, to the extent that we cannot influence it, and part itself a consequence of the actions of men and women. The broad structure described is set out in Figure 2.1. I will go on now to say a bit more about the five main components of the model, and how they interlink. Each will be discussed at much greater length in the chapters which follow.

Each individual has personal characteristics: no two people are the same. Even in identical circumstances (economic and/or non-economic) therefore, each individual may behave differently. Our interest, however, is principally in those personal characteristics which are sufficiently common, and sufficiently dominant, that they strongly influence the behaviour, not only of one or two persons but of many persons, acting individually or in groups of individuals. The available evidence suggests that personal motivation is a key characteristic. We all need to eat and drink, for example, and we require shelter, and we are therefore motivated to try and satisfy these needs. We also have many other needs and wants which influence our behaviour. Motivation, as shown in Baxter (1988) is partly determined by our biological and psychological characteristics, and partly by environmental influences, such as our cultural background.

In addition to motivation, we might also in our study have allowed a role for an individual's personality in determining his or her behaviour. Once again, personality is something with which we enter this world, but it may also alter with the passage of time, in response to personal influences (or, in our terminology, 'environmental' influences). Whereas personality differ-

Figure 2.1 The basic model

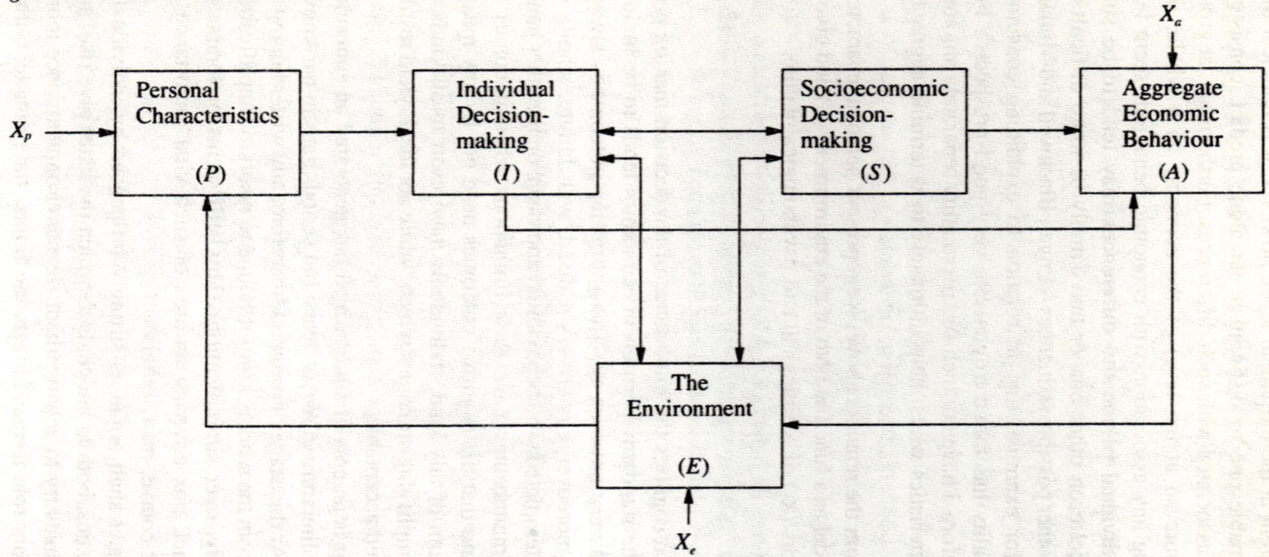

$$P = P(E, X_p) \quad (1)$$

$$I = I(P, E, S) \quad (2)$$

$$S = S(I, E) \quad (3)$$

$$E = E(I, S, A, X_e) \quad (4)$$

$$A = I + S + X_a \quad (5)$$

ences may be apparent at the individual level, however, it is not clear that such differences enable one to distinguish, let alone predict, consistent behaviour patterns associated with such differences. Furthermore, at group level, and even more so at the level of the economy as a whole, the prospects of finding any association with economic behaviour seem less plausible, since individual personality differences may tend to be submerged, or to cancel each other out, or may simply be more difficult to identify among the other possible influences – Engel, Blackwell and Miniard (1990) conclude, for example, that in relation to explaining consumer behaviour, 'personality has failed to generate very good prospects'. For these reasons, therefore, I have not included personality separately amongst the personal characteristics which help ultimately to determine aggregate behaviour.

Following on from the remarks above, we represent personal characteristics (P) in our model as a function both of the environment (E) and given, or exogenous, factors (X_p) of a biological and psychological nature.

$$P = P(E, X_p) \tag{2.1}$$

Our model also recognises the importance of the decision-making process. Here again, the standard approach in economics tends to be limited in its horizons, and very prescriptive. The optimising outcome is always the one selected – moreover it is always realised, with failure, wholly or partially, never contemplated. The behavioural approach, on the other hand, recognises that human beings have their limitations when it comes to decision-making, and that the resulting outcomes need not by any means represent an optimum of any kind. Individuals may resort to all kinds of short-cuts and/or simplifying strategies which, while not ideal, yield results which are considered acceptable.

Decision-making is an area of study which has generated an enormous volume of research literature in recent years, but serious gaps in our knowledge still remain. At this stage of progress, therefore, any writer hoping to draw conclusions from the work is himself bound to resort to simplification (or, more accurately, over simplification). This still seems preferable to leaving a large black box covering an area of such vital importance to economists, and, of course, many others.

Decision-making, I shall argue, is strongly influenced by individuals' personal characteristics, both in the goals to which the latter give rise, and in the ways individuals try to achieve them. The environment, once more, also has an important role to play. It sets the limits, for example, within which decisions have to be taken, be they financial limits, time limits, or whatever. The environment, as we portray it, also includes those powerful social influences to which individuals have always been subject, more so today probably than ever before, given the role which the communications media now play in most people's lives.

Some of the social influences, such as those of the family, may also come to bear more directly on individuals. Most individuals now find that some of their goals are best achieved – perhaps can only be achieved – through participation in what I have called 'socioeconomic decision-making centres', i.e., institutions such as a family, a firm or a trade union. Most people now also look to governments to meet some of their needs, such as security from aggressors. Participation in such decision-making centres usually gives the individual some influence over their activities (in democratic societies at least) but in turn these institutions also exert a profound influence on the lives of individuals. In our model, therefore, individual decision-making (I) is shown as a function of three principal sources of influence: personal characteristics (P), the environment (E) and socioeconomic decision-making centres (S).

$$I = I(P, E, S) \tag{2.2}$$

Our goal in economics is to explain not only individual behaviour, but also aggregate behaviour, whether within groups or institutions, or at the level of the economy as a whole. Our concern, therefore, is not only with individual decision-making, insofar as the sum of these individual behaviours affects aggregate behaviour, but also with the decisions of all those decision-making institutions whose behaviour helps determine aggregate outcomes. The decisions of governments tend to be treated as exogenous in economic models, but a behavioural approach treats government as part of society, both responding to the wishes of members of the society (certainly in democratic countries) and through its actions influencing in turn the behaviour of those over whom it exercises sovereignty.

The family, too, is not simply a group of individuals acting wholly independently. The members form a unit, with its own system of decision-making, and the activities and behaviour of the individuals are inevitably affected by the other members of the family group.

Trade unions constitute another centre of decision-making which we cannot ignore. While the direct expenditure over which they exercise control may not be great, they have an important bearing on the labour market, through their influence on wage claims and settlements, and on the supply of labour.

The activities of firms are dealt with at length in the standard economic models, but a surprising feature of these models is the way in which the entities called 'firms' appear to make and implement decisions all on their own. In practice, as advocates of behavioural theories of the firm have pointed out, it is individuals acting within these firms who actually make and carry out the decisions. When this fact is explicitly recognised, attempts to explain the behaviour of firms assume a very different complexion. The human element must be accorded a central role, and it is our model of individual decision-making that we must resort to in order to obtain some guidance on what factors motivate and otherwise influence human behaviour.

To the decision-making centres listed so far may be added a wide range of groups, such as voluntary organisations, sports and leisure clubs, etc., which are responsible for decisions about how funds are expended (such expenditure is usually classified as part of consumers' expenditure in national accounts). These funds may be derived directly from members, or perhaps via government disbursements, but the main point is that the expenditure is not undertaken by any one individual on his own behalf, but rather by one or more individuals acting on behalf of others. As such, the decisions of the institution may well lead to aggregate outcomes somewhat different from those which would have resulted had the spending decisions been taken only by each individual acting on his, or her, behalf alone.

Socioeconomic decision-making centres function solely as the instruments of their members and, where relevant, staffs. They have no corporate human identity. Furthermore, it seems most unlikely that those individuals acting within decision-making units adopt persona which are wholly independent of, and different from, those which they assume when acting alone, on their own behalf. We should expect to find, therefore, that the factors which influence individual decision-making, such as personal characteristics, also reveal themselves in the decisions taken by individuals within institutions. The goals of firms, for example, are likely to be strongly influenced by the personal goals of managers.

Just as the general environment constrains and bears on the actions of the individual decision-maker, so too will it help determine institutional decision-making. As in the case of individuals, firms, and even governments, are subject to resource constraints and the mores of society. Within our model, therefore, we see socioeconomic decision-making as a function of individual decision-making and environmental factors.

$$S = S(I, E) \tag{2.3}$$

It will be clear by now that we have allotted environmental factors an important causal role in our model, but the direction of causation is by no means all one way. The environment, as we are becoming increasingly aware, is also at the mercy of the activities of individuals and institutions run by individuals. Aggregate behaviour, too, insofar as it affects the principal economic variables, will help constitute the economic constraints, such as those of income, within which all decision-making takes place. It was noted earlier, too, that the environment will include all the social influences which are so important in determining, for example, consumer choice. Class, race, religion and lifestyle are examples of social influences whose bearing on consumer behaviour has been extensively researched. In Baxter (1988) we also saw the importance of reference groups to consumer choice. The introduction of behavioural foundations to economic models also enables modern mass communications to exert their influence, acting often through the medium of reference groups. In the standard economic models such influences are simply introduced ad hoc or they are treated as part of the ubiquitous 'changes in tastes', with the implication that they are of little more than residual importance. The extent of spending on advertising strongly suggests that this can hardly be the case.

Drawing together the various strands of our discussion, we show the environment in our model simply as a function of aggregate behaviour (A) and an autonomous variable (X_e) representing those aspects of the environment which we may take as given, such as natural resources.

$$E = E\,(I, S, A, X_e) \qquad (2.4)$$

I come, finally, to aggregate behaviour. Our model is not an *alternative* economic model. On the contrary, I maintain that the variables discussed ought to be an integral part of all economic models in which individual behaviour is of consequence – and that must include most of economics. I shall show as I progress that the behavioural foundations outlined are relevant to the outcomes in all the major markets of the economy: goods markets, labour markets and the money markets. Personal characteristics, for example, acting through needs and wants, help determine consumers' expenditure. Our model, too provides a better understanding of the activities of firms, and endogenises government actions, rather than assuming that they emerge in some mysterious fashion wholly unconnected with the decisions of those who run the affairs of government. Decisions on labour force participation, wage claims and settlements, savings and personal investment, and much more, are also closely linked with the key variables in our analytical structure.

The behavioural variables highlighted are in the nature of 'intervening variables' (see Katona, 1951), i.e, they are variables which influence the response by individuals to any change in economic circumstances. They intervene, in other words, between changes in an independent economic variable and a consequent change in an associated dependant variable. Behavioural variables have, of course, been introduced in numerous economic studies, as in empirical work on the consumption function, but on an ad hoc basis, and with little or no attempt at theoretical justification. My approach implies that the introduction of behavioural variables ought to be standard practice in economics – accompanied, of course, by adequate theoretical support.

We complete the outline of our basic model by representing aggregate activity in the economy overall, and, within that, in individual markets as the sum of personal decisions (some of which will act directly on economic aggregates) and decisions by socioeconomic institutions (in which individual actions will also play a part).

$$A = I + S + X_a \tag{2.5}$$

All the principal relationships I have identified will be spelled out at much greater length in succeeding chapters. Even at this stage, however, it will be apparent that we are dealing with a very complex, dynamic structure. As usual, a balance will have to be struck between relating the structure to as many potential areas of study as possible and not making it so complex that we become enmeshed in a morass of detail. Not all variables of possible relevance will be included. I shall concentrate on those aspects which appear to have most to offer at the present time, in the hope that as research progresses more complete models might be constructed.

3 Personal Characteristics

We begin our discussion of the principal parts of our behavioural model with an examination of the personal characteristics of the individual, the basic unit of our analysis. These personal characteristics play a central role in determining individual behaviour in a wide variety of settings, including many which are of interest to economists. I shall be concentrating principally on motivation, a large and diverse subject area in psychology, and one within which divergences of view still persist. Many of the differences in viewpoint may be more apparent than real, however, awaiting only the emergence of a unifying structure which will help resolve most of the differences. Psychology, like the other social sciences, is still at a relatively early stage of development, and it seems to be the case that progress in some areas awaits prior advances in allied subjects.

MOTIVATION

In Baxter (1988) I examined a variety of theories of motivation, and decided to pursue four principal aspects of motivation at greater length, since they seemed to hold out hope of providing a better explanation of economic behaviour. These four aspects of motivation were: needs, and their associated wants; equity; goals; and the expectancy-valence or value approach to motivation. There is no need to go over the same ground again, but it is essential to draw together here the conclusions which emerged from the earlier study, since we shall be making use of them.

In reviewing the various theories of motivation I noted how frequently such theories, although expressed in different forms, rested ultimately on the view that personal needs, and the desire to satisfy these needs, were among the prime motivating forces underlying human actions. Personal goals, for example, were generally set with the purpose of satisfying needs and their associated wants. The valence component of expectancy-valence models also rested on the value placed on possible outcomes in relation to their efficacy in satisfying needs. Even the desire for equitable treatment might be represented as evolving from deep-seated needs. In the present study I therefore treat needs, and needs satisfaction, as being among the principal influences which 'energise' individuals and give their actions direction. They also help explain why individuals continue pursuing particular activities, and why they ultimately cease such activities.

Locke and Henne (1986) in a survey article suggest a useful way of integrating and assessing the enormous literature on motivation which helps clarify some of the links noted above. They identify four major concepts in their general model of motivation: needs, values, goals and emotions (with cognition playing a part in all four concepts). Need is regarded as the fundamental motivational concept, but needs theories, they maintain, are unable by themselves to explain human actions. 'They may explain why a person has to act (if he wants to live) and why he often wants to act, but they do not account for the particular action chosen.' Locke and Henne go on to say, however, that 'specifically, need theories do not account for individual differences. By definition, everyone has the same needs . . .'. The latter assertion seems unwarranted, even at the level of basic physiological needs. The need for nutrition, (as we shall see later) varies according to age and sex. To take another example of a rather different sort, some individuals seem to have a strong need to belong to social groups, others are happier for the most part on their own. Locke and Henne appear to be correct, nevertheless, in maintaining that needs alone are only part of the answer to the question of what motivates individuals. Additional explanatory concepts are needed. Cognition, they say, is one (people have different beliefs about what will satisfy their needs) but another part of the answer they assert is that people differ in their values.

Values, according to Locke and Henne:

> are what the individual considers good or beneficial. Values can range in content from basic moral values (right and wrong) to personal preferences in ice cream flavour. While needs are inborn, values are acquired through experience.

The analysis of needs in Baxter (1988) suggested that while needs are indeed inborn, they are also subject to environmental influences, and may change over time. Even such basic needs as those for nutrition have almost certainly changed over the years as lifestyles, and over the longer term climate, have altered. The 'values' of Locke and Henne in fact appear to cover much of what I will treat, in a rather more general fashion, as part of the environment.

Locke and Henne also claim that most work motivation theories are in essence value theories.

> They focus on the influence of one or several particular values, such as achievement or equity (justice) on action or on the effects of values in

general (expectancy theory). Such theories are a step closer to action than need theories but again are incomplete. A given value can be expressed in many different ways in many different situations. To know what a particular person will do in a particular task situation one needs to know how his values are translated into specific goals.

Notions of equity are certainly not something we are born with, although we may be pre-disposed toward one way of thinking about such matters rather than another. Our social environment, however, must again be a powerful influence, acting through the physical and psychological experiences to which we are subjected, with, as argued in Baxter (1988), social comparisons playing an important role. I will have more to say on equity later in the present chapter.

The inclusion of expectancy-value theory under the general value heading makes sense in terms of the framework adopted by Locke and Henne, although I shall be looking at such theories principally as part of the decision-making process. Once again, however, it is certainly the case that expectancy-valence (or value) theories are inadequate on their own as theories of motivation. We must know what gives any course of action a particular value if we are fully to understand, and perhaps also be able to predict, outcomes. That necessarily brings us back ultimately to needs, and their associated wants.

To Locke and Henne, 'Goals are a means of actualising values. They are the mechanism by which values are translated into action'. Goals should therefore 'predict and explain behaviour (at the immediate level) better than needs or values, even though a full explanation of action would involve all these'. This view of goals deriving from needs corresponds with the conclusions reached in Baxter (1988).

Finally we come to emotions, which Locke and Henne regard as both the result of action and an inducement to further action. The actions result in satisfaction or dissatisfaction which feed back into an assessment of the extent to which values have been attained, with the possibility of a reappraisal of goals and further action. This action-appraisal sequence we shall again fit into our own model at the decision-making stage.

A closer look at needs

The above discussion of motivation suggests that before going on to look at the individual's decision-making process we must first examine the factors determining an individual's goals. There appear to be two principal factors at work: first, personal needs; second, environmental factors. The latter act both directly and indirectly (through their bearing on needs) on the formulation of goals. We begin with a closer look at needs, leaving the discussion of environmental factors to Chapter 4. We shall also in the present chapter have something to say about notions of equity, which in certain circumstances, such as wage bargaining, may act as a powerful motivating force.

Needs are difficult to define, and indeed definitions vary. Lederer (1980) distinguished two main schools of thought, one which regarded needs in an objective light, the other treating them as subjective in nature. The two approaches Lederer noted, however, were not necessarily exclusive, and the difference might ultimately prove to be only terminological.

In analysing needs, a number of writers have attempted to classify them, foremost amongst these writers being Maslow (1970). Maslow's work appears of doubtful validity to some commentators, but this has not stopped it being widely cited, probably because it appears to accord with many people's intuition and experiences. One appealing feature is the heavy emphasis placed by Maslow on 'higher order' needs. At the lower level, man's first preoccupation must be with the means of survival: the physiological needs for food and drink (Maslow's first category of needs) and those for safety – security, stability, protection, law and order, etc. (the second category). With Maslow's other three main categories, however, we move on to a higher plane: the needs for belongingness and love; the need for esteem; and, finally, the need for 'self-actualisation', a sort of self-fulfilment. These latter aspects of Maslow's classification hold out the prospect of a fuller, more rewarding lifestyle for men and women as their standard of living improves. Individuals are expected to grow over time, not just in a physical sense (although that might be a part of the total picture) but rather in terms of their outlook, and what they are able to contribute to, and get out of, life. The implied change in emphasis in the pattern of personal expenditure over time has important implications for economists and those who cater for the requirements of consumers.

In addition to the emphasis on personal 'growth', Maslow's work on needs contained a number of other important features. Maslow regarded his theory as holistic rather than atomistic, and dynamic rather than static, combining the two into what he called the holistic-dynamic point of view. The holistic approach leads to a stress on the environment and its influence in the motivation of behaviour. In commenting on Maslow's work, Arkes and Garske (1982) note that 'the interpersonal sphere of the environment is crucial: other people are central in providing satisfaction for needs such as positive regard, love, and esteem, and even for elements of enhancement and actualisation'. Interpersonal relations tend also to be very dynamic, constantly changing as individuals spark responses from each other. This interpersonal feature of the needs-based approach to motivation, and, associated with it, the role of social comparisons, was given prominence in Baxter (1988). As was seen in Chapter 2 of the present study, the importance of these links will be maintained in the analytical structure of the present work.

Needs, it was argued in Baxter (1988) lead to associated wants, and if an economist were to attempt to classify consumers' expenditure he would probably produce a classification which could be fitted reasonably comfortably into that of Maslow. Indeed, Marshall (1961), one of the few economists to attempt the categorisation of wants, produced a classification very similar to that of Maslow (see Haines, 1982) while approaching the task from the point of view of an economist rather than a psychologist.

Another writer much of whose work falls largely under the heading of needs is D.C. McClelland. His early work concentrated on what he considered to be the important need for achievement – the relevant references are given in McClelland (1987). Drawing on a wide range of studies, McClelland (1961) noted that the need for achievement (which he abbreviated to *n achievement*, or *n Ach*) could be said to underlie many of the main characteristics associated with entrepreneurship, including: a willingness to undertake activities with a moderate degree of risk attached to them; energetic, innovative behaviour; a willingness to accept individual responsibility; a readiness to engage in long-range planning and the anticipation of possible future outcomes; the development of organisational skills.

The fact that many of those with high *n Ach* behaved in many of the ways likely to result in successful entrepreneurship led McClelland in turn to suggest that *n Ach* must therefore play a vital role not only in business organisations but in helping explain variations in rates of economic growth between countries. At this stage of his work, the question of whether *n Power* was a further ingredient essential to managerial success was left unsettled, but in his later work power as a motivating force in business assumed much greater importance, along with the need for affiliation.

The need for power was not one of the motivating forces identified by Maslow, but most would probably agree there is at least a prima facie case for considering it. A good deal of research has focused on how people with a strong power motive behave under a variety of circumstances. In particular, researchers have attempted to determine whether such people tend to be more aggressive. A number of problems have complicated the findings. Those assessed as having a high *n Power* were frequently found to be able to curb their aggressive instincts – Winter (1973) found social class played a part in such behaviour. Women with high *n Power* also behaved less aggressively than men, suggesting once again that the power motive does not come into play indiscriminately, but rather is modified or curtailed by other influences which come to bear on individuals. It appears, nevertheless, that McClelland (1987) is correct in concluding that 'What is not in question is the general conclusion that people high in *n Power* strive to be assertive'.

McClelland's need for affiliation, or interaction with other people, appears similar to Maslow's need to belong, although McClelland places greater stress on the role of this need in managerial contexts. After examining the evidence, McClelland (1987) concludes that those high in *n Affiliation* learn social relationships more quickly, engage in more dialogue with others, and also show more evidence of maintaining their connections with other people. The evidence also suggested that men with high *n Affiliation* tended not to succeed so well as others in management, perhaps because they were too prone to avoid conflict and criticism. Small manufacturing firms, or research and development firms headed by men high in *n Affiliation*, also tended to be less successful. On the other hand, there was also evidence that such men were effective in integrating the efforts of management and labour, so that they worked better together.

We now turn to look at another writer on needs, whose work derives directly from that of Maslow, yet differs from it in a number of important respects. Alderfer (1972) uses three categories of human needs, which he calls 'existence', 'relatedness' and 'growth' (described as ERG for short). The existence needs 'include all the various forms of material and physiological desires' (Alderfer, 1972) and therefore comprise Maslow's comparable physiological category, but might also be said to include elements of Maslow's 'safety' needs, to the extent that these cover any physical requirements for safety, such as accommodation. Since Alderfer was especially concerned with human needs in an organisational setting, his definition of existence needs also covers such things as pay, fringe benefits and physical working conditions.

Alderfer's second category, relatedness needs, includes personal relationships with others who are important to the individual ('significant others') such as family, friends (and enemies), co-workers, supervisors and subordinates. A characteristic of relatedness needs is that 'their satisfaction depends on a process of sharing or mutuality'. Once again Alderfer's category straddles those of Maslow, incorporating elements of Maslow's safety, love and belongingness, and also, it would seem, esteem and self-actualisation needs.

Finally, Alderfer's growth need has many similarities with Maslow's self-actualisation need. According to Alderfer (1972):

> Growth needs impel a person to make creative or productive effects on himself and the environment. Satisfaction of growth needs comes from a person engaging problems which call upon him to utilise his capacities fully and may include requiring him to develop additional capacities. A person experiences a greater sense of wholeness and fullness as a human being by satisfying growth needs. Thus, satisfaction of growth needs depends on a person finding the opportunities to be what he is most fully and to become what he can.

Alderfer's ERG theory differs from Maslow's needs theory in that, while it assumes that all three broad categories of needs are active in all persons, the strengths of each will vary from one person to another, and there is not necessarily any fixed hierarchy among them. More than one may operate at any given time, and satisfaction of one need will not necessarily result in a progression to the next higher need.

The individual life cycle of needs

The nature of personal needs indicates that many of these will alter as an individual progresses through his, or her, lifetime. There is, in other words, an individual life cycle of needs. This life cycle may also be discussed within a family context, where the ramifications are even more extensive, and rather than duplicate some of the discussion, I will therefore leave detailed analysis of the life cycle to Chapter 4. For the present, it is sufficient to provide one or two examples of how needs will vary over the individual life cycle.

The clearest example is provided by food needs. Table 3.1 gives official UK recommendations for the average daily intake of nutrients – similar recommendations have been made by the National Research Council Food and Nutrition Board in the United States. The data show quite clearly that for both males and females there is an inverted U-shaped life cycle of food needs. The data, it should be stressed, are averages, and will vary somewhat according to height and weight, the amount of physical activity, and according to differences in physical environment, such as climate, but the life cycle pattern is indisputable.

Physical changes in the individual also mean that clothing needs will alter over the life cycle. Health needs, too, will vary. They tend to be especially high in the early years, when children are subject to many illnesses to which adults have developed some immunity. In later years, health care tends once more to be in greater demand.

The nature of leisure pursuits is also likely to vary over the life cycle.

Table 3.1 Recommended family amounts of nutrients

Age range	Energy MJ[1]	Energy Kcal[2]	Protein g[3]	Calcium mg[4]	Iron mg	Vitamin A μg[5]
Males						
Under 1	3.25	780	19	600	6	450
1	5.00	1200	30	600	7	300
2	5.75	1400	35	600	7	300
3–4	6.50	1560	39	600	8	300
5–6	7.25	1740	43	600	10	300
7–8	8.25	1980	49	600	10	400
9–11	9.50	2280	56	700	12	575
12–14	11.00	2640	66	700	12	725
15–17	12.00	2990	72	600	12	750
18–34[6]	12.00	2900	72	500	10	750
35–64[6]	11.50	2750	69	500	10	750
65–74	10.00	2400	60	500	10	750
75 and over	9.00	2150	54	500	10	750
Females						
Under 1	3.00	720	18	600	6	450
1	4.50	1100	27	600	7	300
2	5.50	1300	32	600	7	300
3–4	6.25	1500	37	600	8	300
5–6	7.00	1680	42	600	10	300
7–8	8.00	1900	48	600	10	400
9–11	8.50	2050	51	700	12	575
12–14	9.00	2150	53	700	12	725
15–17	9.00	2150	53	600	12	750
18–54[7]	9.00	2150	54	500	12	750
55–74	8.00	1900	47	500	10	750
75 and over	7.00	1680	42	500	10	750

Notes:

1. megajoule (= 1,000 kJ)
2. kilocalories (= 4.184 kJ)
3. grams
4. milligrams
5. micrograms (1,000 = 1 mg)
6. moderately active males
7. most occupations

Source: Ministry of Agriculture, Fisheries and Food (1986) *Manual of Nutrition*, London: Her Majesty's Stationery Office (HMSO).

As people grow older, the nature of their pursuits tends to become less active, with reading and walking, for example, perhaps higher in the scale of preferences than in earlier years. These and all other life cycle-associated changes in personal demands will be accompanied by changes in personal consumption behaviour – changes, moreover, which will occur quite independently of any accompanying changes in personal income or in the prices of goods. Clearly, therefore, the individual life cycle is much too important to be ignored in the economic analysis of consumer behaviour.

Considerations of equity

Until now we have given most attention to needs as a motivating force. In some circumstances, however, there may be other motivating forces at work. One of the strongest of these is notions of equity, which, like needs, may determine individual (and group) goals. Considerations of equity frequently arise when individuals interact with each other, especially during exchange transactions, as between employer and employee. Once again I will restrict myself to the basic essentials, since a fuller discussion can be found in Baxter (1988).

The most fully developed theory of equity in exchange is that of Adams (1963, 1965) who presented it in terms of the relationship between employer and employee, while making clear that it was of more general application, covering groups as well as the individual. A person engaged in a social exchange makes a contribution to the exchange – an 'input' in Adams's terms – for which he expects to receive something in return – an 'outcome'. Adams's input includes not only effort but also the contributions of intelligence, experience, education and skill. On the outcome side, while pay is one of the most important rewards, the outcome also comprises job satisfaction, fringe benefits, status, etc. The importance of perceptions is stressed by Adams. Not all inputs and outcomes lend themselves to measurement, and even where they do, differences of opinion, based on different perceptions, may still persist.

Expressed in Adams's terms, equity exists when,

$$\Sigma O_{ip}/\Sigma I_{ip} = \Sigma O_{ia}/\Sigma I_{ia}$$

where O_i and I_i are the weighted sums of outcomes and inputs, and p and a are subscripts denoting Person (the person for whom equity and inequity exists) and Other (any individual with whom Person is in an exchange relationship or with whom Person compares himself when both he and Other are in an exchange relationship with a third party, such as an employer, or with third parties who are considered by Person to be comparable, such as employers in a particular industry or geographic location).

The social comparison process is inherent in Adams's theory, and in other similar theories of equity. The normative expectations of what constitutes fairness have been formed in the process of socialisation at home, school or work, or any other social environment which Person has experienced. These social influences are strongest when they emanate from a reference person (or group) with whom Person is in the habit of comparing himself.

Adams's theory of equity has been subjected to criticism, but generally of a positive kind. It remains a most useful way of looking at the difficult question of equity, and is expressed in a form with which economists can identify (indeed it seems to have taken some of its inspiration from economics). It is, however, worth drawing attention to one crucial point which appears to have been overlooked in the literature on equity theory. I stress it, since it helps explain the problem of inflation, which will be discussed at a later stage.

Although sometimes classified under the general heading of 'distributive justice', equity theory does not tackle the problem of how the total resources of a community ought to be distributed. It could well be the case, therefore, that if we summed the outcomes judged to be equitable, we would find that they exceeded the total resources of the community. It may be that this point has been disguised by the fact that there are both monetary and non-monetary outcomes.

Among the outcomes, pay is likely to constitute much the largest financial cost, but fringe benefits, and even status and job satisfaction, may also have financial costs attached to them, even if employees regard them as principally non-pecuniary elements in the outcomes.

If therefore equity in exchange is to avoid the problem of inflation we have to add the condition that the sum of the cost of all outcomes must not exceed the total resources available at any given time. We would then have a form of distributive justice in the work situation. Whether it would be possible *in practice* to devise such a distribution of resources which is both *perceived* to be equitable by all and at the same time within the limits of the financial resources available is a question to which as yet we have no answer. We can see here, however, the possible seeds of disequilibrium in the economic system.

In Baxter (1988) I also introduced the concept of relative deprivation in our discussion of equity. The notion of relative deprivation has similarities with the theory of equity in exchange, but as I showed, the two approaches are by no means identical. Relative deprivation is concerned only with under-reward. Furthermore, relative deprivation takes into account the *feasibility* of attaining a desired outcome. As well as recognising, therefore, the possibility of fixed resources, as noted above, it may also be forward looking, incorporating the important element of expectations. As currently presented, the latter more dynamic feature is lacking in the theory of equity in exchange. When we come later to apply notions of equity to decision-making processes, we shall therefore also find a use for the concept of relative deprivation.

CONCLUSIONS

In reaching my conclusions I also draw on Baxter (1988). My principal conclusion is that, at the present time, the concept of needs, despite its weaknesses, represents the best foundation for a theory of motivation relevant to economics. Indeed, many of the other theories of motivation, such as that of goals, or the expectancy-valence (or value) approach, are ultimately based on needs. If we think of motivation as a process, the ultimate motivating force within the individual appears to be some concept of needs. It may be that one day progress in the biological sciences will cause us to revise our view of needs, but for the present the concept seems to fit our requirements better than any alternative theory available.

One of the strongest arguments in favour of the needs-based approach, it seems to the writer, is that individuals clearly do have physiological needs which must be met if they are to survive. These needs are even greater if the individual is not merely to survive but to exist as a healthy, robust person. The question then is, does the mind exist independently of the body and bodily needs? The answer must be no. There is plenty of medical evidence available to demonstrate that bodily deprivation ultimately affects the mind adversely. Might the mind otherwise be free of needs, however, or does it too have needs of its own if both mind and body are to remain healthy? There are strong grounds for thinking that the concept of needs is again appropriate. Experience has shown, for example, that individuals who undergo long periods in solitary confinement, totally deprived of interpersonal relations, do suffer mental deterioration. The idea that there is a need for love and belongingness, or relatedness, does not therefore seem at all far-fetched. When we progress into the realms of self-actualisation, or growth, needs, we are, however, admittedly on less firm ground. There is nevertheless a strong *prima facie* case, evident in the great interest shown by many individuals in the arts and other creative activities, and in leisure pursuits generally, for believing that there are also 'higher order' needs which have to be met in order to lead a healthy, rounded existence. It is no coincidence, therefore, that the needs-based approach to motivation has retained such a strong attraction, despite its apparent weaknesses. Quite simply, the theory accords closely with the personal experiences and intuitions of many people.

The empirical evidence available on needs provides little support for the idea of a detailed hierarchy of needs – especially any idea of a rigid hierarchy – as propounded by Maslow. At best, we are able to distinguish at present only between broad categories of needs, such as 'lower order' and 'higher order', or between the three broad types of need identified by Alderfer in his ERG theory, which bear a close resemblance to Maslow's more detailed categories. Furthermore, preferences and priorities in the meeting of needs clearly vary between individuals, and there is plenty of evidence available from studies of consumer behaviour to suggest that preferences and priorities do change over time (a matter I return to later). Once the more 'basic' needs, such as those for food, drink and shelter, have been met, people tend to turn their attention to satisfying 'higher order' needs.

There is also a great deal of evidence to indicate that needs are determined in part by environmental factors – the effects of the physical environment are among the most obvious – and these too may cause needs to alter over time. I shall be examining these environmental influences at greater length in the next chapter. Environmental influences may be even more crucial, however, in determining wants, as well as needs. The importance of the distinction between needs and wants was stressed in Baxter (1988), and its importance will, it is hoped, become even more evident in the present work. The two are by no means synonymous. In later chapters I will be looking at the ways in which needs are transformed into wants.

A needs-based approach to motivation also points to the conclusion that it is not very meaningful to talk about a 'representative consumer', since there are crucial distinctions which must be made between consumers. To begin with, differences in sex account for differences in needs which are too great to ignore. Empirical studies have established that nutritional needs differ according to sex. As one might expect, they also differ according to age. It must follow, too, that needs will differ according to the *number* of individuals, an obvious conclusion, it might seem, but one which it does no harm to stress when we are dealing, for example, with families and larger collectives. A needs-based approach also highlights the importance of the life cycle in determining the changing pattern of an individual's needs; and it points to the *family* life cycle as an appropriate vehicle for analysing both the pattern of family needs and changes in this pattern over time. This latter aspect will be treated at greater length when we come to examine the social environment.

In equation (2.1) we expressed personal characteristics as a function of exogenous (biological and psychological) factors (X_p) and the environment (E). My discussion of motivation and the role of needs suggests we can now be more specific. The variable X_p maps into a vector of individual needs $d_1, \ldots, d_n$, which we denote by D, i.e., $X_p \rightarrow D$. These needs are themselves subject to the influence of environmental factors which will be examined at length in the next chapter. Since needs are in turn a function of the sex of the individual and his/her age, we can be still more specific.

$$D_i = D(a_i, s_i) \tag{3.1}$$

where D_i represents the needs of individual i, and a_i and s_i are the age and sex, respectively, of individual i. The precise mathematical form of the relationships will be determined by empirical research, but it was noted earlier how many needs varied according to the individual life cycle, following an inverted U pattern, and will therefore be non-linear in nature.

It is worth noting at this point that the micro foundations of standard neoclassical economics contain no place for the individual or family life cycles, even although there is growing recognition of their potential importance. At the macro level, their crucial role in the consumption function has long been recognised, and in recent years there has been an interest in the part played by the life cycle in labour supply decisions. Still further recent evidence has been provided by Fair and Dominguez (1991), who have found that the changing age distribution in the United States has significant explanatory power in consumption, housing investment, money demand and labour force participation equations, although they do introduce a number of caveats indicating that more work with age data is required. What is needed first, however, is adequate theoretical justification for introducing the life cycle in the first place. I would maintain that this is only likely to emerge from a more broadly based behavioural approach to economics.

Although not generally listed among classifications of needs, a desire for equitable treatment is also, I maintain, one of the strongest motivating forces, and there is a good deal of empirical evidence to this effect. Notions of equity are likely to be especially important in the work situation, particularly in matters of pay, and I shall return to this aspect in later sections of the present study.

Finally, I draw attention to an important feature common both to notions of equity and to my earlier discussion of needs: individuals have a habit of comparing themselves with others (including *groups* of others, as we shall see later). The need for esteem, for example, will frequently require reference to others as a basis for that esteem. The process of self-actualisation will also often require social interaction and social comparisons. In making judgements about equity, comparisons are made with the inputs and outcomes of others. In sum, social comparisons are crucial to any analysis of how individuals behave. When we come to examine the social environment in Chapter 4, we shall see, furthermore, that social influence is often exerted via a social comparison process.

Part II
The Environment

INTRODUCTION

Individuals, informal groups and institutions exist within a general environment which both exerts powerful influences upon them, and is in turn greatly influenced by them. Within this general environment we may distinguish an economic environment, comprising those conventional economic variables, structures and institutions which have been of primary interest to economists, such as financial flows of income and expenditure, and market structures within which goods are bought and sold. In effect, it would include all those variables one would expect to find in a conventional model of an economy. Our general environment also includes a physical environment, such as the availability of land and other natural resources, the state of technology and the important element of time – all variables which economists have tried to take account of, in some degree at least, in their economic models.

There is, however, one additional dimension of the general environment to which economists have conventionally paid scant attention, namely, the social environment. Traditionally, this has been regarded by most economists as the preserve of psychologists, sociologists and other social scientists, and of only passing interest, since it did not appear to have any measurable or predictable influence upon the principal economic variables. It is my intention to demonstrate, however, that the social environment exerts much too powerful an influence upon economic affairs for its neglect to be allowed to continue. Indeed, as improved communications and growing economic interdependence bring the peoples and nations of the world closer together, the social dimension of the environment is becoming ever more important. Allied to a growing recognition of the true nature of the physical constraints confronting the world, economists face an environmental challenge with which they must grapple more successfully if they are to continue to have anything of real import to say.

I will now examine the nature of the social environment and its many influences at greater length. I shall then go on to discuss in turn the physical and economic dimensions of the general environment, attempting all the while to draw out the interrelationships between the different dimensions of the environment, and between the environment and the other principal sectors of our model.

4 The Social Environment

The social environment exerts its influence at different levels of social aggregation. At the simplest level we have the lone individual, who may influence the way another individual, or even a group of individuals, behaves in the process of taking decisions about such matters as how (and indeed whether) to spend his, or her, money. Similarly, a group of people may influence the decision-making of a lone individual, or decision-making by other groups. At a more aggregated level still, there is evidence, as we shall see, that social stratification exerts an influence on the consumer behaviour of individual members of the different social classes. Finally, at the most aggregated level of all, that of cultures, and within them subcultures, there may again be powerful influences at work, although the somewhat amorphous nature of the concept of culture makes it difficult to identify meaningful proxy variables which would enable tests to be made of the precise impact of the cultural factor. There are nevertheless specific aspects of culture which seem to lend themselves to empirical testing.

While I will be arguing that each of these levels of the social environment plays some part in determining the behaviour of both individual and socioeconomic decision-making units, it is also appropriate to ask about the precise *means* by which these influences are transmitted. In Baxter (1988) I examined the role played by the social comparison process in influencing personal and group behaviour, and in particular the part played by reference groups. The term 'reference group' embraces not only small groups of people but also larger and looser collectives, such as social classes. It is therefore relevant at each of the levels of aggregation we identified above. I shall start my analysis of the environment by looking at the social comparison process, especially the use of reference groups, since these provide an important vehicle by which interpersonal influences are transmitted. I shall also be looking, however, for other important ways in which personal influences are transmitted, especially where there is supporting empirical evidence.

SOCIAL COMPARISONS AND REFERENCE GROUPS

Work on reference groups grew out of studies of the social comparison process carried out in the early years of the present century. Both streams of work therefore exhibit many similarities, and ought, it seems, to be discussed together. Festinger's 1954 study marks an important stage in the more recent work on social comparisons. He attempted to set out a rigorous and more fully developed theory of self-evaluation, resting on the enunciation of a number of hypotheses which could be subjected to empirical testing. The attention of most commentators has centred on Festinger's tenets regarding the choice of others for the purposes of comparison. His hypothesis III states: 'The tendency to compare oneself with some other specific person decreases as the difference between his opinion or ability and one's own increases'. Corollary IIIA further maintains that 'Given a range of possible persons for comparison, someone close to one's own ability or opinion will be chosen for comparison'.

The desire to assess one's own abilities and opinions was therefore, in Festinger's view, among the principal reasons why individuals engaged in interpersonal comparisons. With regard to abilities, Festinger opined that there would be little point in a person making discrepant comparisons, since this would be a poorer guide to the potential for action on his part than comparisons with others whose abilities more closely resembled his own. This somewhat restricted view of the alternative courses of action was later criticised by, among others, Latané (1966) who suggested that a novice chess player might, for example, wish to compare his abilities with those of the Grand Masters of the game, in order to understand better just what could be achieved, and how far short he fell of the best.

A further study by Gordon (1966) concerning opinions also found that those who were uncertain of the correctness of their opinions, and wished a basis for comparison, tended to compare themselves with those holding similar opinions. The old adage that 'birds of a feather flock together' appears therefore to have its counterpart where matters of personal opinion are concerned.

Festinger was able to cite empirical evidence in support of his hypothesis, although not all the evidence was unambiguous. His work on self-evaluation has been continued, however, by other researchers, and a useful review of this work can be found in Suls and Miller (1977). From the point of view of this study, the work is valuable in providing evidence of the importance to individual behaviour of the social comparison process. I will now turn to look at the related work on reference groups, where further evidence will be found of the vital importance of social comparisons.

The term 'reference group' was coined by Hyman (1942) in a study of status. Later writers have refined and developed the idea, and a definition now widely used is that given by Sherif (1953), who described reference groups as: 'Those groups to which the individual related himself as a part or to which he aspires to relate himself psychologically'.

I am concerned here simply to outline some of the main features of reference groups and their workings. A fuller statement can be found in Baxter (1988). I noted earlier in the present section that reference groups may occur at different levels of aggregation. Pollis (1968) has suggested that we ought to distinguish three such levels: first, the psychological level, where we are primarily concerned with the motivation, personality, perceptions, etc. of the individual; second, the sociological level, where we are dealing with two or more individuals, and we are interested in group, institutional and collective influences; finally, the social psychological level, where we are concerned concurrently with individual and social behaviour of all sorts. It will be apparent, therefore, that although reference groups are frequently discussed in the context of group behaviour, their applicability is much broader, and is relevant, in effect, at all levels of social aggregation. This point will emerge clearly as our analysis in the present section progresses.

Reference groups are often divided into *comparative* and *normative* groups. The former entails comparisons with others, generally groups with which the principal actors come into contact, such as friends, relatives and those at work. The comparisons are frequently made for the purposes of self-evaluation, and also for the evaluation of others.

Normative reference groups, as the term suggests, are groups from which a person takes his standards. A number of studies have shown, for example (see Newcomb, 1943) that a member of a group will frequently tend to identify with the norms of that group, even if at the outset his norms were different, or if he held no relevant norms.

It is now accepted that some overlap may occur between comparative and normative reference groups, but the distinction nevertheless seems useful and worth retaining. A third type of reference group is sometimes distinguished in the literature, namely, an 'informational reference' source (see, for example, Ofshe, 1972). Such a reference group may well be relevant in decision-making when the search process comes into play.

The classification of reference groups outlined above provides useful guidance on the criteria likely to determine the selection of reference groups. The self-evaluation function indicates that reference groups will only be selected if they are *relevant* (Turner, 1955). There would be no point in an individual or group selecting a reference group which was so dissimilar that no useful conclusions could be drawn from comparisons. Associated with the requirement of relevance is that of *similarity*. Festinger

(1954), while not employing the concept of reference groups, concluded from a review of the evidence that when comparing their abilities and opinions with those of others, individuals tended to select others whose abilities and opinions were reasonably close to their own. Hyman (1942) in his celebrated study also concluded:

> The rare occurrence of the total population as a reference group and the great frequency of more intimate reference groups are characteristic of the process of judging status.

In the selection of normative reference groups, *relevance* will also be an important consideration. A further factor frequently mentioned is *saliency*, which has a bearing not just on the selection of reference groups, but the relative importance attached to each. Stafford and Cocanougher (1977) state that:

> The available empirical work on salience indicates an individual may make decisions or resolve conflict in the direction of the references that are most prominent or salient for him at a particular point in time. This suggests that situational factors, such as psychological proximity or time sequence, may be of substantial importance in explaining the differential effects on an individual's behaviour.

Stafford and Cocanougher go on to quote a number of examples of saliency arising from research work.

My principal interest in the subject of reference groups in the present study lies in the extent to which such groups *influence* individual and group behaviour, and in the manner in which this influence is exerted. The discussion above indicates that some reference groups will exert much more influence than others, with those meeting the criteria of relevance, similarity and saliency likely to have the greatest impact. A number of writers, however, have distinguished other means by which groups and individuals may make their influence felt. These means of bringing influence to bear do not apply only to reference groups, but they are certainly relevant to them.

The exercise of *power* is one of the other means by which influence may be exerted. Power is a subject about which a great deal has been written, yet much uncertainty and disagreement remains over its precise nature. I shall touch on this subject again in later sections, but for the present I will confine my attention to one study, by French and Raven (1968), which identified five bases of power which seem important, and which have featured in numerous studies. First, *reward power*, which, as the term suggests, is based on the ability of a social agent (*O*) – who may be a person or a group – to reward a person (*P*). *Coercive power* is similar to reward power, but there is now a threat of punishment rather than reward as the means of exerting influence. *Legitimate power* is defined as the power which *O* is able to exercise because *P* has values which dictate that *O* has a legitimate right to exercise his influence. Moreover, *P* feels obliged to be guided by the power exerted. *Referent power* is probably the most obviously applicable of the five to reference groups. It arises when *P* identifies with *O*, is attracted to *O* and wishes to be closely associated with *O*. Finally, *expert power* is based on *P*'s perception of *O*'s expertise – expertise which he values – either in relation to *P*'s own knowledge or to some absolute standard of measurement.

A further source of group influence which we shall encounter again in later sections – and one which seems closely linked to the idea of reference groups – is *leadership*, either by a single person, or by a person or persons representing a group. The group leader is usually the member who is best able to initiate and maintain the expectations of, and interaction within, the group. Once again there is a good deal of empirical evidence to substantiate the view that leadership has an important influence on personal behaviour.

We move on now to examine the different levels of social aggregation from which the influences on personal and group behaviour emanate. I will start with the influence of one individual upon another, because it is interpersonal relationships of this nature we first encounter as very young persons, and because such relationships remain among the strongest social influences upon us throughout our lives. Starting with individual relationships we might also hope to be able to construct common building blocks which we can utilise when we go on to look at more complex interpersonal relationships, such as those within social groups like the family or work group. At all times I shall be trying to keep in mind my primary objective, which is to explain the influences on personal behaviour which are of economic significance. Seen in this light, we are really looking for ways in which one individual may stimulate another to act in a particular way, perhaps by consuming one product or brand rather than another, or perhaps by consuming rather than saving.

INDIVIDUAL INFLUENCE

Observation informs us that individuals are social beings. Very few choose to lead a life of total isolation from their fellows. Why should this be so? The answer must be that we all feel a *need* for social relationships. We choose to interact with others during much of our daily lives, otherwise we would see more signs of attempts to shut ourselves off from society. Other evidence of the need for social contact, as was noted earlier, is the deleterious physical and mental effects which most humans experience if kept in total isolation from their fellows for long periods.

In order for one person, or a group, to influence an individual, they must somehow communicate with that individual. The communication may be oral or it may be by visual means, perhaps in writing or by a form of sign language. Studies of the nature of social influence generally concentrate on three types of influence, which mirror those we examined when discussing reference groups, namely, normative, comparative and 'informational' social influences. In persuading potential customers to buy their products, those engaged in marketing attempt to harness all three forms of influence, using the media as an aid. Over the years, a number of models of communication- and influence-flow have been developed to help improve our understanding of the process. The earliest model envisaged a one-step (and one-way) process of communication from the marketer to consumers, with the media interposed as the *vehicle* of communication. Such a simple model, however, did not adequately reflect the different means of communication in use, and Lazarsfeld *et al.* (1948) suggested a somewhat more sophisticated model which allowed for the fact that the media frequently exerted their influence, not directly on purchasers, but indirectly, via an opinion leader (or leaders). Once again, however, the flow of influence was envisaged as occurring in one direction only, whereas research showed that purchasers also *initiated* the search for information – Arndt (1968), for example, found that up to 50 per cent of all word-of-mouth communication was initiated by consumers seeking information from opinion leaders. Later multi-step models therefore allow for a more dynamic pattern of communication, envisaging a two-way flow of information and influence between an opinion leader and other consumers, and between individual consumers themselves.

The above models of communication and personal influence lay great stress on two linked features: word-of-mouth communication and opinion leadership. The importance of word-of-mouth communication is now well documented. In an early study of purchases of consumer durable goods, Katona and Mueller (1955) found word-of-mouth to be one of the most important sources of information and influence, with more than 50 per cent of those sampled consulting with friends prior to purchase. An extensive review of the literature by Dichter (1983) concluded that as much as 80 per cent of all purchases could be attributed to word-of-mouth influence.

Why should word-of-mouth be so important, and potentially more effective in many instances, it seems, than expensive advertising campaigns? In another review of the literature, Arndt (1967) concluded that there were three principle reasons: first, consumers found word-of-mouth to be more reliable and trustworthy than the alternatives – in effect a means of reducing the risk entailed in purchasing; second, they valued the social support and approval provided by their personal contacts when making a purchase; third, having made recommendations, there was social pressure from those giving the advice to see that it was followed. All three reasons demonstrate the importance of personal contacts, in contrast to the impersonal nature of much mass advertising, even if it attempts to transmit a very personal message.

We have viewed word-of-mouth communication in a positive light until now, but there may also be a strong negative side to it. News of defects in a product can be transmitted very rapidly by word-of-mouth, as many enterprises have found to their cost. When the Coca Cola Company (1981) investigated the role of word-of-mouth communication among customers who had registered complaints, it found clear evidence of association between the two. The negative consequences were especially great if the customers were dissatisfied with the company's response to their complaints.

The second major link in the communication models we looked at above – and one related closely to word-of-mouth influence – was opinion leadership, since interpersonal communication requires both a transmitter (generally the opinion leader) and a receiver (usually the follower). Leadership appears to be exercised principally in relation to specific products, or quite closely related groups of products, such as small and large household appliances (see, for example, Myers and Robertson, 1972). There is little empirical support for the idea of a 'know-all' opinion leader with expertise covering a wide range of products.

On the question of the characteristics associated with opinion leaders, they are, as one might expect, similar in many respects to those of the persons on whom they exercise most influence. They are usually from the same social class, and are frequently friends, neighbours or work associates (Summers, 1971, Price and Feick, 1984). Physical and social proximity, in other words, are important. In purely personal terms, it is not surprising that many opinion leaders tend to be gregarious, self-confident and of much the same age as those they influence. While certain key characteristics of opinion leaders have been identified, however, no 'identikit' figure emerges from the literature on the subject.

Other research work has also established that the purchase of certain kinds of products is more susceptible to personal influence (see, for example, Robertson, 1971). Products which are very conspicuous to the public eye, such as clothing, or which may be tried or tested against objective criteria, or which are complex, or entail a high degree of risk (of failing, or not working as intended) are all more subject to the effects of personal influence on the purchaser. The risk aspect is likely to be especially important in the case of new products, and there is now a good deal of evidence that personal influence plays a key role in facilitating new product innovation and the spread, or diffusion, of new products throughout the population. An extensive discussion of this feature of consumer behaviour can be found in Loudon and Bitta (1984).

The above discussion is sufficient to demonstrate that interpersonal influence dovetails closely with the operation of reference groups, as outlined earlier. Word-of-mouth communication and opinion leadership, both well documented, and closely interlinked, provide good examples of the informatory and normative characteristics of reference group behaviour. There can be little doubt that these factors improve our understanding of the reasons underlying consumer purchases. They ought therefore to feature in any attempt at a reasonably comprehensive explanation of the factors determining consumer behaviour, especially at the micro level. At the macro level, the consequences of such factors as word-of-mouth communication and opinion leadership may well be more difficult to demonstrate. At this level of aggregation, the more general concept of reference groups seems likely to be of greater importance. It was suggested in Baxter (1973), for example, that a broadening of reference groups, possibly associated with the growing influence of the media, might have been a factor giving rise to the more severe wage pressures of the late 1960s and early 1970s in the United Kingdom.

We go on now to discuss the *family*, which, although a group, we discuss separately from other groups, since it has important characteristics in its own right, and, particularly in the early years of life, has a very powerful influence on individual behaviour.

THE FAMILY

We must first establish precisely what we mean by 'family', and how it relates to the broader term 'household'. Definitions vary somewhat, but one of the most commonly adopted is that employed by the US Bureau of the

Census in compiling its statistics. The Bureau defines a household as all the persons who occupy a 'housing unit', which may be a house, an apartment, a group of rooms or a single room constituting separate living quarters.[1] In the United Kingdom, the corresponding official definition is: a single person or a group of people who have the address as their only or main residence and who either share one meal a day or share the living accommodation.[2] The nuances are slightly different, but the essential idea is the same.

The family is described by the Bureau as a group of two or more persons related by birth, marriage or adoption who are living together in a household.[1] The UK definition is narrower, placing the emphasis principally on the institution of marriage: a family is a married couple, alone or with their never-married child or children (of any age), or a lone parent together with his or her never-married child or children.[2]

A further distinction is often made between a *nuclear family* and a *single parent family*. The former consists of two adults of the opposite sex living together, generally in a socially approved relationship, and usually with one or two children (either their own or adopted). The single parent family may either be headed by a married parent whose spouse does not reside in the same household, or by a single, widowed or divorced parent.

Although declining in relative importance (for reasons outlined below) families are still much the most important form of household, accounting for around two-thirds of the total number of households in the US, and almost three-quarters in the United Kingdom. In the remainder of this section I shall therefore be concentrating my attention on the family unit, principally because it is the behaviour of families which is most important in determining consumer spending, but also because up until now relatively little attention has been paid by researchers to the purchasing behaviour of other types of household, and information about them is therefore limited.

Bearing in mind that my ultimate objective is to demonstrate how the social influences exerted by the family have an important bearing on the real economy, I will now go on to examine certain features of the family which are especially important in this regard. I will look first at the family life cycle, which establishes many of the parameters helping to explain family behaviour. I will then go on to examine the changing structure and nature of the family unit itself, and how this has affected, and continues to affect, both consumers' expenditure (and the distribution among its different components) and the associated spending by businessmen. I will then go on to look at the ways in which influences relevant to economic behaviour are brought to bear within the family, and how the family exerts influence beyond its own bounds.

The family life cycle

In discussing the personal characteristics of individuals I stressed the importance of the life cycle of needs, and their associated wants. In a family context, where two or more individuals are brought together, the individual life cycle still functions, but the needs and wants of the group are no longer simply the sum of individual needs, as they would be if individuals lived independently of their family. Moreover, the needs and wants of each family will differ according to the age and sex composition of the family, as I demonstrate in a later section. We have here once again a social institution whose economic consequences are not adequately caught by the traditional economic emphasis on the effects of income and price changes.

I draw here on the more extended discussion of the family life cycle in Baxter (1988). There we saw that, while there is general agreement that the family life cycle begins with the marriage of a couple, and that certain events, such as the birth of the first child and retirement, mark important stages in the cycle, there is much less agreement when attempts are made to break down the cycle into more detailed stages.

Opinions on the appropriate number of stages in which to sub-divide the family life cycle have changed with time. Murphy and Staples (1979) give a useful summary of the development of these ideas. I will concentrate principally on a study by Reynolds and Wells (1977) which contains a wealth of data, and which yields plenty of evidence on why the different stages of the family life cycle are important to consumer behaviour, even if the study does not settle the question of just how many individual stages it is appropriate to identify in the cycle.

Beginning with the 'early years', Reynolds and Wells emphasise how early childhood (from birth to around five years of age) is characterised by rapid physiological change, requiring an increasing food intake – I noted earlier how the recommended intake of nutrients follows an inverted U-shaped curve as a person progresses over the life cycle. Growth also requires frequent changes of clothing as children outgrow their existing clothes, often well before they are worn out, as parents know to their cost. The nature of the food intake also alters, as the young person progresses from soft foods to a more solid diet. Illness is also quite common at this stage, and medical needs tend therefore to be high. Socialising begins at this stage too, and one can already detect the influence which one child exercises upon another.

Reynolds and Wells continue their analysis of the different stages in like vein, moving progressively through later childhood (from around five years to the early teens), the era of the 'young consumers', sub-divided into early adolescence (puberty to about the age of 15) and later adolescence (from about 16 to 20 years), and then to the 'young adults' stage covering the age range from 18 to 35.

The *family* life cycle usually begins with marriage, which has an important bearing on people's needs, and even more, it seems, on their wants. Marriage itself helps meet human needs, through the sense of belonging which it brings. It also gives rise, however, to new and changing needs, one of the most important being for joint accommodation. A further important consequence of setting up a new home is the requirement for a number of major durable goods, many of them expensive. Reynolds and Wells quote figures to the effect that over one-half of sterling flatware (cutlery), about one-quarter of bedroom furniture sales, around 40 per cent of stereo and hi-fi equipment, and high proportions of many other durables are purchased by those about to be, or who have just recently, married. The arrival of the first child has other important repercussions on family life.

Young adulthood is followed by the 'middle years', from age 35 to 54 years. A feature of both these stages noted by Reynolds and Wells is the heavy demands placed upon family finances, especially by the needs of growing children. There tends to be a drop in financial optimism and there is heavy use of credit. These financial pressures are in turn linked with decisions about work which we shall return to at a later stage. As was shown in Baxter (1988), the return of a housewife to the labour force is closely associated with the presence of children and the age of the youngest child. It is in the family life cycle, in other words, that we must search not only for many aspects of consumer behaviour, but also for some of the most important determinants of labour force trends.

We come, finally, to the 'old customers', those aged 55 and over according to the definition used by Reynolds and Wells. The mental and physical changes accompanying old age lead to still further changes in needs and wants. There is an increased need for medical care, and labour saving devices become more important. Interests and activities, partly through necessity, become increasingly home-based. The most important turning point in this age group is retirement, when income suffers a sharp drop. Financial outlays also fall, however – house mortgages are likely to have been paid off, national social security contributions are not any more required, and the costs of working no longer have to be met, etc. – and as private pension provision improves, the retired are increasingly better prepared. It has even been suggested (see, for example, Kotlikoff and Summers, 1981) that saving during the life cycle may now have as its goal the provision of bequests rather than the financing of consumption in old age.

Although differences of view still persist over the appropriate divisions of the life cycle, empirical evidence shows that the concept, in a variety of forms, is helpful in explaining purchases of individual products. It may well be the case, therefore, that particular forms of the life cycle are appropriate to particular products. There is no reason why one version of the cycle should fit the purchases of all products, convenient though that would be.

Before turning, finally, to examine some of the empirical evidence, it is worth noting that critics of the life cycle concept have drawn attention to the way in which the standard nuclear family, to which most research applies, has become less relevant in recent years, as I remarked earlier. Divorce, separation, cohabitation, etc., require a 'modernised' life cycle, and some writers, such as Murphy and Staples (1979), have suggested appropriate stages for a life cycle of this nature.

Of the numerous studies of the life cycle, we select a number which tested not only for the effects of the cycle itself, but also at the same time for other related variables. Hisrich and Peters (1974), for example, tested simultaneously for the effects of the life cycle, age, income and social class on the use of entertainment facilities. The results of the study showed that stage in the family life cycle was more closely related to the use of leisure facilities than either age or social class. Further tests based on the *frequency* of use of the same facilities (a better indicator of regular, as opposed to just occasional, use) showed a strong association with all four explanatory variables, confirming that income by no means provides the sole explanation of consumer behaviour for this class of expenditure.

A further study by Fritzsche (1981) again showed that in simultaneous tests with an income variable, the life cycle contributed to an explanation of spending on energy consumption. Both the life cycle models tested (those of Wells-Gubar and Murphy-Staples) showed total energy consumption following an inverted-U pattern, being lower amongst the younger married without children, reaching a peak in the middle-aged married with children stage, and declining thereafter. A life cycle variable also helped explain consumption of individual types of fuel, and consumption at regional level.

One study by Wagner and Hanna (1983) has contradicted the generally favourable test results of the life cycle, but is itself open to a number of criticisms (see Baxter, 1988). Some of their test variables appear to overlap, for example, and the role of a number of the variables is also ambiguous. From the evidence available, it seems fair to conclude that the life cycle of needs and wants – or the 'consumption life cycle', as I call it – can make an important contribution towards explaining certain categories of consumer expenditure. I shall return to this topic later.

The changing nature and structure of the family unit

In addition to the rise in *total* population which has taken place in most countries, adding to the total of needs and wants, and therefore to total consumption, there have been a number of other changes affecting households and families which have also had an important bearing on consumption. We looked in the previous section at the nature of the family life cycle, and it will be apparent from the discussion, first, that any changes affecting the total *number* of families, or for that matter households, will affect demand for many items of personal consumption. The more households and families, the more units of accommodation will be required. There are implications here for the construction industry, depending upon precisely how the additional accommodation needs are translated into demand for physical units of accommodation. The additional accommodation then has to be furnished, and there will consequently be additional expenditure on a whole range of consumer durables – furniture, refrigerators, washing machines and telephones, for example. Predictions of the demand for such consumer items must therefore allow for expected changes in family and household formation.

Table 4.1 shows how the total number of households, and the number of family households, has increased markedly in recent years in both Great Britain and the United States. In Great Britain, the total number of households increased from 16.2 million in 1961 to 19.5 million in 1981, and 21.2 million in 1987. Projections show a further increase to over 23 million by 2001. Over the same period, family households also rose appreciably in number, but at a slower rate. Similar trends were evident in the United States.

These overall changes in family and household formation reflect complex *social* changes. The higher divorce rate has added greatly to the number of one-parent families. Young people are also leaving their parents earlier and setting up homes of their own, either alone or with friends. The lengthening average life span has also meant, too, that much greater numbers of the elderly are now living alone after the decease of a spouse. There have also been marked fluctuations in the birth rate – high after the Second World War, then declining, then rising again to a peak in 1964 in Great Britain, declining once more to a trough in 1977, followed by a partial recovery. All these social trends have consequences for needs and wants which are far too important for economists to omit from their analysis.

It is not, however, just the total number of families and households which affects personal consumption. The *pattern* of personal consumption, as we saw earlier, alters over both the individual life cycle and the family

Table 4.1 Household and family trends

Great Britain	*1961*	*1971*	*1981*	*1987*	*1991*[1]	*2001*[1]
Households (million)	16.2	18.3	19.5	19.4	22.0	23.3
average size (persons)	3.09	2.89	2.71	2.55	2.50	2.42
Family households (million)	13.5	14.2	14.3	13.8		
as % of all households	83.2	77.8	73.5	71.0		
Lone parent families[2] – as % of all households	2.5	3.5	5.8	4.7		

[1] Projected.
[2] With dependent children, but may also include some non-dependent children.

Source: Social Trends, General Household Survey.

United States	*1960*	*1970*	*1980*	*1987*
Households (million)	52.8	63.4	80.8	89.5
average size (persons)	3.33	3.14	2.76	2.66
Family households (million)	44.9	51.5	59.6	64.5
as % of all households	85.1	81.2	73.7	72.1
Lone parent families – as % of all families	12.8	13.2	17.5	20.1

Source: Statistical Abstract of the United States.

life cycle. Any change in the age distribution within families or households, taken as a whole, could therefore be expected to alter the global pattern of consumption among the different products, other things remaining equal. The high birth rate in many countries after the Second World War produced a boom in the demand for consumer goods needed by children. We now have the contrary situation, with a growing population of elderly people beginning to have a major impact on the demand for many products. The demand for retirement homes, health services, and ultimately funeral services, have all been significantly affected, and entrepreneurs have been quick to reap the benefits.

The sorts of changes we have been examining are often described simply as 'demographic changes', and are sometimes introduced into economic models on an ad hoc basis, without any theoretical justification, simply because they are too important to be omitted. We must, however, try to pin down more precisely why it is that 'demographics' matter. My answer is that needs vary according to age and sex, they have a particular pattern over the individual life cycle, and there is an associated pattern over the life cycle of the family. Any change in the demographic pattern will therefore alter both total needs and the pattern of associated wants. It is therefore once more the concept of needs to which we must ultimately turn for an explanation of how social changes have important economic consequences.

Family influence on decision-makers

I shall be concentrating here not so much on *family decision-making*, which I will leave until a later chapter, but on ways in which family members exercise influence on each other, and on those outside the family. I find it helpful, therefore, to distinguish between *intra* family influence i.e., a family's influence on its own members, some or all of whom are likely to undertake purchases primarily for their own use, and *extra* family influence, i.e., influence exerted by the family on decision-making units (individual or socioeconomic) outside the immediate family.

Families usually consist of husband and wife, and frequently also children. Much of the work on family influence has concentrated upon the relative influence of husband and wife in a variety of contexts, and in pursuit of different ends. The relative influence of the spouses varies, for example, according to the products under consideration. It also varies according to the stage of the decision-making process being considered. In certain circumstances, too, children may also influence buying behaviour. I will therefore look at each of these aspects of family influence in turn.

One of the principal studies of the relative influence of husband and wife is that by Davis and Rigaux (1974), who investigated both changes in relative influence over the stages of the decision-making process and from one product to another. The study has a number of weaknesses, especially the small sample size, but it also has the virtue of having been carried out in considerable depth. Davis and Rigaux employ a diagram (reproduced as Figure 4.1) displaying all decisions simultaneously. One axis is a scale of the relative influence of husband and wife, the other a scale of role specialisation, as measured by the percentage of families reporting that a decision was made jointly. Following a procedure adopted by others in earlier studies, the purchasing decisions in respect of 25 products were divided into four categories: husband-dominant, wife-dominant, syncratic (if more than 50 per cent of families made a decision jointly) and autonomic (if less than 50 per cent made a joint decision). The decision process was also divided into three stages: Phase 1, dealing with problem recognition; Phase 2 on the search for information; and Phase 3 when the final decision was taken.

Figure 4.1 is based on averages across all three phases, and shows that insurance decisions were husband-dominant, whereas decisions regarding kitchenware, household cleaning products, wife's and children's clothing and food were all wife-dominant. Decisions in each of these areas of activity conformed to the same pattern in each of the three decision phases when taken individually, but in the case of *other* decisions there was a

Figure 4.1 Husband-wife roles in purchase of 25 products

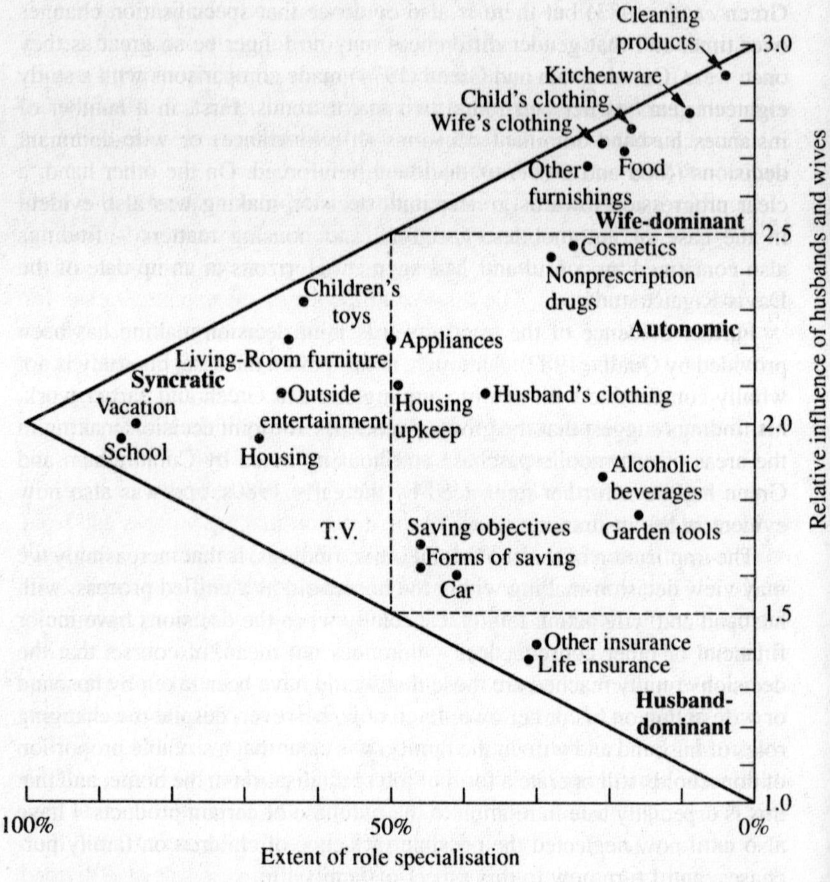

Source: Davis, H.L. and Rigaux, B.P., 'Perception of Marital Roles in Decision Processes', *Journal of Consumer Research*, 57 (1974).

significant change in the final phase. Thirteen were classed as syncratic in Phase 3, compared with only six or seven in the earlier stages. A contrasting change was apparent among those classed as autonomic in Phase 3 (five decisions, compared with ten and nine, respectively, in Phases 1 and 2). The results suggest that in the case of many products there is a change in marital roles as the decision-making process progresses – a finding supported by the fact that spouses confirmed that they did in practice distinguish between the phases when taking buying decisions.

Other studies confirm the existence of a degree of role specialisation in family decision-making (see, for example, Woodside and Motes, 1979, and Green *et al.*, 1983) but there is also evidence that specialisation changes over time, and that gender differences may no longer be so great as they once were. Cunningham and Green (1974) made comparisons with a study eighteen years earlier and found two major trends. First, in a number of instances husband-dominant decisions (life insurance) or wife-dominant decisions (food and groceries) had been reinforced. On the other hand, a clear progression towards greater joint decision-making was also evident in the case of automobiles, vacations and housing matters – findings also confirmed by consultants Management Horizons in an up-date of the Davis-Rigaux study.

Further evidence of the trend towards joint decision-making has been provided by Qualls (1982). Although, as is so often the case, his study is not wholly comparable with that of Cunningham and Green and earlier work, his findings suggest that the growing tendency for joint decision-making in the areas of automobile purchase and housing noted by Cunningham and Green had been further reinforced by the early 1980s, and was also now evident in life insurance.

The implication of the above, and other, findings, is that increasingly we may view decision-making within the household as a unified process, with husband and wife acting jointly, especially when the decisions have major financial or other consequences – this does not mean, of course, that the decisions finally reached are those that would have been taken by husband or wife acting on his or her own. Even now, however, despite the changing roles of husband and wife in the family, it is clear that a sizeable proportion of households still operate a form of job specialisation in the home, and that this is especially true in relation to the purchase of certain products. I have also until now neglected the possible influence of children on family purchases, and I turn now to this aspect of family life.

Although children today are subject to a wide variety of influences, including strong pressures from peer groups and the mass media, the family remains one of the central influences on their lives. Reviewing the literature on the consumer socialisation of children, Moschis (1985) concluded that parents could influence the purchasing behaviour of their children *directly* through several communication processes, including overt interaction about consumption matters (such as purposive training), using reinforcement mechanisms (both positive and negative), and providing opportunities for a child to observe its own consumer behaviour. The family can also affect consumer learning *indirectly* by influencing a child's interaction with other sources of consumer influence. A study by Ward, Wackman and Wartella (1977) showed, however, that parents do not on the whole consciously try to instruct their children about consumer behaviour. Few mothers engage in purposive 'consumer training'. The training, such as it is, arises from children modelling themselves on parental behaviour, and through such activities as checks by parents on how children are spending their pocket money. Children also initiate interaction when they request products.

The above suggests that the influence of parent(s) on child is dominant, but there is also evidence that children influence the consumer behaviour of parents. In effect, there is interaction between parent and child. Ward and Wackman (1972) showed how children's attempts to influence their parents, and the degree of success achieved, varied by product. The choice of breakfast foods, in particular, but also the choice of snack foods, sweets, soft drinks and children's toys, were all heavily influenced by children. In a follow-up study of cereal purchases in supermarkets, Atkin (1978) confirmed a high degree of parental yielding to child requests.

Adults are often separated from younger children in research studies, partly because there is evidence that parents tend to yield more readily to the views of children as they grow older (Ward and Wackman, 1972, and Ward *et al.*, 1977). The influence of peer groups also tends to weigh more heavily with older children. Nevertheless, the influence of the family still appears to predominate. Moschis and Moore (1980) in a study of purchase influences on 734 adolescents, covering eight product categories, found that by a majority of almost two to one the adolescents preferred parents to friends as a source of information – the purchase of sunglasses was an exception to the rule. The influence of parents was especially strong in the case of the more expensive products, such as wrist-watches. Moschis and Moore also found evidence, however, that the older teenagers become, the more information sources they tend to draw upon, and the greater becomes peer group influence on their purchases. It seems not unreasonable to surmise, nonetheless, that some vestige of parental influence remains, even after a young person has 'flown the nest'.

Looking back now at our discussion of family influence as part of the social environment in which purchasing decisions are made, a number of features stand out. First, the family has exerted, and continues to exert, a number of direct influences on purchasing decisions. The family life cycle, as we saw, has a bearing on the consumption of certain products, such as energy and leisure facilities, which is independent of family income, age or social class. Moreover, the important structural changes which have taken place within households and families have also had direct effects on purchases. The large increase in the total number of households and families has affected demand for accommodation, to take but one example, and changes in the age-sex composition of families have meant additional changes in family needs and wants. In our basic model, these factors will affect spending decisions by the family as a *socioeconomic unit*, acting on behalf of its members.

The family also exerts indirect influences on purchasing decisions. The actual *pattern* of the spending on products by the family unit, and doubtless also total spending, will be determined by the network of interpersonal relationships within the family, the principal ones being the influence of parents on younger children and adolescents, and, in the reverse direction, the influence of children on their parents. Family members, in effect, use their own families as an important reference group. Even when an individual leaves his family, he may still use it as a reference group. In terms of our basic model, therefore, the indirect influence may be felt both at the level of the *individual* and at the *socioeconomic* level of the family acting as a unit.

GROUPS

Groups are more than mere aggregations, or collectives, of individuals. They are social institutions which both modify the behaviour of group members and are in turn influenced by their members. They cannot therefore simply be regarded as a mere collection of individuals, each of whom continues to act as he, or she, would have done had they not joined the group. Moreover, as we saw earlier, groups may influence the behaviour of non-members. Economics has not yet been able to incorporate these important facts into the main body of theory. In consumer economics, for example, there is uncertainty and confusion about whether consumption should be analysed in terms of individuals, families or households. Sometimes all are treated synonymously. Nor is there generally any mention of the expenditure of non-profit making groups, or organisations, such as clubs, whose expenditure is classified in national accounts as *consumers' expenditure* – even if only a relatively small part of the total. If economics is to make better sense of the workings of society, it must take greater account of the basic structure of society and how it functions. The framework of analysis we adopt will, it is hoped, go some way towards sorting out the confusion by showing how groups fit into the general pattern of economic behaviour.

Definitions of groups differ in detail, but usually they embrace a number of common features. Members of a group generally identify with it, and perceive themselves to be *affiliated* to it, even if there are no formal procedures for affiliation. This helps give groups a certain cohesiveness which is lacking in mere aggregations of people. *Communication* between group members also helps foster *cohesiveness*. There is, too, a degree of *interdependence* among group members, in terms of obligations and the outcomes of group activities. Members usually also share common norms, motives and interests. One of the principal reasons for membership of groups is the attainment of personal goals, which are closely linked to individual needs and wants. Group membership, for example, may help satisfy the need to belong, or the need for self-actualisation, as with membership of an art class or music circle. Membership of groups may also assist consumers in making decisions about personal expenditure, or perhaps in furthering their economic interests, via, for example, membership of a staff association or trade union.

Group classifications also take many forms, but once again certain common denominators tend to emerge. Groups are often delineated according to whether they are *primary* or *secondary*. The former describes groups with which an individual interacts regularly, usually face-to-face. The family group, which we looked at earlier, would fall under this heading, as would leisure groups, work groups, church groups, and so forth. Secondary groups are those with which an individual interacts only occasionally, and they tend therefore to be less important to him.

Since groups are essentially social institutions, they cannot function without some form of structure, even if only a very loose one. Groups are therefore often classed as *formal* or *informal*. A formal group would tend to be characterised by an operational structure which sets out members' rights and duties, perhaps in the form of a constitution, with members performing clearly defined roles, especially those holding formal office, as in the case of chairman, secretary and treasurer. At the other extreme, we might find peer groups, say of students, regularly participating in apparently anarchic groups, but groups which nonetheless operate according to certain conventions, and within which members again tend to play certain *roles* – leader, follower, entertainer, spokesperson, etc.

Possibly linked to the formal-informal dichotomy, a distinction is also often drawn between *membership* and *non-membership* groups. At one extreme, members of a formal group might be given a token of membership, such as a card or key; but less formal membership is also possible. It is sufficient simply for a member to 'belong', i.e., to participate in the activities of the group, which might be, for example, a neighbourhood group, or perhaps a group with a common enthusiasm for veteran automobiles. In contrast to such groups, an individual may identify himself with a group without having any formal part in its activities, or he may aspire to future membership. Such might be the case with a sports team, or a group whose activities tend to be costly, and at present beyond the reach of the individual.

The group interaction process

Given the voluminous work on groups, we must of necessity be very selective, touching only on those aspects which seem most relevant to our study. Even then, selection is made difficult by the fact that research work on groups has tended to be segmented, with no over-arching theory which unites the different strands of work. In an attempt to provide some measure of unity, McGrath (1984) has, however, identified four common 'inputs' to the group interaction process. First, there are the group members, each of whom has *personal characteristics*, such as motives (including needs and goals), personality and attitudes. These group members exist within an *environment*, which constitutes the second input. The environment comprises a physical environment and a social environment (which might include, for example, inter-group conflict), and for our purposes we would also wish to include an economic environment.

A third input is that groups have different *structures*, with different patterns of relationships among the individuals comprising the groups. These structures may be defined in a variety of terms – for example, by the division of labour within the group, by the system of communication, by the distribution of power, or by interpersonal relations. Finally, the nature of the particular *task(s)* that a group is trying to carry out is yet another factor that must be taken into account in trying to understand, and predict, group interaction. Adoption of a task implies the existence of a goal, or goals.

In addition to these inputs to the interaction process, group interaction may itself give rise to additional forces which in turn influence the interaction process.

In my present study I touch on each of the major inputs to the group interaction process. I have already examined personal characteristics, noting the key role of motivation, which helps determine personal goals, which are in turn likely to have a close bearing on group tasks. I discuss the environment at some length in the present section of my study. Group structure is discussed later in the present section, and again when I come to examine group decision-taking, where it is of central importance.

Consumer-relevant groups

Until now I have talked in a general fashion about 'groups', but can we be more specific about which particular groups of the many in existence are relevant to our analysis? In the case of consumers, who account for over one-half of total final expenditure in most countries, Schiffman and Kanuk (1987) identify six basic consumer-relevant groups: the family, friendship groups, formal social groups, shopping groups, consumer action groups and work groups. The *family* I have already discussed separately, owing to its special importance. *Friendship groups*, which are usually classed as informal groups because they tend to be unstructured, with no specific levels of authority, are normally the next most powerful influence on consumers after the family. Such groups are likely to include friends bonded together by such factors as similarity of outlook, trust and a community of interests. Together with the family, friendship groups are very important in satisfying an individual's need for belonging.

Formal social groups also help satisfy needs and wants, and their associated goals. They are very common in leisure-related activities, such as sport, cultural pursuits and travel, but may also be a means of fostering one's work career, even if the activities of the group (such as a country club) are not always directly work-related. In Maslow's terminology, many of these activities could be described as forms of 'self-actualisation', and therefore help satisfy important higher order needs.

Membership of formal social groups is also important in that it may influence a consumer's behaviour in significant ways. Members of such groups frequently exchange views on consumer products relevant to group activities (and perhaps also on products not directly relevant), such as golf clubs and tennis racquets, and perhaps books, interesting new travel venues, and so forth. Once more, in effect, we have an example of groups which serve as reference groups. A further important feature of these formal social groups is that they may themselves act as purchasing agents on behalf of group members (and are therefore also decision-making units in their own right). It is for this reason that expenditure by such groups, as was noted earlier, is classified as *consumers' expenditure* in national income and expenditure accounts.

The fourth type of consumer-relevant group identified by Schiffman and Kanuk was *shopping groups*. Two or more people often engage in shopping expeditions. These groups will often, but not always, be offshoots of family or friendship groups. There may therefore be some overlap, but shopping expeditions may sometimes be for specific purposes, such as the purchase of items of clothing, for which the opinion of the other member(s) of the shopping group may be considered important. Schiffman and Kanuk cite evidence that two or more people shopping together are likely to buy more than if they had shopped alone.

Shopping groups sometimes use a member's house as a base from which to operate. These in-home shopping groups are often a means of marketing the products of a particular producer or vendor. The stamp of approval given by other members of the group seems to be a powerful sales aid.

Consumer action groups have now become very active in the US, UK and other countries. The subjection of consumer goods to scientific (and sometimes not so scientific) tests is a useful aid to decision-making, and via the media the influence of some groups extends well beyond the confines of members. These groups are often instrumental in bringing about improvements in the quality of goods, leading to greater satisfaction for consumers after purchase.

Finally, Schiffman and Kanuk draw our attention to the importance of *work groups* to consumer behaviour. Work groups may sometimes exist in a formal sense, where employees work together as a team, or they may consist of less formal associations of members brought together through working at the same site. Given the large proportion of their lives which employees spend at work, it is not surprising that work groups should be influential in determining consumers' purchases.

The structure of group influence

We have now reached a stage where we are able, by drawing upon our earlier discussions, to construct a general and more formal representation of group influence, and to show, in particular, how such a structure would fit into our overall behavioural model. Figure 4.2 sets out the likely structure. I distinguish, first, between an *environment group*, which is part of the social environment, and the *individual* and *socioeconomic* decision-making units which the environment group may influence – an environment group may, of course, also be a decision-making group, but there will be instances where this is not the case, as with friendship groups. Within the environment group there may also be *intra-group influences* (between members within the group) in contrast to *inter-group influences* (between members in the environment group and members in decision-making groups – and perhaps also members in other environment groups).

The principal intra-group influences have much in common with the individual (person-to-person) influences we looked at in an earlier section. We saw that word-of-mouth communication is of central importance, and closely linked with the role of opinion leaders. In the case of a group with more than just one line of communication, there will, of course, be a more complex web of communication, even in quite small groups, but there is no essential difference in principle. In Figure 4.2 I have taken a simple example of a four-person environment group, comprising an opinion leader *Elm* (where the letter *l* denotes leadership and *m* that the leader is male) and three other individuals, with *i* also being male and *j* and *k* female. The directions of the arrows indicate the person(s) to whom each member of the group tends to turn for a valued opinion. All turn to individual *l*, and we suppose that *l* therefore exercises opinion leadership. Empirical investigations of such networks of influence (sometimes referred to as 'sociograms') have in practice been able to identify opinion leaders. Coleman's (1959) study of doctors taking advice from each other on the introduction of a new drug is an example often cited.

Since members of a group are often members of other groups, or in contact with members of other groups, word-of-mouth communication also plays a part in *inter-group* communication as well as intra-group communication. Given the common interests and purposes of a group, however, it seems likely to be a more powerful influence in the case of the latter.

Another important phenomenon which is important both to intra-group and inter-group communication is the *diffusion* process by which a *new* product is accepted and spread throughout a market. Word-of-mouth communication again proves to be the vital mechanism by which the diffusion process works in practice, and studies have shown, too (see, for example, Engel *et al.*, 1990) that opinion leaders tend to be to the fore in accepting the new products (and therefore in this context are sometimes described as *innovators*).

In the example in Figure 4.2 I show the environment group (E_g) exercising two kinds of influence. First, as in the case of families, there is the influence arising from social comparisons, with the environment group acting as a reference group, both for the individual decision-making unit (I) and the socioeconomic decision-making unit (S_g). Given that the members of the environment group look to individual *Elm* as opin-

Figure 4.2 The structure of group influence

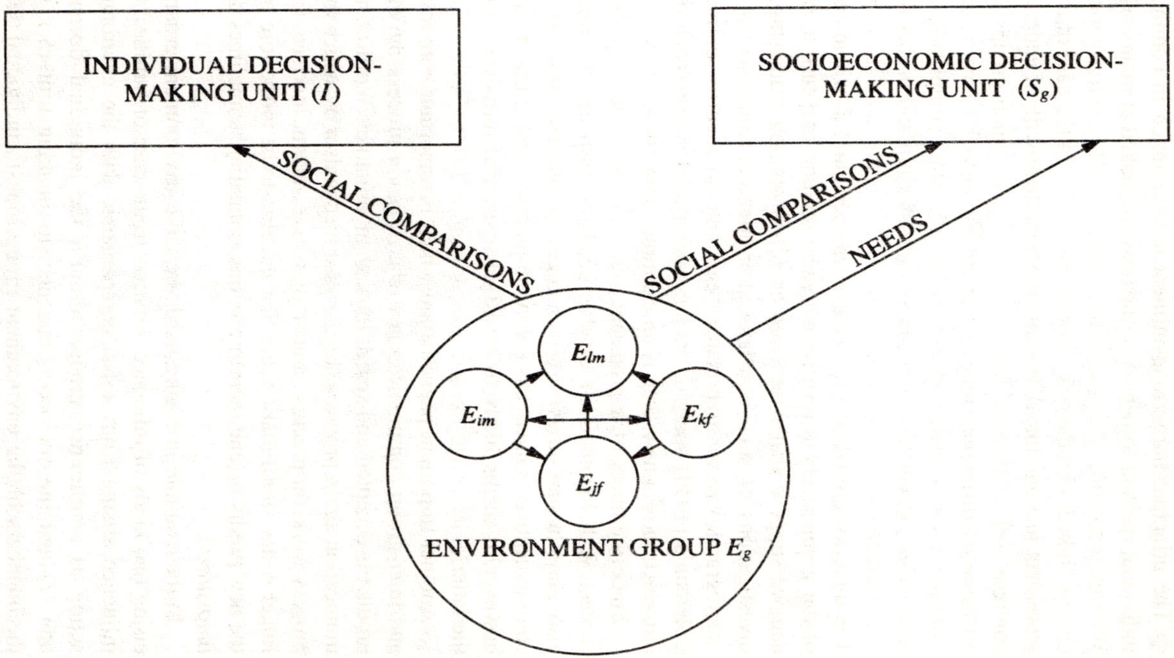

ion leader, and innovator for new products, we can, in effect, represent the influence of E_g by that of *Elm*. Given, too, that there is evidence, as we saw in Baxter (1988), that reference groups influence both product and brand selection by consumers, we can show consumption by *I* as a function of consumption by *Elm*, as in equation 4.1.

$$I^x = \mu E^x lm \qquad \mu > 0 \tag{4.1}$$

where the superscript *x* denotes consumption of product *x* and μ is a constant.

Using the same reasoning, we could also show

$$S_g^x = \mu E^x lm \qquad \mu > 0 \tag{4.2}$$

It may be the case, of course, that individual *Elm* does not himself consume product *x*, but only influences its consumption. In that case, a more complex formulation based on consumption by the group would be necessary, but there is no difference in principle.

It may also be the case that an environment group is at the same time a decision-making unit, so that E_g and S_g are the same body. In such instances, we could still show consumption by the group as a function of consumption by the group leader.

Until now I have discussed the social comparisons of the environment group's influence solely in the context of consumer behaviour, but social comparisons also have other very important consequences for decision-making. I showed in Baxter (1988) that social comparisons, allied to notions of equity (a very potent source of motivation) have a close bearing on wage behaviour. There is a great deal of empirical evidence confirming that in assessing the adequacy of their pay, and therefore the pay rises which they feel are justified, groups of employees (whether organised in trade unions or not) compare themselves with other (reference) groups. Trade unions form one category of socioeconomic decision-making unit we shall be considering later. For the present, I wish only to note that social comparisons have repercussions extending beyond that of consumer behaviour.

The second form of influence exercised by the environment group E_g has its origins in the needs, and the associated wants, of its members. I am thinking here, in effect, of the case referred to above, where E_g and S_g are the same body, but for the purposes of our model acting in different capacities. We can illustrate the case by reference to the group's needs. These needs, as we saw earlier, vary according to age and sex, and, in the case of a family group, according to the stage of the family life cycle. If we consider E_g to be a family group, we can show very clearly how its purchases of foodstuffs are likely to vary with the passage of time. Using the data from Table 3.1, which gives official recommendations for the average daily intake of energy, protein, certain minerals and vitamins according to age and sex, we can calculate how family needs will alter over, say, a five year period. For one family only, such changes will have a relatively marginal effect on its total expenditures if expressed on an annual basis; but if we were to aggregate the data for all families, then such annual variations could have a considerable impact on consumption of certain products, and therefore on the overall pattern of consumption, if there were at the same time sizeable changes in the age-sex composition of the population. Such changes have indeed taken place in many countries since World War Two. We are assuming here, of course, that family wants, or preferences, do reflect, in some degree at least, changing family needs, but this does not seem an unreasonable supposition.

The results of the calculations are shown in Table 4.2. We can see clearly that family needs for food will indeed vary over time.

In non-family groups, the passage of time may cause similar changes in preferences, although it will really depend again upon how the age-sex composition of groups alters. Assuming the membership of a group remained unaltered, however, the ageing of the group would have consequences for expenditures. A leisure group, for example, could be expected increasingly to favour less active pursuits; a shopping group might become less concerned with buying the latest fashions and pay more attention to the quality and durability of clothing; while an action group might show increasing concern for measures which would enhance personal safety and security. Such changes in preferences may obviously have significant effects on the pattern of personal expenditure, and, what is more, these changes may occur quite independently of any accompanying changes in income and prices.

SOCIAL CLASS

I now move further up our ladder of social aggregation, this time to a much larger collective, that of social class. Whereas families and groups may generally be determined with some degree of precision, delineating a social class is much more problematic. Although class is more frequently associated with sociological discussions, the term also has a long and interesting pedigree in economics. Foster (1987) in the *New Palgrave* traces its ances-

Table 4.2 Recommended daily food needs of a family of four

		Year *t*						Year *t*+5					
		Energy		Protein	Calcium	Iron	Vitamin A	Energy		Protein	Calcium	Iron	Vitamin A
		MJ[1]	*Kcal*[1]	*g*[1]	*mg*[1]	*mg*[1]	*µg*[1]	*MJ*[1]	*Kcal*[1]	*g*[1]	*mg*[1]	*mg*[1]	*µg*[1]
	Males												
Age	60	11.50	2750	69	500	10	750	10.00	2400	60	500	10	750
	14	11.00	2640	66	700	12	725	12.00	2900	72	500	10	750
	Females												
Age	54	9.00	2150	54	500	12	750	8.00	1900	47	500	10	750
	17	9.00	2150	53	600	12	750	9.00	2150	54	500	12	750
Total Family Needs		40.50	9690	242	2300	46	2975	39.00	9350	233	2000	42	3000

[1] Definitions given in footnotes to Table 3.1.

try through the Physiocrats, Ricardo, Marx and Engels up to the present day. Max Weber, whose ideas have had a profound influence on the more recent discussions of class, proposed three dimensions for the analysis of social position: 'class situation', which referred to a person's material 'life chance', or economic advantages, within any market situation, whether as consumer, employee or landlord; second, 'status situation', or the social respect accorded particular social groupings; finally, 'power', which defined the degree of a group's access to the legitimate use of force.

In my discussion of the social environment, I am most concerned, it would seem, with the second of Weber's three dimensions of social position, although aspects of each of the three dimensions are relevant. Status certainly seems to be one of the most important dimensions of class. But status is itself determined by a variety of factors. Among those most commonly identified are occupation, education, income and ownership of assets, of which property is the most obvious manifestation. These factors are, of course, all interrelated in some degree, and this is one of the difficulties in trying to decide which criteria are most important in determining social class.

'Values' and 'lifestyle' are sometimes listed in the consumer behaviour literature as being strongly associated with social class. Values cover shared beliefs about how people should behave in society. How, for example, children should be brought up, the importance to be attached to education, behaviour at work, religious practices, etc. Lifestyle is a wide-ranging concept which most people probably feel they recognise, even if they may find difficulty in defining it in practice. I shall have more to say about it later.

The problems encountered in defining social class inevitably raise practical difficulties when attempts are made to measure social class, but progress has been made in this field, and it is worth looking briefly at some of this work, since it constitutes an essential tool in testing the importance of social class.

Measuring social class

A distinction is often drawn between subjective, 'reputational' and objective means of measuring social class. The first of these entails the subjects categorising themselves according to class, but it has been found that people tend to avoid the extremes at each end of the classifications, so that doubt has been cast on the validity of this method. Reputational measures rely on participants judging the social class of *others*. Once again the large subjective element inseparable from such an exercise may cause problems.

Furthermore, since a good deal of knowledge about the subjects of study has to be available if the procedure is to work at all, this method of classification may be more appropriate to localised studies. Most attempts at classification have therefore looked for suitable objective measures of social position.

Objective systems of classification sometimes rely upon a sole measure of class, but composite indices are more common. An interesting example of the former variety is the status ordering of a wide range of occupations by Treiman (1977). The study was doubly interesting in that Treiman was able to devise an international classification of occupations. The findings showed that the topmost status ratings were accorded to physical scientists, college professors, lawyers and chemists, in that order. At the other extreme of the range, listing from the bottom up, were mail clerks, receptionists, clerk-typists and dental hygienists. Treiman's scales have proved useful in statistical analysis, but more use has been made of composite measures of social class.

Among the composite measures, greatest use has been made of Warner's Index of Status Characteristics (ISC). This index combines four variables, using a seven-point rating scale (the weights are given in brackets): occupation (4), *source* income (3), house type (3) and dwelling area (2). Warner based his work on six social classes: upper-upper, lower-upper, upper-middle, lower-middle, upper-lower and lower-lower. Later work, however, has suggested fewer principal groupings. Coleman (1983) has drawn attention to the way in which two other important studies, working from different perspectives, have arrived at surprisingly similar classifications. Coleman and Rainwater (1978), following Warner's social-psychological approach, constructed a hierarchy based upon status, in which identification with each class was influenced most heavily by educational credentials and occupation, but also in varying degrees by social skills, family history, recreational habits and other social indicators. Coleman (1983) groups their hierarchy into a three-fold classification (with the percentage of the total population in each given in brackets): Upper Americans (14), Middle Americans (70) and Lower Americans (16).

The other study, by Gilbert and Kahl (1982), was primarily a sociological work, in which most weight was given to capitalist ownership and the occupational division of labour. Status and values were then treated as derivatives of the two primary variables. Once again Coleman found that the Gilbert-Kahl classification fell readily into a three-fold grouping, each similar in size to that which emerged from the Coleman-Rainwater study: Upper Americans (15), Middle Americans (65) and Marginal and Lower Americans (approximately 20). While each of the groupings could be sub-divided according to the classification employed, looking at the issue from the consumer behaviour point of view, Coleman concluded that only a sub-division of Middle Americans into Middle Class and Working Class was clearly warranted, since each still represented distinct social worlds with different behavioural norms and lifestyles. Lower Americans are, however, sometimes sub-divided into two classes (as they were by Coleman-Rainwater and Gilbert-Kahl) distinguishing between those in work and those who survive on government transfer payments.

One outcome of Coleman's (1983) work was a Computerised Status Index (CSI) which has been extensively used in consumer research for business enterprises.

Social class versus income

There has been for some time concern that the use of social class as an explanatory variable for consumer behaviour might be superfluous, since its effects could be more readily captured by income. After all, there is bound to be some overlap between income and the use of occupation and education as indicators of social class. On the other hand, it is not difficult to point to instances of relatively low incomes being associated with relatively high status (or vice versa) – the academic professions are an oft-cited case. It is therefore worth considering whether social class does indeed have something to add to an explanation of consumer behaviour which income does not fully catch.

Martineau (1958), Coleman (1960) and Levy (1966) were early adherents to the view that social class was more important than income in determining consumer behaviour. Levy maintained that 'social class variations are variations in lifestyle', and could not be adequately captured by income differences alone. Subsequent research cast doubt on this argument. Slocum and Mathews (1970), for example, found that if income was held constant, social classes (as measured by an index similar to that of Warner) did not exhibit a large number of different buying preferences (using credit cards as the means of payment). In a study which also dealt specifically with the social class versus income issue, Myers *et al.* (1971) found that in the case of seventy-eight products out of a total of ninety-one tested, income proved to be more closely associated with buyer behaviour than class. Since the study related only to toiletries, drugs and cosmetics, soaps, paper, drinks and a range of foodstuffs, Myers and Mount (1973) carried out a further study covering purchases of a range of durable goods and services – again with similar results.

Hisrich and Peters (1974) have drawn attention to a major weakness of the last two studies listed. Both asked only for information on whether or not the product had been used, not *how frequently* it had been used. Moreover, many of the products (wine and whisky, for example) were of such a nature that frequency of use might well have been associated with social class. Hisrich and Peters demonstrated (using Warner's ISC) that in the case of entertainment activities, while the use/non-use results did indeed suggest that income was a superior explanatory variable to social class, when frequency of use was tested, the results were reversed, and social class became the superior correlate.

A form of the relative income hypothesis has also surfaced in the social class versus income debate. Coleman (1960) maintained that *within* a social class some members were 'overprivileged' and others 'underprivileged'. In other words, some within a class had a relatively high income, others a relatively low income, and this determined both the types and the range of products purchased. Higher income individuals would tend, so the argument ran, to buy better quality and higher-priced durable goods, whereas those on relatively low incomes would have to make do with smaller, fewer or less costly goods. Peters (1970) provided support for this relative income hypothesis in a study concerned solely with automobile purchases. He found that the buying behaviour of relatively well-off blue-collar workers was more like that of affluent white-collar and professional workers than that of the less well-off blue-collar workers.

Our discussion indicates that the social class versus income debate is rather more complex than was at first supposed, but out of the conflicting claims and approaches some sort of consensus now appears to be emerging. In an attempt to resolve many of the issues, Schaninger (1981) tried to determine the product classes for which social class, income, or a combination of the two, were superior, using statistical techniques which enabled the influence of each to be judged. The study also tested for frequency of use, and covered an exceptionally broad range of consumer goods. Schaninger's findings were, first, that social class was superior to income for those segments of consumer purchases that did not entail high financial outlays, but did reflect underlying lifestyles and values not captured by income – these comprised a whole array of non-durables, including consumption of instant, frozen and canned convenience foods and beverages, snack foods and wines. Income was generally superior for major kitchen and laundry appliances requiring substantial expenditures, but whose use was now more widespread, so that they no longer appeared to serve as the status symbols they once represented.

A combination of social class and income was found by Schaninger to be generally superior for product classes that were highly visible, served as symbols of social class or status-within-class, and required either moderate or substantial expenditure – examples included clothing and make-up, automobiles and television sets. There was also support for the importance of relative income as an explanatory variable in the case of automobile ownership, and to a lesser extent in ownership of television sets, but there was, too, some evidence of 'status incongruence' – inconsistent, or non-conformist, purchasing behaviour. It was found, for example, that

> Lower income upper middle class housewives are more likely to purchase low priced dresses, and lower income upper middle and lower middle class housewives are also more likely to take advantage of grocery pricing promotions than housewives of the same classes in higher income quartiles – indicating a willingness to compromise their social class tendencies to cope with low relative income.

The featuring of 'lifestyle' as a factor closely associated with class is an interesting development we noted earlier. The belief that lifestyle is a key explanatory variable in consumer behaviour has led to the search for an operational measure of the concept, usually referred to as 'psychographics', or AIO (activities or attitudes, interests and opinions) – a good discussion of the topic may be found in Engel *et al.* (1990). It may yet prove to be the case that lifestyle rather than social class is the appropriate explanatory variable, but the two seem to be interlinked, and the theoretical underpinning which would clarify the basis of each appears to be lacking at present. The danger is that, in the absence of adequate theoretical foundations, we end up with no more than the best correlates, subject to the instabilities that implies.

Other evidence of the role of social class in consumer behaviour

The preceding section dealt specifically with the issue of whether social class or income (or some combination of the two) was the most powerful determinant of consumer behaviour. Having established that there is a strong case in favour of social class, in the purchase of at least some goods, we now go on to look at other studies which provide yet further evidence of how the use of social class can improve our understanding of consumer behaviour.

Given the importance of the home to most people, if social class were to be important we would expect to find it reflected to some degree in purchases for the home. This proved to be very much the case in an interesting study by Laumann and House (1970), which analysed the contents of living rooms, the part of a house which probably best represents the image householders wish to convey to outsiders. Fifty-three living room objects or characteristics were classified according to their high or low social status (as indicated by the status of those who purchased them) and according to whether they were modern or traditional (again as indicated by the type of purchaser). The results are given in Figure 4.3, and show for example, that those with high social status and a traditional bent tend to purchase traditional furniture and pianos, and to have fireplaces. Those of the same social class, but with a 'modernist' inclination, were found to favour modern furniture, sculpture and abstract paintings. Among those of lower social status, religious objects, translucent curtains, floral carpets and wall mirrors were especially popular with the more traditionally minded, whereas animals, mixed furniture, floral curtains and televisions were more commonly found among those with more modern tendencies.

A number of studies have also demonstrated class differences in leisure pursuits. Coleman and Rainwater (1978), in a study to which we referred earlier, found that those with higher social status tended to travel more widely and more frequently, and to engage in the more expensive forms of recreation. Other researchers have shown that upper class consumers spend most on attendance at cultural activities, such as the opera, ballet, concerts and visits to museums, whereas lower class consumers tend to prefer fishing, baseball and television viewing (see, for example, Cotton, 1972, and Robbins and Robbins, 1979). Sporting activities show similar divergences. Tennis, ice skating and bridge are associated principally with upper class behaviour, while boxing, bowling and pool or billiards are primarily lower class preoccupations (Bishop and Ikeda, 1970).

We may conclude from the above discussion, it seems, that whereas social class may not have a universal role in helping us understand consumer behaviour, it does have a role independent of consumer income in explaining particular forms of behaviour, and should not therefore be ignored. We move on now to the broadest social collectives of all – cultures and sub-cultures – where the concepts are much more amorphous, and the problems of trying to ascertain their significance for consumers multiply. An eclectic approach may nonetheless yield some dividends.

CULTURE AND SUB-CULTURE

Generally speaking, as we have moved progressively from smaller to larger collectives, the problems of defining the relevant environmental constructs

Figure 4.3 Social status attributes of living-room objects

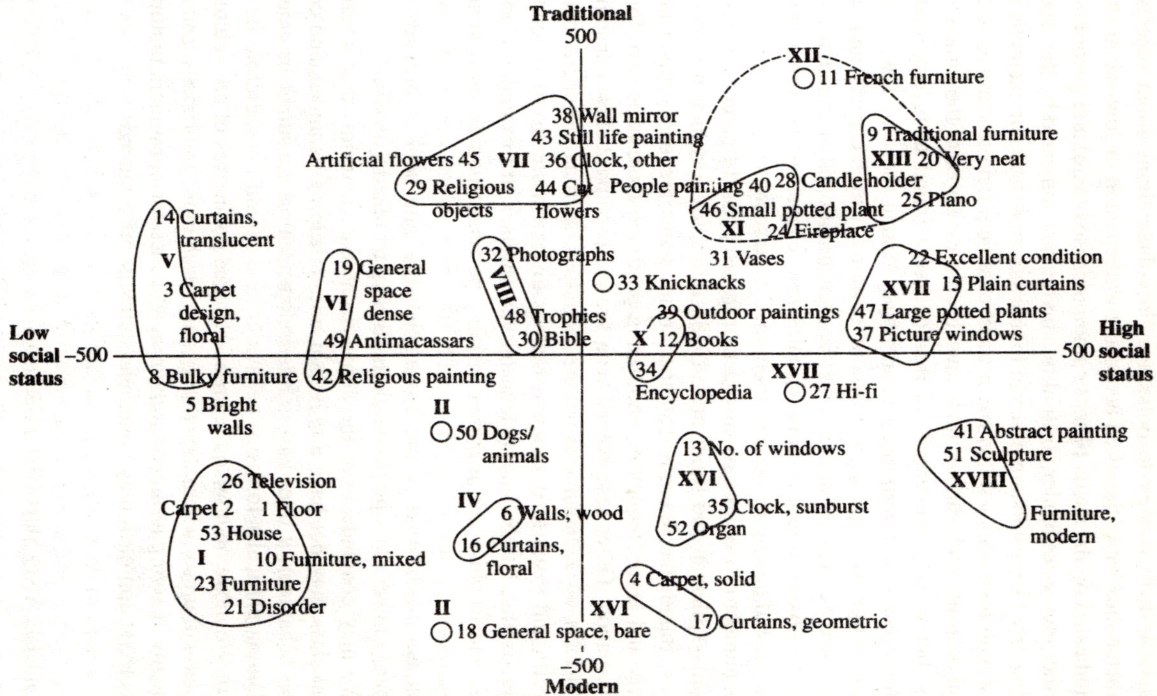

Source: Laumann, E.O. and House, J.S., 'Living Room Styles and Social Attributes: The Patterning of Material Artifacts in a Modern Urban Community', *Sociology and Social Research*, **54** (1970).

have increased. In discussing culture we are not dealing with a single, simple entity, but rather with a complex of influences which appears to be important in determining economic behaviour. Definitions do vary, but as with social class there seems to be a fair measure of agreement about the principal features of culture. First, a culture tends to have shared *beliefs* – a belief being what we know, or think we know, about an object. This does not mean that every single individual in the society must share the beliefs, but that they are sufficiently widely held for their impact on society to be of some significance. The beliefs may cover a wide variety of matters, ranging from religious beliefs to the form the political system ought to take, or the appropriate role for the State in economic affairs.

Some beliefs are, of course, likely to be more important than others in shaping society. The most important are sometimes given the status of *values*. The belief that certain personal liberties should under no circumstances be subjugated by the State would, for example, constitute a value judgement about how society should be organised. Some parents, to take another example, believe that private education has a high value – not simply in the monetary sense. This leads many such parents to spend large sums of money educating their children in private institutions.

Beliefs are also closely linked with *attitudes*. If we believe that the inhabitants of a particular country are friendly, or that they can generally be relied upon to produce goods of high quality, then we are likely to be favourably disposed towards purchasing the products of that country, and we may also wish to spend money visiting the country on business or on holiday.

Cultures also tend to be characterised by behavioural *norms*. These cover a wide range of activities, such as the timing of meals (very late in the evening in Spain, relatively early in Britain) the nature of these meals (frequently a cooked breakfast in Britain, a very simple breakfast in France) and the drink taken with them (often wine in France, Italy and other Mediterranean countries).

Taken together, the beliefs, values, attitudes and norms create marked contrasts in the ways people of different cultures live, and the ways in which they satisfy their needs and wants. It is, however, one thing to say that such cultural differences must inevitably be reflected in differences in the behaviour of consumers and businessmen, quite another to demonstrate empirically the practical consequences. A number of attempts have been made to investigate the relationship between values and consumer behaviour, many of them drawing on the work of Rokeach (1973). It seems fair to say, however, that work of this nature is still at an early stage, and has also been the subject of some criticism. At the present time, the work of probably the greatest significance has been carried out at what is usually referred to as the 'sub-cultural' level. While it is difficult to sum up complex cultures in terms of a few key variables, fairly distinct groups can nevertheless be identified within cultures which enable comparisons to be drawn between these sub-cultures and society as a whole – and indeed between the sub-cultures themselves. Most of the work has focused on two principal racial groups, both in North America: namely, the black sub-culture and the Hispanic sub-culture. A few studies have also concentrated on religious sub-cultures, particularly that of Jews in the United States. We go on now to look principally at the black and Hispanic sub-cultures.

The black sub-culture

In attempting to assess the influence of the black sub-culture on economic behaviour (really consumer behaviour, since there seems to be little evidence relating to other economic behaviour) one has to bear in mind that what appear to be differences in behaviour compared with other racial groups may be due to some of the social influences we examined in earlier sections. The median age of the black population in the United States is appreciably lower than that of whites, for example, therefore one would expect this to be reflected in differences in needs and wants. Black incomes are also lower, on average, than those of whites, and so too is educational attainment, as measured by years spent at college. Even when allowance is made for such differences, however, research evidence suggests there are still sufficient variations in product purchase behaviour to justify treating blacks as a separate sub-culture.

Loudon and Bitta (1984) in a survey of the relevant literature identified three major findings in relation to black consumer behaviour:

1. Blacks save a higher proportion of a given income than do whites.
2. For a given level of income, black consumers also allocate their expenditure differently from whites. They spend more on clothing and non-automobile transportation and less on food, housing, medical care and automobile transportation.
3. At comparable income levels there is no racial difference in expenditures on recreation and leisure, or on home furnishing and equipment.

Even these findings, however, are not entirely unambiguous. The above-average expenditure on non-automobile transportation may simply reflect the fact that a high proportion of blacks live in urban areas and are heavily dependent on local utilities for transport. The poor urban housing of blacks also appears to be a factor in their low demand for home furnishings, and in their low ownership of major domestic appliances.

A strong feature of black consumer behaviour which has emerged from empirical investigation is a concern for goods which give a degree of status to the buyer. 'Socially visible' products, such as fashionable clothes, are very popular, and blacks also seem readier to experiment and set new trends (Sexton, 1972, Harting, 1980).

Investigations of brand loyalties suggest that blacks are also much more loyal than whites, and in the case of some brands may be prepared to countenance sizeable price rises without reducing their consumption (Wellington, 1981). Quite why there should be such strong attachment to certain brands is not entirely clear, but it may be something to do with different exposure to media influences, some of which are targeted at black consumers.

The Hispanic sub-culture

My cautionary words about the need to be wary of attributing differences in behaviour to sub-cultural influences when they may simply reflect the other social influences we have already identified, are again relevant. Once again, too, my comments relate to the United States, although many of the Hispanic population are recent immigrants, and many do not even appear to consider themselves American. Other features of the Hispanics are in many respects similar to those of blacks. The median age is below average, and families are larger than average. The proportion completing High School is relatively low, and, partly as a consequence, the median income is well below that for the rest of the population.

In their survey of sub-culture influences, Loudon and Bitta (1984) again found distinct differences between Hispanic and non-Hispanic purchases of consumer goods – although some aspects of Hispanic behaviour were similar to those of blacks. Food purchases by Hispanic families tended to be about 10 per cent above average, in part because of the large size of families, and average consumption of beverages, both alcoholic and non-alcoholic, also tended to be higher. Greater use of fast-food outlets and a proclivity towards packaged foods were also evident.

As in the case of blacks, some purchases, such as those of automobiles and jewellery, indicate a strong concern with status, which is not really surprising in groups still trying to establish themselves more firmly in society. Hispanics also appear to be very open to the influence of advertising, and they show brand loyalty once persuaded to buy. They also seem very ready to experiment with new products coming on the market.

While there is obviously scope for much further research, there is already sufficient evidence to indicate that analysis of sub-cultural influences can help us gain an improved understanding of consumer behaviour. The principal evidence at present pertains to the blacks and Hispanics, but the work is also being extended to other sub-cultures. Hirschman (1981), for example, using cohort analysis, has provided evidence suggesting that American Jews form a sufficiently cohesive community, based on the intermingling of culture and religion, for their behaviour as consumers to be analysed separately. Her findings – which were controlled for the possible effects of age, marital status, income, education and occupation – indicated that Jewish ethnicism was positively related to consumer information gathering, use and dissemination.

CONCLUSIONS

In Chapter 3 I showed how personal characteristics were important in giving rise to a variety of needs, and how these needs varied over the individual life cycle, and according to the sex of the individual. I also noted that needs appeared in some degree to be subject to environmental influences. From the point of view of the economist, however, who is interested in the behaviour of the individual as it affects the demand for goods and services, it is the individual's wants, or preferences, which are ultimately of greatest concern. Needs, such as that for drink, may often be satisfied in a variety of forms, and it is the individual's wants which determine the precise product or brand selected, and whether he will indeed consume more than the satisfying of his needs requires. Needs therefore give rise to wants – although the two terms are often used synonymously, despite being far from identical.

Just as the general environment in which a person lives may have some bearing on his needs, and changes in these needs over time, so too does the environment influence a person's wants. Since needs, however, are largely inborn – to the extent, for example, that we all have certain physiological needs – it is principally wants which are influenced by the environment, and changes in it. In the interest of simplicity, therefore – and because in reality we appear to have little knowledge of how the environment affects needs – our model concentrates on the effects of the environment on wants.

Figure 4.4 shows in somewhat greater detail than in Figure 2.1 the various links in our model, as I have constructed it so far. Following my discussions in the present chapter, we are now in a better position to put some flesh on the bare bones. The basis of individual wants is personal

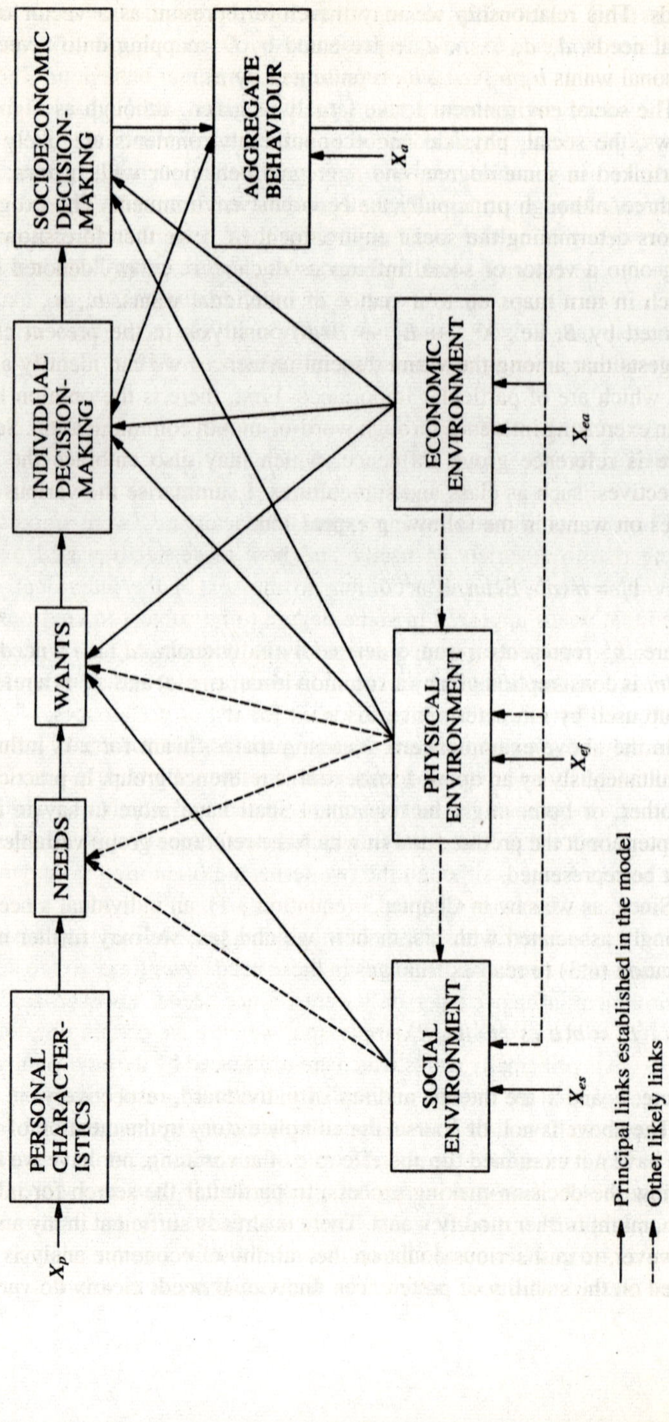

Figure 4.4 Needs, wants and environmental influences

needs. This relationship we may therefore represent as a vector of personal needs, $d_1, d_2, \ldots, d_n$, represented by D, mapping onto a vector of personal wants $b_1, b_2, \ldots, b_n$, represented by B.

The social environment I take largely as given, although as Figure 4.4 shows, the social, physical and economic environments are likely to be interlinked in some degree; and aggregate behaviour will, in turn, affect all three, although principally the economic environment. The exogenous factors determining the social environment (X_{es}) we therefore show mapping onto a vector of social influences $es_1, es_2, \ldots, es_n$, denoted by E_s, which in turn maps on to a vector of individual wants, $b_1, b_2, \ldots, b_n$, denoted by B, i.e., $X_{es} \rightarrow E_s \rightarrow B$. My analysis in the present chapter suggests that among the various social influences we can identify at least two which are of particular importance. First, there is the opinion leader, often exercising influence through word-of-mouth communication. Second, there is reference group influence, which may also embrace the larger collectives, such as class and sub-cultures. I summarise the various influences on wants in the following expression:

$$b_i^x = b\,(d_i^x, E_i^x lm, R_i^x) \tag{4.3}$$

where, b_i^x represents a want x desired by individual i, d_i^x is i's need for x, $E_i^x lm$ is consumption of x by an opinion leader (male) and R_i^x is a reference group used by i in determining his want for x.

In the above example I am assuming that i's want for x is influenced simultaneously by an opinion leader and a reference group. In practice, one or other, or both, might be relevant. I shall have more to say in a later chapter about the precise form in which the reference group variable might best be represented.

Since, as we saw in Chapter 3 (equation 3.1), an individual's needs are strongly associated with his, or her, age and sex, we may further modify equation (4.3) to read as follows:

$$b_i^x = b(a_i, s_i, E_i^x lm, R_i^x) \tag{4.4}$$

where, a_i and s_i are the age and sex of individual i, respectively.

The above is not, of course, the complete story in the creation of wants. We have not examined the possible role of advertising, nor have we looked at how the decision-making process, in particular the search for information, might further modify wants. There is already sufficient in my analysis, however, to cast serious doubt on the validity of economic analysis predicated on the stability of preferences. Individual needs clearly do vary over the life cycle, and they vary according to sex. Individuals therefore have strong time preferences for many products. In relatively short-term studies of individual behaviour, the age factor might possibly be discounted without too much loss, but in more aggregated studies, the effects of age changes on the demand for a product may be appreciable even in the short term. It is surely time, too, that economic theory recognised gender differences. There are certain products, such as lipstick, which few males make much use of, because they do not feel the need for them, and others, such as perfumes, which they may use, but not nearly so frequently as women – even if social conventions are changing. The income and price effects will therefore differ appreciably between the sexes.

The use of different opinion leaders and reference groups must also account for differences in individual behaviour which are too important to ignore. Not only might these sources of influence help explain why people at the same income level have different preferences, but they are also likely to play a part in explaining different reactions to price changes. Moreover, while there does appear to be some stability in the use of opinion leaders and reference groups, changes do occur. Throughout their lives, individuals move in and out of groups as they change friends, move to another part of the country, switch jobs, or simply age. In the aggregate, many such differences may cancel out or be submerged, but even at this level important changes occur. There does seem to be a tendency, for example, in many of the more advanced industrial countries, for class differences to decline, or at least to be less widely felt. Such differences may be difficult to catch statistically, but it is hoped that sufficient evidence has been produced in the present chapter to indicate that the effort would be worthwhile. What we can definitely say is that, from both theoretical and empirical standpoints, there are strong grounds for questioning any analysis resting on the constancy of tastes and preferences.

I will now go on in Chapters 5 and 6 to examine the influences of the physical environment and the economic environment on wants, and the constraints they place on decision-making.

5 The Physical Environment

Although most space is devoted in the present study to the social aspects of the general environment, since they have been grossly neglected by most economists, there is a growing recognition that economists have also failed lamentably to take adequate account of the physical environment in their deliberations. These sins of omission have given rise to heightened concern as the twentieth century has progressed and social and environmental problems have multiplied. In the environmental field, there were signs in the late 1960s and early 1970s that some economists at least were prepared to try and swim against the tide, and numerous articles and books were devoted to environmental economics. The Organisation for Economic Co-operation and Development (OECD), representing the more advanced industrial countries, even established an Environmental Directorate, and in 1971 went so far as to arrange a seminar on environmental economics, with the aims of clarifying the issues of greatest concern and formulating common goals among its member states. Unfortunately, these various initiatives did not have the desired impact – perhaps because much of the work undertaken stuck rigidly to the neo-classical tradition, encountering the many problems associated with that approach, to which I shall return below.

The nub of the problem is that the physical environment cannot just be treated as another input which can be precisely costed and used accordingly in economic calculations. In many instances there are, or ought to be, physical constraints which cannot be exceeded, and therefore limit economic output. Moreover, the physical environment, quite simply, is hideously complex, we do not possess full information about it, and it consequently gives rise to conditions of true uncertainty in much decision-making with an environmental input – and this means a large and rapidly growing proportion of all decision-making. In such circumstances, the adoption once more of (rather conservative) simplifying decision rules seems preferable, I shall maintain, to the often partial analysis which is at present so common.

I begin this Chapter with a look at the neo-classical approach to environmental issues, and some suggested alternatives. No attempt is made to treat the subject of environmental economics at any length, although I hope to draw attention to many of the key issues. Fuller discussions can be found in the studies by Mishan (1971), Daly (1972), Baumol and Oates (1975),

Pearce (1976), Dasgupta and Heal (1979), Fisher (1981) and in numerous other texts.

ALTERNATIVE APPROACHES TO ENVIRONMENTAL ISSUES

The neo-classical approach

Economic discussion of the environment has tended to concentrate on three principal issues: the treatment of externalities, in which the problem of pollution looms large; the appropriate policies for exhaustible resources, such as oil and mineral reserves; and how best to treat renewable resources, such as fish stocks and areas of woodland, which may become exhausted if over-exploited. The first of these issues has been presented in a variety of forms, but the basic principles are the same. In producing goods for consumption, firms may also produce harmful by-products, such as gases or poisonous chemicals. In the standard utility function only the benefits from the goods are considered: the harmful effects (or 'bads') are ignored. The environmental argument is that both sets of effects must be taken into account, otherwise we may be given a very misleading indication of the changes in social welfare associated with production. Stated formally, the conclusion is that each firm should pollute only up to the point where the marginal utility from so doing is just equal to the marginal social costs, or disutility. Another way of expressing this is to argue that firms ought to be taxed according to the cost of their pollution ('the polluter pays' principle). It is then possible to derive the tax required for a Pareto optimum.

A problem with the neo-classical analysis is that while simplified examples can be given of how a tax might be used to combat harmful environmental externalities, in practice the conditions for application of the theory often simply do not hold. In a typical case of river pollution, for example, there are likely to be many polluters, and the effects may be felt by whole communities, rather than by just one or two downstream users of water. In such instances, the information to enable proper costing of the full effects of pollution is most unlikely to be available. On perhaps the grandest scale of all, how are we to establish the cost of burning fossil fuels which release carbon dioxide into the atmosphere, thereby threatening the ozone layer?

Even in relatively simple cases of harmful externalities, organising a system to measure, monitor and administer taxes may be beyond the capabilities of the private sector, and the costs of the system may themselves be so high as to render it unusable.

The exploitation of a *non-renewable* resource is presented as being no different, in principle, from the constrained utility maximising problem of standard neo-classical economics, with consumption being spread over time in an optimum fashion. Unfortunately, such a model, while it provides a useful yardstick, suffers from a number of fatal weaknesses when attempts are made to apply it in the world as we find it. There is, first, the difficulty that, in practice, many of the relevant markets are very far from being competitive. Oil production, to take just one obvious example, is largely controlled by a cartel (the Organisation of Petroleum Exporting Countries – OPEC). Supplies of many other exhaustible commodities are controlled in various ways – for example copper, bauxite and natural diamonds – or there may be only a few producers. Economic theory suggests that in such circumstances output will be lower than under competitive conditions, and prices are likely to be higher. The evidence available tends to support these predictions.

The single biggest difficulty in exploiting non-renewable resources is, however, the uncertainty surrounding such operations. This is in part a consequence of the sheer complexity of the issues involved, and of the lack of full information on which to base calculations, but the uncertainty also has other origins. Fisher (1981) makes the point that in an Arrow-Debreu economy markets exist for every commodity at every date, and in every state of the world. Uncertainty will not therefore be a problem, since the resource owner will know future prices as well as current prices; but in the real economy forward markets do not exist for all commodities. In these cases resource owners must form their own expectations about future prices, and with so little firm information to go on, there is little doubt that, even in the relatively short term, they face conditions of true uncertainty – that is, circumstances which are so uncertain that it is impossible to calculate the probabilities of different outcomes. If the resource owners overestimate future prices, they will also be overestimating the supply of the resource they wish to make available later, and underestimate what they wish to provide now. The reverse, of course, is also true.

Future demand for a commodity, and therefore its price, may be affected by a whole host of factors, especially if, as is usually the case, the commodity is internationally traded. On the supply side, exploration tends to be a continuing activity, and new finds may be much greater or much less than expected. Improvements in technology also have a bearing on the supply side, since they may enable existing finds to be more fully exploited, or new finds to be exploited which would not previously have been worthwhile – commercially viable means of exploiting tar sands would enormously increase the recoverable reserves of oil, for example. Technological improvements also affect demand. Less of the commodity may be required per unit of output (as is the case with steel in the production of automobiles and ships) or competing commodities may be able to encroach on markets previously secure. Political uncertainties and the ever-present threat of war further complicate any attempt to take a forward view of markets. We should remember, too, that one of the principal conclusions from our examination of the influence of the social environment on individual needs and wants was that personal preferences are by no means as stable as economists assume. This may, of course, have implications for commodities – even if gold has until now retained much of its lustre, can we really be sure that, in an artificial market, 'diamonds are forever'?

One way of trying to cope with uncertainty is to use a higher discount rate, thereby depleting the non-renewable resource more quickly. This does not, however, overcome the problems referred to earlier, and it still leaves open the question of what the appropriate rate should be, which remains uncertain. Furthermore, Pearce (1976) makes the point that in theoretical models the discount rate employed is the *private* rate of discount, so that if the *social* discount rate differed from it, resources would not be optimally allocated – nor is the appropriate social discount rate something that can be determined with certainty.

Yet another problem relating to non-renewable resources is the appropriate treatment of future generations. Looking at the issue purely from the efficiency viewpoint, the assumption might be made that consumption by future generations is a public good to members of the present generation. There is plenty of evidence, however, as in the burning of fossil fuels and the treatment of rainforests, that the present generation cannot be relied upon fully to look after the interests of future generations. There is, in reality, not just an efficiency problem but also a very real problem of intergenerational equity. What is efficient from one point of view need not be equitable – as many commentators have indeed noted with regard to the Pareto optimum.

Turning, finally, to renewable resources, in certain respects the problem is simpler than that for non-renewable resources, since the time horizon may be shorter. The strategy will usually be to try and maintain a steady state which permits an optimal, sustainable yield. When, in the case of a resource like fish stocks, renewal can take place quite quickly (at least if the resource is not unduly depleted) past errors might be remedied quite quickly – although this is not true of resources like rainforests, where the maturation process extends over many years.

At the heart of the problems concerning many renewable resources – true again of fish stocks – is the existence of common property rights. Outside the confines of national waters, the seas are effectively in common ownership. In theory, rational individuals might be expected to co-operate and agree on fishing to maintain the desired steady state, but in practice – as we have seen in the North Sea off the coasts of Western Europe – there are benefits to be gained by those who take only a short-term view and are not influenced by thoughts of inter-generational equity. It is difficult, too, to preach inter-generational equity to peasants cutting down the rainforests of South America if it is the only way of ensuring the survival of the present generation. In such cases, the notion of equity has to be extended beyond the confines of the rainforest, but that will not be a message easily transmitted to the peasants. The answer, it seems, must be to offer them adequate compensation for their forbearance.

Given the numerous difficulties, theoretical and practical, with the neo-classical approach to environmental affairs, it is not at all surprising that those seeking better ways of combating threats to the environment have turned to governments for support. As we shall see below, this does not by any means solve all the problems, but there seems little doubt that governments have an important role to play.

The role of government

Where externalities are a problem, the neo-classical system may admit a role for government if the solution seems to require the imposition of taxes, say on polluters, or the provision of subsidies. The government's role is a very passive one, however, since it does only what is necessary to facilitate the maximisation of profits, or utility. Given that, in practice, we are generally quite unable to calculate the Pigovian tax or subsidy levels – we simply do not in most instances have the necessary information – various writers have suggested a more active role for government. Baumol and Oates (1971) have proposed a formal 'environmental pricing and standards procedure' which, while not aspiring to anything like an optimal allocation of resources, does posses some important optimising properties.

The procedure proposed by Baumol and Oates entails the selection of 'somewhat arbitrary' standards for an acceptable environment. The standards are only 'somewhat arbitrary', insofar as they would be based on the best available evidence concerning such matters as the effects of unclean air on health, of polluted water on fish, or of harmful noise levels on hearing. In the first of these, maximum levels of sulphur dioxide or lead in the atmosphere might be set; in the second, minimum levels of oxygen could be required, and in the third a maximum number of decibels insisted upon. The imposition of such standards would be designed to achieve a 'reasonable quality of life'. The standards need not be set for all time, but rather adjusted in the light of new evidence and changing circumstances.

Baumol and Oates were at pains to emphasise that the price system (in the form of taxes) could still function under their proposals, and that the use of unit taxes (or subsidies) to achieve specified quality standards would at least satisfy one important property of optimisation: that it would be the least-cost method of achieving the set standards. In response to a unit tax on its emission of smoke, for example, a cost-minimising firm would cut back on the emissions until the marginal cost of a further reduction in smoke was just equal to the tax. Furthermore, since all firms in the area would be subject to the same tax, the marginal cost of reducing smoke emissions would be equalised across all activities. Finally, Baumol and Oates stressed the practicality of their approach. The standards set might not be optimal but they would be clear, and for the most part easily monitored and policed.

In practice, environmental policy in those countries where it exists has largely been based on laying down standards, much along the lines recommended by Baumol and Oates. In effect, in the absence of any practical means of ensuring optimum outcomes, we are for the most part obliged to seek government intervention; and governments in the face of the complexities involved, the lack of information and all the uncertainties are in turn forced to resort to a variety of *rules*. These rules are 'somewhat arbitrary', but for the most part draw upon the latest scientific information available. Increasingly, too, rules are being adopted internationally, under the auspices of the United Nations, and, in many European countries, in response to pressure exerted by the European Community. There is a growing recognition that externalities are often international in scale, as when large waterways such as the Rhine and the Danube flow through a number of countries.

Government rules are by no means confined to externalities like pollution. The Norwegian government, for example, has regulated the rate of exploitation of its non-renewable resources of oil and gas in the North Sea; and OPEC members have done the same, acting as a cartel. Members of the European Community have also acted jointly to try and preserve fish stocks in the North Sea. The policy of setting quotas and minimum mesh sizes for fishing nets has been pursued against bitter opposition from fishermen, who, while recognising the need to conserve a vital renewable resource, argue that in the short term the fishing limits threaten to put them out of business. Many crews, it seems, have invested in expensive modern fishing boats with the help of bank loans, and can only hope to repay these loans if they maintain the high levels of fishing catches to which they have become accustomed. It is not at all clear how in such competitive circumstances renewal of resources could be ensured without government intervention and the imposition of rules and regulations – even with government intervention, via the European Community, the political pressures may be such as to force the setting of catch levels too high for steady state renewal.

Governments (local and national) have been among the principal supporters of a relatively new technique which draws its inspiration from the potential Pareto improvement rule of neo-classical economics, and tries to overcome some of the practical difficulties which arise in implementation. This is the so-called cost-benefit analysis (CBA). In its pure form it relies for its measurement techniques on consumer surplus theory, and for its aggregate decision rules on Kaldor-Hicks compensation tests (see Pearce, 1976). By no means all applications of CBA keep to these rules, however. Even where they do, CBA cannot hope to be more than a partial solution, since familiar problems keep re-surfacing: in practice we just do not have all the information required to determine an optimum outcome; and since in many situations there are gains as well as losses, the need for interpersonal comparisons of utility arises.

A recent example of CBA from the United Kingdom illustrates the sorts of problems which arise. A study for the Forestry Commission of the environmental effects of afforestation recommended planting conifers because they were economically viable, whereas native broad-leaved woodlands were not. The findings, which horrified conservationists, were reached by pricing the timber, recreation and carbon-fixing values of each type of forest (carbon-dioxide gas apparently being implicated in the threat of global warming) and judging the benefits against land values. Left out of the analysis, unfortunately, were the conservation values of the landscape and the animal wildlife which would disappear (conifers being much criticised for their detrimental effects on the landscape and the manner in which their dense coverage is unsuitable for many kinds of wildlife). These aspects essential to a comprehensive CBA were found to be 'too difficult to value'. Findings based upon such partial analysis may be the best that can be achieved in the circumstances, but we should be clear about the very real danger that they might lead to decisions which would conflict with those taken had a full analysis been feasible. At best, therefore, the use of CBA seems advisable only in those cases where there is the possibility of reaching reasonably accurate values for all the major costs and benefits involved. This leaves many instances where governments will have to fall back on 'somewhat arbitrary' rules.

IS THERE A CONFLICT BETWEEN GROWTH AND THE ENVIRONMENT?

One of the central issues which has arisen in the field of environmental economics is whether continued economic growth is consistent with the safeguarding of the environment. Mishan (1971) is often credited with highlighting the growing costs of economic growth, in the form, for example, of harmful externalities. His general conclusion was, 'that the continued pursuit of economic growth by western societies is more likely on balance to reduce rather than increase social welfare'. He gave weight to his argument by enumerating a set of conditions which, if met, would ensure a *positive* relation between economic growth and welfare:

1. That the economy be highly competitive in structure in all its branches, or else so organised that in all sectors the outputs of goods are such that their prices tend to equal their corresponding marginal costs (these conditions, he stressed, are sufficient, though *not* necessary).
2. That all the measurable effects on other people or firms arising in the production and use of any good – other than those effects which already register on the market mechanism in the form of alterations in product and factor prices – be brought into the cost calculus.
3. That in increasing *per capita* output over time the process of economic growth does not bring about a less equitable distribution of income.
4. That the consuming public be fully conversant with the comparative qualities and performances of all new goods coming on to the market.
5. That the public, regarded as producers, become no worse off in adapting themselves to new techniques of production.
6. That the so-called relative income hypothesis does not hold; or, less stringently, that an overall increase in real income *per capita* will have more than negligible effects in making some people feel better off without making others feel worse off.
7. That the welfare experienced by men from sources other than goods produced by the economic system is small enough to be neglected.

Unsurprisingly, Mishan maintained that none of the conditions was likely to be met in today's wealthy societies.

Beckerman (1972) has been one of the severest critics of the anti-growth school. He argues that, implicit in the notion that there is a conflict between economic growth and the environment is the belief that there is something in the nature of a fixed technical relationship between the rate of growth and the degree of 'pollution' (standing for all the 'bads' associated with growth). If this were so, it would then be possible to select an optimum rate of economic growth (for some, such as Daly, 1972, it would be zero growth) determined by the usual marginal conditions, i.e., where the technical trade-off line was tangential to the indifference curve linking pollution and the growth rate. Beckerman maintains that there is no evidence to support the existence of a technical relationship between growth and pollution – or that such a relationship, even if it were to exist, would be rigidly fixed and impervious to remedial action.

Beckerman goes so far as to claim that it is even possible to stand the argument on its head and maintain that economic growth, because it is associated with technological progress, such as improved heating systems, might result in less pollution. Policies to reduce pollution, since they might well stimulate new investment, could even serve to accelerate growth. Growth, of course, also provides the resources to finance pollution control, although such use would probably have to be a conscious act of policy.

Closely linked with the technological argument is the working of the price mechanism, which, even if it does not adequately catch all the costs of pollution, can be expected to come into play as resources diminish. As Pearce (1976) points out, the role of the price mechanism is often neglected by the critics of growth. When raw materials become unduly expensive, the search for replacements, or more efficient means of using existing materials, will be likely to stimulate technological advances. Even pollution, if it became too bad, might be expected to generate growing opposition – as indeed we have seen in the past in respect of atmospheric pollution in cities, and are now seeing in the case of rivers and beaches – and result in moves to charge the cost of remedial action to polluters. Rising prices associated with economic growth therefore constitute one of the main constraints which the physical environment will impose on decision makers when considering alternative courses of action.

Given the complexities of the issue, the existence of true uncertainties, and therefore our inability to reach definitive conclusions, the inevitable outcome, it seems, will be increasing resort to decision-making rules which at least appear to point in the right direction. Beckerman (1972) is prepared to make at least two concessions to the environmental lobby. First, he accepts that the Pigovian assumption that what contributes to economic welfare also contributes to human welfare in general is less convincing now that the 'most pressing of conventional needs' (in our terminology the 'lower order needs', it would seem) have been satisfied – at best true only of the more advanced industrial countries, and probably not true even in them. Second, Beckerman accepts that the failures of the market system due to externalities have become increasingly obvious.

Implicit in Beckerman's concessions is the need to develop better means of measuring the costs of economic growth, and probably also the need to devise broader measures of general welfare. For a time it did in fact seem that progress was being made in these directions. Programmes for the development of social indicators were started, for example at the OECD, and under the auspices of the Social Science Research Council (as it then was) in the United Kingdom, but these fell victim to changing sentiment in the late 1970s and 1980s, when opinion swung in favour of the operation of free markets. There is a need now to appreciate that these matters are by no means peripheral: rather they are essential to informed decision-making.

CONCLUSIONS

My brief look at the physical environment is sufficient, it is hoped, to bring out a number of points relevant to my study. First, conventional neo-classical economic analysis, while it may provide some theoretical guidance on how to take decisions in matters concerning the environment, in practice cannot provide the answers needed. Most practical problems are, quite simply, too complex, requiring in most instances information essential to decision-making which just is not available. Conclusions may be reached by the use of techniques such as cost-benefit analysis, but where such analysis is of a partial nature, as it usually is, there is no assurance that the recommendations will lead to the most beneficial effects on the general welfare. The best that can probably be hoped for in most instances is the adoption of rules which seem to point in the right direction, and which take account of the best scientific information available.

The lack of adequate information makes informed discussion of the economic growth versus the environment issue well nigh impossible, but the potential dangers are too important to be discounted altogether. At the very least, there is a need to take account, so far as is practicable, of all externalities, and to develop better measures of economic, and the general, welfare than can be provided by existing systems of national income and expenditure accounts. We ought also to play safe if there is any doubt about the rate at which renewable resources should be exploited – as in the case of fishing for certain types of whale – or when it is feared that the rate of depletion of non-renewable resources might be unduly rapid.

It follows from the above that economic decision-making is (or ought to be) subject to environmental constraints. The direct constraints are those imposed by the availability of physical resources and the state of technology. Linked to these, and acting indirectly, is the constraint exercised by the price mechanism. If not distorted artificially, the latter will often provide early warning of environmental pressures, and help bring about the economic and technological changes essential to the preservation of the environment. Ultimately, however, given all the uncertainties and inadequacies, we are also likely to be dependent on governments to intervene and impose constraints, in the form of rules, where these seem essential to our survival.

6 The Economic Environment

[illegible]

OBJECTIVE ASPECTS

[illegible]

6 The Economic Environment

The principal features of the economic environment will doubtless be familiar to most readers, and I shall not therefore dwell on them at any length. I shall, however, be drawing attention to those features which have received inadequate attention from economists, usually, it seems, because they are believed to fall outside the customary remit of economics. Such outdated notions of subject boundaries are gradually crumbling, but the process still has some way to go.

The economic environment divides into objective factors, upon which economists place greater stress, and subjective factors, among which expectations are of especial importance. It is a matter of some interest, and wonderment, that whereas many economists have strenuously upheld the need to retain what is seen as the purity of economics, they have been prepared to admit the subjective world when necessary. Expectations are in a different category altogether from the standard economic variables, such as incomes, prices and output. Expectations are subjective in nature (as indeed is the notion of utility), even if they have their links with the objective world – two individuals faced with the same objective situation may form different expectations. They have nevertheless become part of the normal economic repertoire, no doubt because it was appreciated that they were simply too important to be left out. Economics bereft of expectations is unthinkable. What is difficult to understand, however, is why the subjective should be admitted in the form of expectations, yet so vigorously resisted when it is proposed that other psychological concepts should also be incorporated in economic analysis.

OBJECTIVE ASPECTS

The objective factors in the economic environment at any given time are for the most part the consequences of decisions taken earlier, both by individuals on their own behalf and by those participating in socioeconomic decision-making units. We can discuss these objective factors under the customary headings of the goods markets, the money, or financial, markets and the labour markets. Within the goods markets there is a price structure which, according to economic analysis, is determined by the supply of and demand for individual goods, although, as we shall see later, it is also determined to a significant extent by the exercise of decision rules by businessmen.

In the financial markets, the widespread use of decision rules is again evident. It might be assumed that government decisions about the money supply and budget revenue and expenditure are taken in accordance with some master maximising plan, but in reality complexity, lack of information and true uncertainty frequently oblige governments to resort to simplifying decision rules. Governments must also, to some degree at least, respond to the wishes of voters, who have their own needs and wants, and to the wishes of interest groups, such as employers and trade unions. Government behaviour, and its consequences for the economic environment, are therefore in some measure a response to influences brought to bear by other parts of the socioeconomic system. The customary practice of treating government as exogenous to the economic system may be convenient for the purposes of economic analysis, but it is unrealistic, and glosses over much that is of interest to economists.

While government actions have powerful effects on the state of the financial markets, private sector decisions on such matters as saving and borrowing also serve, of course, to determine the level and structure of interest rates. Supply and demand are again to the fore in explaining the cost and availability of funds, but if we attempt to look behind the supply and demand schedules, psychological influences are almost always present. The demand for money for precautionary purposes, for example, or for the purchases of assets, may depend on aspects of personality, such as how averse a person is to taking risks. Swings in consumer sentiment also seem to affect the readiness of consumers to borrow.

In the labour market, the supply of labour, and its quality in terms of skills and training, are further important ingredients of the economic environment. So too is the cost of this labour – both the general level of wages and salaries and their structure across industries, occupations and regions. The institutional aspects are touched upon below.

An important achievement in economics has been to bring out the significance of different market structures for the pricing, output and other strategic decisions of firms. An understanding of the significance of these differences has been important not just for businessmen but for governments. Much less effort has gone into assessing the effects of different institutional arrangements on economic affairs. A significant issue in labour markets, for example, is the question of whether industrial unions are more conducive to improved economic performance than general unions. Another issue of some importance is whether governments should intervene in labour markets, and if so, in what form.

We have also had numerous demonstrations in recent years of the importance of the regulatory framework governing economic affairs in a country. Changes in beliefs about the efficiency of free markets have resulted in changes in attitudes towards regulation in countries such as the US and the UK. The 1980s was in large measure a decade of de-regulation in these countries. The results, unfortunately, did not always live up to the expectations of the proponents of de-regulation. Relaxation of the activities of the Savings and Loan Associations in the US, for example, appear to have been instrumental in facilitating the excessive lending which led to many of these institutions becoming insolvent. In the United Kingdom, relaxation of regulations governing banks and building societies helped fuel the excessive growth of mortgage and consumer lending in the late 1980s. Had the possible consequences of all these changes in regulations been better appreciated, much greater caution would have been shown, and much pain and sorrow avoided.

The principal features of the economic environment, as outlined in the examples above, are crucial to decision-making, since they both help determine the scope of the opportunities available to decision makers and the constraints within which they must work. If we take factor inputs, for example, the supply of labour, the availability of land and the size of the capital stock – and the effectiveness with which these are all combined – these limit the output of goods and services produced in a country within any given time period. The rewards to factors of production, on the other hand, provide both the opportunities for the satisfaction of needs and wants and place limits on the extent to which needs and wants may be gratified.

SUBJECTIVE ASPECTS

While objective factors are of great importance in the economic environment, we should by no means neglect the subjective, which on occasions clearly dominate, as in times of major crisis. The subjective and objective are likely, of course, to be linked. Expectations, for example, do not change in a vacuum. As interest rates fall, perhaps in response to a decision by government to increase the money supply, business sentiment and the expectations of consumers and businessmen about the future may become more buoyant and optimistic. The link between the change in the objective environment and the change in sentiment and expectations need not, however, be uniform. A change in business sentiment may feed on itself. Businessmen are always talking to each other, and as more become optimistic, that may in itself be a cause of still greater optimism. Subjective factors may then begin to dominate. In effect, subjective factors may begin to play a role of their own, acting as intervening variables between the original objective change and the subsequent actions of individuals.

It seems true to say that the field of expectations formation and change has not been a central concern for psychologists in the way it has been for economists. Whereas the latter have treated expectations in a very mechanistic and prescriptive manner, as with adaptive expectations and, more recently, rational expectations, psychologists have tended towards greater flexibility. Newcomb (1972) notes the tendency of psychologists to distinguish between *expectancy* and *expectation*. Among social psychologists 'expectancy' seems, in general, to stress a psychological *state*, whereas 'expectation' commonly refers to the *content* of what is expected. On the question of *how* the two terms are used, Newcomb found that nearly all usage fitted fairly well into two broad classes: intrapersonal and social. In the case of the former (usually concerning expectancy) the emphasis is on psychological states of 'set', involving some sort of preparatory adjustment to anticipated events or situations – among examples of other specific uses of the expectancy concept Newcomb included 'subjectively expected utility'. Social influences were associated, amongst other things, with learning the expectations of a society – as part of its culture. Social structure included patterns of action bound by rules of expectations. Katona (1960), as Newcomb noted, also viewed expectations as in important ways the outcomes of group influences – which could be exerted indirectly as well as by direct interaction.

Expectations, I conclude, originate in a variety of environmental influences – economic, social and physical – and appear also to be subject to differences in personal characteristics. Quite how all these factors come together to determine expectations, and changes in them, is a matter, however, about which we as yet appear to have little knowledge. Given the importance of expectations, it is surprising just how little basic research has been undertaken in the field. The consequence for my present study is that, while recognising the key role of expectations for both individual and socioeconomic decision-making, this important variable does not feature prominently in our analysis.

The lack of an adequate theory of expectations has not precluded empirical testing of a variety of anticipatory variables. Surveys of consumers' and businessmen's intentions with respect to consumer spending, investment, housing starts, sales, prices and employment, etc., are now commonplace, and as data have accumulated over time have become a feature of most econometric models of national economies. Lack of a proper theoretical base has meant, however, that the reasons for including some indicators are not always clear, other than their apparent contribution to explaining past movements in dependent variables. Anticipatory variables are often treated simply as auxiliary variables in standard behavioural equations; but, as I noted earlier, we need also to know what factors, in turn, determine anticipations.

A further problem is that anticipatory variables have been shown to be very volatile, and are therefore really only suitable for short-term predictions stretching at most one year ahead – and in most instances remaining firm probably only three to six months ahead (see, for example, the discussion by Adams and Klein, 1972, of experience with the Wharton Model in the US).

Most progress in developing psychological explanations of expectations, and changes in expectations, has been in the consumer field. An early pioneer was Katona (1951, 1960, 1975 and numerous other texts) working principally with attitudinal variables. It is probably fair to say that, while this work has not contributed greatly to the explanatory powers of formal models at the macro-level (Adams and Klein, 1972) Katona's survey approach – which is still being developed – has nevertheless proved to be a useful complement to econometric models. Survey work facilitates more in-depth analysis of the reasons for changes in consumer behaviour than can be undertaken with econometric models, and is especially useful when new circumstances emerge which mark a major departure from the past.

Although I have not made great play of anticipatory variables in my analysis in the present study, many of the social influences bearing on consumers, upon which Katona and others have laid such great stress, have been caught by my analysis of the effects of the social environment. The social, physical and economic environments are all strongly interlinked within the general environment, and although it is helpful for many purposes to study them separately, in practice they merge imperceptibly with each other, forming a complex, dynamic mosaic.

Part III
Individual Decision-Making

7 The Individual Decision-Making Process

In previous chapters I have examined the importance of personal characteristics and the influences on individuals of the general environment within which they live. During much of these discussions individuals have assumed a rather passive role, but real life is characterised by the need for individuals to be constantly active in taking decisions. My previous discussions, I hope to show, will provide us with a better understanding of the nature of many of the key decisions which have to be taken. In Part three I will bring the whole issue of personal decision-making to centre stage. We cannot hope, it must be stressed, to cover all potentially relevant aspects of the voluminous work on decision-making which has appeared in recent decades. Instead, I shall concentrate on those aspects which seem most useful to our purposes. This will mean cutting a number of corners, and omitting material which some readers might consider of crucial relevance, but the approach adopted here can always be supplemented and extended by those who find the general approach useful.

I will begin by taking a preliminary look at the goals which individuals pursue in the light of my analysis of personal characteristics and the role of the general environment.

THE INDIVIDUAL'S GOALS: A PRELIMINARY LOOK

In Chapters 3, 4 and 6 I analysed the principal factors determining wants. In essence, the personal characteristics of individuals give rise to needs, many of which follow a pattern over the individual life cycle. It is these needs which in turn give rise to wants, in association with strong environmental influences. I summarised these determinants of wants in equation (4.4), which showed that the age and sex of the individual, opinion leaders and reference groups all had key roles to play. The problem facing the individual is how best to satisfy the vector of wants, represented by B, given that certain constraints act on the individual. In particular, for most people there is a real income constraint, since his/her financial resources will be limited, and constraints of time and physical availability may also apply.

It is not just an individual's *absolute* income which influences his/her behaviour, but also that person's *relative* income. It was stressed in Baxter (1988) that *differences* in incomes are often crucial in determining the choice of goods available to the individual. It is not surprising, therefore, that individuals are very conscious of, and attach considerable importance to, differences in absolute incomes. This is likely to be especially so in the case of any difference between a person's pay and the pay of those with whom he habitually compares himself, i.e., his reference group(s). The satisfaction (or utility) which a person is obliged to forego because of his lower income (and therefore the narrower choice of goods available) might be quite disproportionate to the difference in income. The importance of relative income can be demonstrated still more forcefully by reference to what Hirsch (1977) called 'positional goods', i.e., goods which, 'are either scarce in some absolute or socially imposed sense or subject to congestion or crowding through more intensive use' – one example, in countries where land is scarce, and therefore expensive, being a house with a garden.

Wants comprise, as it were, the demand side of our analysis. On the supply side we have 'satisfiers' which, when obtained by the individual, are capable of extinguishing, or satisfying, a want – even if often only temporarily. In such instances the satisfied want will no longer motivate the individual to action.

As a general rule, goods purchased by individuals will not be synonymous with satisfiers, since most goods will be able to satisfy more than one want. An item of food, for example, will not only have nutritional value, it will probably also have taste, and possibly colour, all of which may contribute towards satisfying a person's total wants for food. In this important respect our analysis, as was pointed out in Baxter (1988), is akin to that of Lancaster (1966, 1971) with his emphasis on the characteristics of goods.[1]

In order to meet his wants, the goal of the individual will be to purchase matching satisfiers – some satisfiers may, however, derive from an investment of time as well as, or instead of, money, as Michael and Becker (1973) have demonstrated. In standard consumer theory, the problem is seen simply as one of maximising utility from consumption of goods, subject to an income (and time) constraint. In recent years, however, a good deal of new work, often by psychologists and others working outside the mainstream of economics (see for example, Shackle, 1972), has cast further doubts on the universal applicability of the maximising approach of the standard economic theory of decision-making, and attempted to develop alternative approaches which I shall be looking at below.

It has to be stressed that even within the economics field alone the literature on decision-making is voluminous, and it is not the intention here to try and survey it all – excellent surveys are, in any case, already available, for example that of Schoemaker (1982) on which I draw – but it is necessary at least to identify its principal features and weaknesses, in order to contrast them with the 'behavioural' approaches which I will also examine.

MODELS OF DECISION-MAKING

Much of consumer demand theory in economics assumes conditions of *certainty*. The consumer maximises his utility, within an income constraint, without having to worry about the risk or uncertainty[2] which in reality surround many decisions. Growing interest in decision-making has, however, now shifted the emphasis of theory increasingly towards situations in which risk and uncertainty are dominant considerations. In economics the foremost paradigm is expected utility theory, and I start by looking briefly at this theory. I shall focus in particular on the telling criticisms which have been made of the theory in recent years, and which have given rise to a wide ranging search for alternatives.

The expected utility model

Initially, expected utility theory was concerned to facilitate choice by enabling comparisons to be made between the alternative monetary values associated with decisions. The principle is usually illustrated with examples taken from gambling, including the renowned 'St Petersburg paradox'. The paradox may be explained in terms of a game in which a 'fair' coin is tossed until it comes down heads. If this occurs on the *n*th occasion, and the player receives 2^n dollars, the game could then be continued with numerous possible outcomes. The interesting question is, how much would individuals be prepared to pay to participate in such a gamble, since the game would pay off handsomely if continued? The player has a probability of $\frac{1}{2}$ of winning \$2, $\frac{1}{4}$ of winning \$4, $\frac{1}{8}$ of winning \$8, and so on for an infinite number of tosses of the coin, with an expected value of infinity. In practice, the evidence indicated that players would only be prepared to pay between \$2 and \$4 to participate in the gamble, despite the expectation of infinite gain.

The expected monetary value (*EV*) of a gamble we may represent as:

$$EV = \Sigma_i p_i x_i \qquad (7.1)$$

where p_i represents the probability of the *i*th outcome and x_i is the associated gain or loss.

In an effort to explain the St Petersburg paradox, Bernoulli (1954) advanced the proposition that what people maximise is not the expected monetary value but expected utility (*EU*). The psychological value of money to an individual, he maintained, did not increase in proportion to the sum of that money. His suggested function therefore took a logarithmic form, linking diminishing utility to increasing quantities of money. He then went on to show that with such a function the total utility obtainable was finite. Bernoulli's approach we may represent as

$$EU = \sum_i p_i \, u(x_i) \qquad (7.2)$$

where *EU* is the expected utility and $u(x_i)$ now becomes the utility of outcome *i*.

Another development of the expected utility model was achieved by von Neumann and Morgenstern (1947). Adopting an axiomatic approach, they were able to demonstrate that with the use of only a few basic axioms which might be said to describe rational behaviour on the part of individuals – for example, the existence of a clear set of risk preferences for each individual, and transitivity between these preferences – then the maximisation of expected utility could be shown to be 'rational' behaviour. Moreover, this was shown to hold true not only for a series of decisions, such as in the examples used earlier, but also for a single decision.

In the von Neumann and Morgenstern model of expected utility the assumption is made that *objective*, or objectively measured, probabilities of an event occurring are available to the individual in making decisions. Ramsey (1931), de Finetti (1937), Edwards (1954, 1955), Savage (1954) and others have, however, developed versions of the *EU* model in which probabilities are subjective, based upon *degrees of belief* about the likelihood of an event. Simultaneous estimation of utility and probability have been achieved using decision-makers' revealed preferences. The flexibility of the expected utility approach has made it a popular research tool, but as we shall see below, its validity has increasingly been called in question.

In an extensive review of the empirical evidence, Schoemaker (1982) highlighted a long catalogue of deficiencies in the *EU* approach (other surveys of the evidence can be found in Ford, 1987, and Machina, 1987), and in what follows I draw heavily on this study. Looking first at the basic axioms on which the theory rests, he showed, for example, that the requirement for stable preferences does not appear to be satisfied – Mosteller and Nogee (1951) found that repeated measures of the preferences of subjects did not always yield the same answers. In another study, Tversky (1969) found violations of the transitivity axiom – that if A is preferred to B and B to C, then A must be preferred to C – in its stochastic form. Coombs (1975) also found that the 'in betweenness axiom' – that a lottery offering outcomes A and B should have an attractiveness level intermediate to those of A and B separately – only held true with regard to about one-half of the subjects who participated in his study.

The *EU* theory axiom which assumes invariance of preference between certainty and risk, other things being equal, has also been called in question. Following in the same vein as Maurice Allais's (1953) well-known paradox, Kahneman and Tversky (1979) showed that people attach undue weight to outcomes that are considered certain, relative to outcomes which are merely probable – a phenomenon which they called the 'certainty effect'. When negative prospects were introduced by reversing the signs of the outcomes, so that gains were replaced by losses, the preference between negative prospects was found to be the mirror image of the preference between positive prospects – hence the term 'reflection effect' which they applied to it. The implication is that risk aversion in the positive domain is accompanied by risk seeking in the negative domain – a finding also confirmed by other researchers.

Still further evidence of the violation of the *EU* axioms has been provided by Maya Bar-Hillel (1973) who in experiments based on withdrawals of marbles from a bag found that people tended to overestimate the probability of conjunctive events and to underestimate the probability of disjunctive events.

It might be objected that the above evidence of violation of the expected utility axioms is based on hypothetical situations, or is unrepresentative of decision-making in the real world, but the evidence available from field studies is no more supportive of the *EU* model. Quite a number of these concern the insurance cover taken out by individuals. Kunreuther *et al.* (1978) found, for example, that in spite of US government subsidies of up to 90 per cent for flood insurance, the majority of eligible home owners in areas subject to flooding were uninsured.

Further signs of weaknesses in the expected utility approach are provided by solid evidence that when faced with the necessity of making decisions under conditions of uncertainty, individuals resort to a variety of heuristics, or rules of thumb, to guide them. Researchers such as Kahneman, Tversky and Slovic have amassed a good deal of reliable evidence not only that such heuristics are widely used, but that they lead to biases in decision-making. Such findings again raise serious doubts about the 'rational', maximising man at the centre of the expected utility model. I shall be looking at the evidence at greater length when I discuss the use of decision rules in a later section.

Although brief, the above discussion is sufficient to highlight key weaknesses in the expected utility model. Given the strength of the evidence against it, one can but wonder at the hold which the model still exercises over academic and other professional circles. The answer lies, perhaps, in Coombs' (1980) conclusion: 'A theory that provides good approximations, even though it is wrong in principle, is going to be used until a more useful theory comes along'.

I will now turn to another category of models which holds out some real hope of overtaking the expected utility approach. This work draws heavily on the field of psychology, and it is interesting, as Slovic *et al.* (1988) have noted, that some of the most recent extensions of the *EU* approach, such as Regret Theory (Bell, 1982, and Loomes and Sugden, 1982) and Prospect Theory (Kahneman and Tversky, 1979) have formed part of a trend towards introducing more psychological considerations into the *EU* model. A similar tendency is apparent in other work on decision-making under uncertainty (e.g. Shackle, 1952, Ford, 1983, 1987 and 1991).

Process, or behavioural, models of decision-making

The expected utility model is often described as a *normative* model, since, in common with neoclassical economics, it assumes that maximising utility is the only 'rational' goal of the decision maker. Moreover, given the decision maker's tastes and preferences, it shows how that goal should be attained . Expected utility theory is also sometimes referred to as a *descriptive* theory, in that it attempts to model the decision process underlying risky choice. The modelling of decision processes in *EU* models is, however, of a much more limited nature than that undertaken in what are usually referred to as *process* (or sometimes *behavioural*) theories of decision-making. At the level of the individual, process theories are grounded in psychology, and analyse the successive steps, often in great detail, of the decision-making process. At the level of the group, or the organisation, which I will leave until later chapters, the contributing disciplines are much more numerous, as one might expect, embracing not only psychological (principally social psychological) but also sociological, political, administrative and other concepts and ideas.

At this point it is helpful to introduce certain important distinctions between the types of choice problems which face an individual. In theoretical decisions and in applied research work, the greatest emphasis is placed upon an analysis of *complex* decision-making. Under this heading would fall what is often referred to as 'extensive problem solving' (EPS) in the consumer behaviour field – see Howard and Sheth (1969) and Howard (1974). In such decision-making there are numerous stages in the decision-making process, and each stage may be analysed in some depth. Such decision-making also requires the availability of a great deal of information – sought from external sources as well as internal (stored in the mind) – and numerous alternatives are likely to be available for choice.

At the other extreme from complex decision-making lies *simple* decision-making, often of a routine or habitual nature. In the simple case it is usually assumed that the succeeding stages of complex decision-making are gone through, but very quickly, or they may be telescoped or represented in a reduced form. Little information is likely to be required (especially from external sources) and there will generally be few alternatives to consider.

Between the two extremes is sometimes interposed an intermediate form of decision-making in which the problems of choice are neither simple nor complex. But since the lines of demarcation are in any case difficult to draw, and there is in practice likely to be a continuum of degrees of complexity, I shall concentrate principally on simple and complex problems.

Complex decision-making

The dominant influence in the study of the process of complex decision-making has been the rapidly developing field of cognitive psychology. It is this approach which has placed stress upon the individual as a thinking person, not only reacting to external stimuli but approaching problems in a logical fashion, searching for additional information when necessary, and assessing the outcomes of decisions once taken. A crucial feature of this cognitive approach is that it recognises the mental limitations of individuals. They may therefore have to recast problems in a simplifying way which enables them to take a decision, even if not necessarily in accordance with the maximising tenets of standard economic theory.

Complex process theories of individual behaviour have been developed in the consumer behaviour field. One of the models most used is that of Engel-Kollat-Blackwell (EKB), or Engel-Blackwell-Miniard (1990) in its most recent form. Other popular models, each with something different to contribute, are those of Howard and Sheth (1969) and Nicosia (1966). The EKB model is reproduced in Figure 7.1. It breaks down the decision-making process into four principal stages.

The first stage is referred to as 'need recognition', which in turn has three principal determinants: individual differences (or, as I have described them in the present study, personal characteristics), environmental influences and information stored in memory. The second stage is the search for information relevant to the decision, which may be sought from internal (memory) sources or external sources. In this stage, environmental influences and individual differences may again play some part. Once the relevant information has been collected and processed we enter the third stage, in which there is an evaluation of the alternatives available to the individual. At this stage, the attributes of different products are likely to be weighed, and judgemental rules may be brought into play. The final stage is the act of purchase and further evaluation, this time of the outcome, leading either to satisfaction or dissatisfaction.

A problem with consumer behaviour models is that some of the boxes shown in complex flow charts are really more in the nature of 'black boxes', since knowledge about them and the parts they play in decision-making is very limited. Knowledge about the nature of the links between many of the boxes is often even scantier, and the links not therefore adequately specified. Nevertheless, empirical tests of some of the models have been undertaken. The Howard-Sheth model, for example, was tested by Farley and Ring (1974) and Farley and Lehmann (1977) with encouraging results.

A further difficulty with complex models of decision processes, such as those in the consumer behaviour field, is that they still seem to imply an ability on the part of each individual to process large volumes of information, even if not on the comprehensive scale of the expected utility model. Simon's (1957) criticism of such an assumption, and his claim that individuals are subject to bounded rationality, remains valid, and a good deal of emphasis in recent years has therefore been placed upon the need to try and determine just how *in practice* individuals make choices. Evidence has steadily accumulated that individuals do in fact try to simplify complex decision-making problems by adopting *decision rules*. Rather in the same vein as the individual faced by an enormous volume of information, we are therefore now going to try and achieve our own goals by simplifying our tasks, and concentrating our attention principally on these decision rules, in the hope that they will provide us with sufficient guidance on individual decision-making for our own purposes. An early writer who stressed the importance of simplification to decision-making was Carter (1953).

Figure 7.1 A complete model of consumer behaviour

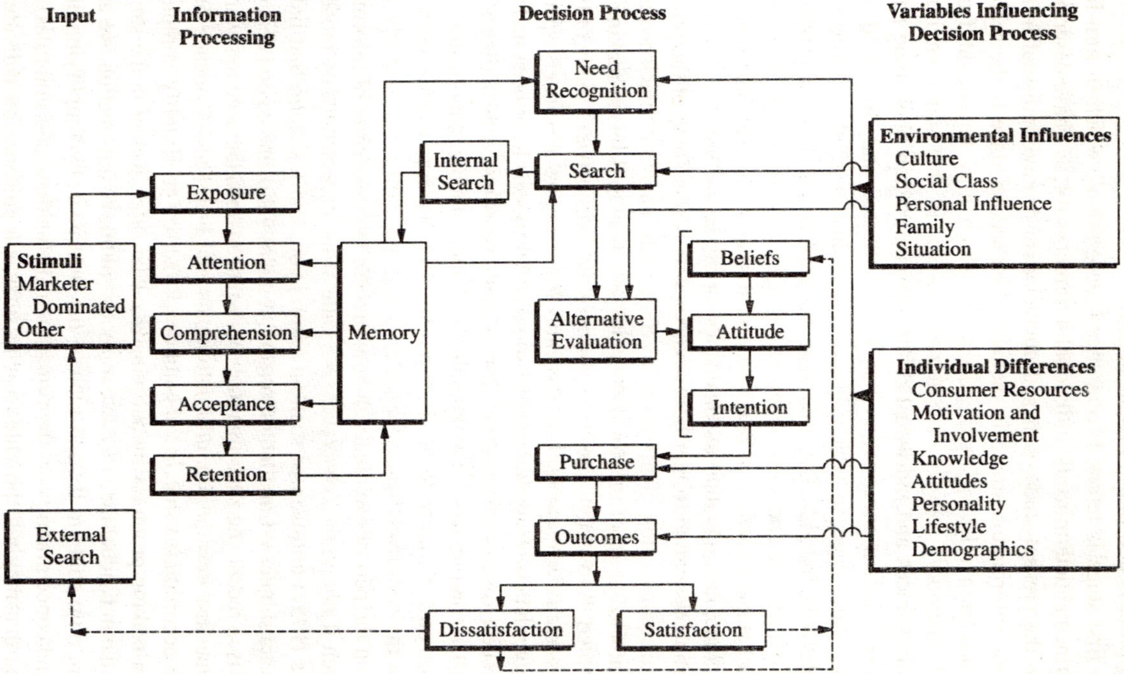

Source: Engel, J.F., Blackwell, R.D. and Miniard, P.W. (1990) *Consumer Behaviour* (London, Dryden Press).

A useful distinction in discussing decision rules is that between *compensatory* and *non-compensatory* models (see, for example, Bettman, 1979). In the former, a high score on one dimension, say, can be offset by a low score on another, i.e., there may be a trade-off between dimensions. In non-compensatory models, on the other hand, there is no such trade-off. I will now go on to look at each of these principal classes of models in turn.

Compensatory decision rules

The general linear compensatory model may be expressed in the following form:

$$\underset{i=1}{\overset{n}{E}} jk = \sum_{i=1}^{n} W_{ik} \; V_{ijk} \tag{7.3}$$

where, E_{jk} is individual k's overall evaluation of product (or brand) j; W_{ik} is the weight given to the individual attribute i (of n) by individual k; V_{ijk} is k's *belief* about the extent to which an attribute i is offered by product j.

An alternative to the above linear additive version of the model is the linear averaging version in which equal or differential weights sum to 1.

The basic dimensions of the model are *attributes*, and one of the attractions is that it permits evaluation of multi-attribute products, or brands. The model is, however, applicable in general to all activities having attributes, not only to the purchase of commodities. It may also be applied in non-linear as well as linear form. The general rule implicit in the model is 'choose the best' (Bettman, 1979).

As Earl (1983) has noted, the compensatory decision model has similarities with Lancaster's 'characteristics' approach to consumer decision-making in economics. The latter, however, is in the prescriptive neo-classical tradition, so that the consumer is assumed always to maximise his utility. There is no such assumption in the compensatory approach. In the Lancaster model, all the information relevant to a decision is available when the decision is made. In the compensatory models this need not be the case. Individuals act when they think they have sufficient information to make a choice, which is not necessarily the same thing as saying that all relevant information will be available. In Lancaster's model, bounded rationality is not a problem; in the compensatory model it invariably will be.

An early example of the compensatory approach was Rosenberg's (1956) expectancy value model. Tests by Hansen (1969) and Bither and Miller (1969) of its predictive accuracy in the consumer behaviour field found that it performed quite well. The most widely adopted compensatory model in recent years, however, has been that of Fishbein (1963, 1975). His model postulates that *intention*, viewed as the immediate precursor of *behaviour*, is determined by a combination of an attitudinal, or personal, component and a normative, or social, component. The most recent version of his model may be expressed as follows:

$$B \sim BI = (Ab)w1 + (SN)w2 \qquad (7.4)$$

where, B is the overt behaviour and BI is the behavioural intention to perform B;
Ab is the attitude toward the act B;
SN is the person's subjective norm concerning the activity;
$w1$ and $w2$ are empirically determined weights, usually interpreted as representing the component's importance in determining intent;
the sign between B and BI signifies that behaviour and intentions will not be precisely equal, since intentions do not always lead to corresponding acts.

The attitude Ab is formed under a particular set of circumstances, and is defined as:

$$Ab = \sum_{i=1}^{n} b_i \, e_i \qquad (7.5)$$

where, b is the belief that behaviour B leads to consequence i;
e_i is the person's evaluation of consequence i;
n is the number of salient beliefs (assumed by Fishbein to be limited).

The component SN is treated as an individual's perception of whether or not people who are important to him think he should engage in a particular activity. Fishbein defines it as:

$$SN = \sum_{j=1}^{n} NB_j \, MC_j \qquad (7.6)$$

where, NB is the person's normative belief that referent j (a reference group or individual) thinks he should or should not perform the act;
MC_j is the person's motivation to comply with referent j;
n is on this occasion the number of relevant referents (since there may be more than one reference group or individual).

A number of features of Fishbein's model are of particular interest to my own study. It will be recalled that in equation (4.4) I concluded that an individual's wants were a function of his needs (and these were in turn linked to the individual life cycle, for which a person's age and sex might be used as proxies) and the influences arising from the social environment (of which reference groups and opinion leaders were of major importance). In Fishbein's model, the independent variable *SN* in equation (7.4) comprises two elements, of which the first is *NB*, the individual's belief about the likelihood that members of a given reference group expect him to perform the behaviour in question. The second element of *SN* is *MC*, the individual's motivation to comply with the reference group's expectations. If motivation is seen as having a firm basis in personal needs, then there would appear to be strong similarities between the independent variables in equations (4.4) and (7.4). In both equations reference group(s) and needs influence the two dependent variables: wants and overt behaviour (in the latter case assuming *B* and *BI* are indeed closely linked, for which there is empirical evidence, as we shall see below).

The only major difference between equations (4.4) and (7.4) is the attitude of the individual, *Ab*, implying that it is principally attitude which determines the progression from a want to an associated act to satisfy that want. It is worth noting, however, that although the attitude and normative components of Fishbein's model are shown as separate and additive, the two may not in practice be quite so separate as is made out (Ryan and Bonfield, 1975). Media influence may also provide a common link, and it could also be said to have a bearing on the e_i component (the individual's evaluation of consequence *i*) of attitude *Ab* in Fishbein's model.

Yet another interesting feature of Fishbein's model from our point of view is its attempt to cater for the problem of bounded rationality (Earl, 1983). The salient attributes to be considered in relation to any activity are limited in number to a maximum of 7 ± 2, since Fishbein accepts that a simultaneous attempt to assess a large number of attributes would lead to information overload.

Finally, Fishbein notes that the salient attributes to be considered will vary according to the type of activity in view.

Since the form of Fishbein's model lends itself readily to regression analysis, and since suitable survey data can be compiled to represent the independent variables, it is not surprising that the model has been widely tested. Surveys of the various empirical results can be found in Ajzen and Fishbein (1977) and Ryan and Bonfield (1975). Generally, the conclusions are supportive, although some studies suggest that multicollinearity between the independent variables is a problem, and there have therefore been attempts to reformulate the model and re-specify some of the independent variables – with an apparent improvement in performance (Ryan and

Bonfield, 1975, Warshaw, 1980, Miniard and Cohen, 1983). Non-linear compensatory models have also been formulated, not just for use in the consumer and marketing areas.

Non-compensatory decision rules

With non-compensatory decision rules it is not possible to compensate for low values on one attribute with high values on another, since all are considered important. To facilitate choice, some studies have tried, however, to attach weights to different attributes, as we shall see below. We look now at a number of the most common decision rules, and some suggested variations of these.

Conjunctive rule Under this rule, each activity, say the purchase of a good, is assessed along a number of dimensions, or attributes. Each of these attributes is required to meet a minimum level of acceptance. In considering the purchase of an automobile, for example, the buyer may want a relatively powerful one, with a minimum brake horsepower, or a minimum rate of acceleration. A more cautious and cost conscious driver, on the other hand, might specify a minimum number of miles per gallon (MPG) of petrol consumed – unacceptable if MPG < 40, for example – and lower horse power and acceleration requirements. The price of the car might also be introduced as a relevant consideration, and treated simply as another relevant dimension.

Only if *all* the minima (or, if it is the case, the maxima) are met will the vehicle in our example be considered for purchase. A difficulty with this formulation, however, is that more than one vehicle may meet all the criteria laid down, and no guidance is provided beyond the binary evaluation of acceptable or not acceptable. A *satisficing* procedure might simply be to choose the first acceptable alternative, i.e., the first to meet all the criteria. Alternatively, a two-stage system of choice might be instituted along the lines considered in the example below.

Disjunctive rule In the case of the disjunctive rule, the individual decision maker attaches overriding importance to one attribute – although in some versions minimum criteria might be laid down for the others. Pursuing our analogy of the automobile buyer a little further, if the consumer is a car fanatic he may insist on a minimum rate of acceleration. Here the disjunctive rule may encounter the same problem as the conjunctive rule, in that more than one good may satisfy the minimum conditions for the key attribute. The next step in the choice process is not clearly specified. One simple way of breaking the deadlock would be for the consumer to choose whichever good possessed the key attribute to the highest degree. For many consumers, price might be a vital consideration, especially if working within an income constraint, but it seems most unlikely to be a general rule for all products or activities, since it would largely negate the whole concept of choice.

Lexicographic rule The lexicographic rule differs from the others considered so far, in that choice is based upon a ranking in order of importance of all attributes of interest to the decision maker. The alternative courses of action are then each considered in relation to the attribute placed first in order of importance. If a number of the alternatives should prove equally attractive in respect of the first attribute, the procedure then to be followed is not clearly specified, and several variations on the basic lexicographic rule might be adopted. The second attribute might, for example, be brought into play, and if this still did not produce a clear winner, the other attributes might be brought in in order of importance until a winner did emerge.

Tversky (1969), Earl (1980, 1983) and others have proposed further variations of the lexicographic rule. In what he refers to as the 'lexicographic semiorder heuristic', Tversky (1969) cites an example concerning selection from job applicants. An employer may be interested in the attributes of intelligence and experience, but rank the former more highly than the latter. Aware, however, that intelligence ratings are not totally reliable, he may decide that only if IQ scores differ by > 3 points will he regard one applicant as more intelligent than another. If the difference in scores between two candidates is < 3 points, therefore, the candidates will be judged equally intelligent, and the more experienced of the two will then be selected. The same process may be used for further attributes if one alternative still does not emerge a clear favourite. This method of selection, as the example suggests, is especially appropriate where the relevant dimension is 'noisy', i.e., not subject to precise measurement. It is also worth noting that the lexicographic semiorder rule may be used to demonstrate intransitivity in choices – as Tversky (1969) shows.

In a later study, Tversky (1972) proposed another sequential elimination rule which he described as 'elimination by aspects'. Aspects, or attributes, are assumed to have differing weights, and one alternative is then chosen with a probability proportional to its weight. All alternatives not having better values than the selected attribute are eliminated. A second attribute is then selected, again with probability proportional to its weight, and the process is repeated. The assumption is that one alternative will eventually emerge as the clear winner.

Earl (1980) proposed a development of what he referred to as the 'behavioural lexicographic model'. People are assumed not only to rank attributes, or characteristics, according to their priorities but to set targets for the attributes. This enables the decision maker to avoid considering trade-offs between characteristics, and to attempt independently to pursue as many characteristic goals as possible. If decision makers run out of relevant attributes before filtering out all but one scheme, they can always resolve the choice problem by using the criterion of cheapness (where it is a relevant consideration) to choose the course of action expected to perform best in respect of the lowest dimension, or search for other relevant attributes which might be taken into consideration. This type of lexicographic model is developed further in Earl (1983).

Heuristics under conditions of uncertainty

The heuristics discussed above do not specifically tackle the problems of decision taking under conditions of uncertainty. A substantial body of research work has concerned itself, however, with the behaviour of individuals faced with such circumstances. The findings, as we noted earlier, add weight to the criticisms of the expected utility model. The results of the studies are surveyed in Kahneman *et al.* (1982). In sum, the studies show that, in order to cope with the uncertainty surrounding decision-making, individuals resort to a variety of heuristics, the most common of which are: representativeness; availability; and anchoring. Furthermore, the use of these heuristics leads to judgemental biases, such that any idea of rational, maximising behaviour on the part of individuals must be abandoned.

Since the findings are important, it is worth saying a bit more, even if only briefly, about each of the heuristics listed. The representativeness heuristic comes into play when an individual is required to judge probabilities of the following sort: that object A belongs to class B, that event A originates from process B, or that process B will generate event A ('process' here refers to a sequence of stages, as in a decision-making process). Faced with such problems, the individual will often base his/her decision on the extent to which A resembles B, or is highly representative of B. Tversky and Kahneman (1974) give examples relating to people's occupations. If the stereotype of a librarian is that they are quiet and studious, or that salesmen are outgoing extroverts, then people may judge the likelihood of an individual belonging to either occupation by how closely he or she accords with the stereotypes. A danger with such procedures, of course, is that other factors ought to enter the assessment of probabilities. One such factor is the base rate frequency of the outcomes, which, in the case of a librarian, for example, would be affected by the fact that librarians form only a small proportion of the total population.

The availability heuristic concerns cases in which the frequency of a class (say sex) or the probability of an event occurring is often judged according to the ease with which previous instances can be brought to mind. Tversky and Kahneman (1974) cite the results of an experiment in which subjects were read lists of well-known personalities of both sexes. Some lists contained more names of men than women, and in some lists the men were relatively more famous than the women. In the case of each of the lists, the subjects erroneously judged that the class (sex) having the more famous personalities was the more numerous. Another example cited was that the subjective probability of traffic accidents rose temporarily for those recently exposed to such occurrencies.

The term 'anchoring' is applied by Tversky and Kahneman (1974) to evidence that people make estimates under conditions of uncertainty by starting from an initial value that is adjusted to yield the final answer:

> The initial value, or starting point, may be suggested by the formulation of the problem, or it may be the result of a partial computation. In either case, adjustments are typically insufficient (Slovic and Lichtenstein, 1971). That is, different starting points yield different estimates, which are biased towards the initial values.

I have given a sufficient account of decision rules in use, it is hoped, to make clear a number of points. First, there is sufficient evidence to confirm that heuristics are commonly employed by individuals in a wide variety of decision situations. The nature of the heuristic used will vary from one set of circumstances to another, and is also likely to vary from one individual to another (quite why, is an interesting question requiring study). This poses problems for anyone hoping to arrive at a simple, unified view of how decisions are made. It may be that further research will enable a number of especially common, and more than usually significant, heuristics to be identified, or enable the available heuristics to be more closely integrated. One thing seems certain, however: the widespread use of heuristics is impossible to reconcile with the expected utility model of decision-making, since, on the basis of the evidence cited above, heuristics clearly mean biases, even bad mistakes, in judgement. It may nevertheless be the case that for some classes of problems the expected utility model will remain useful, given the enormous breadth of decision-making situations.

The above suggests a field of study in a state of some turmoil, and one might wonder why, if decision-making is so complex and diverse, the social, economic and political situations are not even more unstable than we find them. The answer seems to be that by no means all decision-making – in fact perhaps only a relatively small part – is concerned with complex problems. Much is of a relatively simple nature, often based only on habit, and we go on now to look at this key aspect of decision-making.

Simple decision-making

From the economic point of view, decision-making by the individual is concerned principally with purchases of items falling under the heading of 'consumers' expenditure'. It also includes, however, labour force decisions (for example, whether or not to work, and, if so, for how long) and decisions over such matters as wage claims and settlements. I shall consider all these aspects at some stage, but for the present I will concentrate principally on consumers' expenditure.

In the consumer field, complex decisions will mainly entail the larger, more important and more expensive items of expenditure. Good examples are automobiles and other consumer durables such as TVs, fridges, dishwashers, etc. – although even for such items, as we shall see below, simplified decision procedures are often used. Purchase or renting of accommodation is generally of even greater importance. Much consumers' expenditure, however, is of a fairly simple, routine or repetitive nature, and in the decision-making literature is described by a variety of terms, such as 'routinised response behaviour' (RRB), or 'low involvement' decision-making – it may also, it seems, include an element of 'limited problem solving' (see below).

Research in the area of simple decision-making has been much more limited than that into complex decision-making. The reasons are easy to appreciate. Complex decisions hold more scope for researchers, since they contain more detailed stages in the decision process; they also involve thinking human beings, with the greater challenge of understanding and detecting underlying patterns of behaviour. Once explained, it would then appear to be a simple matter to relate the model developed to less complex decisions. Finally, the idea of a thinking, responding human being has much greater attraction for marketers and others who hope to influence the purchasing behaviour of individuals.

Despite the greater attention paid to complex decision-making, consumer purchases of a straightforward, routine nature are likely to be just as important, if not more so, than purchases associated with complex decision processes. There is a *prima facie* case for thinking that it is the less complex, habitual purchases which make up the bulk of consumers' expenditure, and account for its relative stability compared with other categories of demand in an economy. Complex decision-making, on the other hand, insofar as it concerns such items of spending as major consumer durables, will tend to be 'lumpy', and may therefore be especially important in determining cyclical *changes* in consumer spending. In explaining simple decision-making I shall bear these considerations in mind, and return to them again when I come to look at consumers' expenditure in the context of aggregate economic behaviour.

When introducing their model of buyer behaviour, Howard and Sheth (1969) noted that it could be used to analyse three different types of buyer decision-making, of which the simplest was routinised response behaviour (RRB). Their definition of this form of behaviour was fairly specific, in that it related to situations in which the buyer's preferences were fixed – one implication being, as Howard (1974) noted, that economists' treatment of consumer behaviour is concerned only with RRB, and not even with limited problem solving (LPS) let alone extensive problem solving (EPS). In the case of RRB, choice can still be influenced by the information available at the time of purchase – assumed to be very limited in scope at this level of analysis – so that, even although brand and product class concepts are fixed, the outcome of choice is not. The extent of the information available, and used, is one of the principal criteria serving to delineate the three classes of buyer behaviour. As we move from RRB to LPS and eventually to EPS, the availability of information, and generally also the options open to the buyer, increase.

It will be apparent from the above that routinised response behaviour is a somewhat restricted category of decision-making, and I would include it under my broader definition of simple decision-making. One further message is clear: complex decision-making concerns only one particular type of buyer behaviour, even if an important one. It should not therefore be studied to the exclusion of other decision-making.

Other writers have also argued in favour of focusing more attention on simple decision-making. Krugman (1965) advanced the notion of 'low involvement decision-making', and his ideas have gained support from a variety of later writers – see, for example, Maloney and Silverman (eds), 1979. Krugman was concerned to explain the effects of television advertising. On the basis of his findings, it appeared to him that individuals did not undertake an extensive processing of advertising information, but rather absorbed the information through being subjected to frequent repetition. In effect they underwent a process of *passive learning* which affected their behaviour without any change in attitude taking place.

Following on from Krugman's work, Ray (1973) presented empirical evidence suggesting that the standard cognitive → affective → conative sequence of communication effects (sometimes represented as awareness attitude behaviour) is appropriate only to high involvement decision-making. In low involvement cases, the sequence appears to be cognitive conative affective, which is in tune with Krugman's notion of passive learning without attitude change. Any change in attitude occurs *after* behaviour (say the purchase of a good) rather than preceding it. From Ray's research the reason seems to be that low involvement behaviour is associated with situations in which few alternatives are available – for example, when the differences between products are unimportant. Low involvement was found by Ray to be most prevalent in respect of convenience foods. The repetition of advertising messages for such low-commitment products mainly acted to increase recall and purchase intentions, with minimal effects on attitudes. This suggests that selection of brands and products, and even switching between them, might occur without attitudes being changed, or even formed.

Difficulties in defining precisely what is meant by 'involvement' have so far limited the low involvement line of enquiry (see Ray, 1974) but additional evidence in support of the view that individual behaviour, in particular individual consumer behaviour, frequently does not follow a complex choice process has been provided by Olshavsky and Granbois (1979). They applied two key criteria in reviewing evidence on the nature of decision-making: did purchasing behaviour occur in the *absence* of *external* search; was *internal* information frequently either not available, not relevant or not consulted? The nature of internal processing meant that the second criterion could only be studied indirectly, but it was felt nevertheless that sufficient evidence was available to reach a reasoned judgement. The primary purpose, however, was to assess the evidence relating to *external* search.

Olshavsky and Granbois (1979) analysed consumer behaviour under four headings: budget allocation (savings/spending and allocation across broad expenditure categories); generic allocation (expenditure on specific products and services); store patronage (shopping and purchasing at specific shopping centres, stores, etc.); and brand purchase. With regard to the first of these, the authors concluded on the basis of the work reviewed that only about one-quarter to one-third of all consumers showed evidence of any *systematic* planning and decision-making in respect of saving; the majority were not 'deliberate choosers'. One exception appeared to be newlywed couples. Ferber (1973) found, for example, that half of such couples interviewed after marriage reported definite savings plans.

The consumption life cycle which I discussed earlier would not appear to support the view that there is a *general* lack of budget planning. Many people obviously do save in their middle years to support a higher level of consumption later in life. Much of this saving is contractual, in the sense that it takes the form of contributions towards organisational pensions, which are often a condition of employment. The more advanced industrial countries also generally require employee contributions toward State pensions. Much saving, too, is associated with the purchasing of housing. Such a commitment is likely to be long-term, and once again could hardly be regarded as unplanned.

In sample surveys carried out to determine, amongst other things, the purposes of savings, Katona (1975) and his associates at the Survey Research Center of the University of Michigan found that slightly under half of all respondents saved for rainy days (emergencies, illness and unemployment), around 30 per cent for retirement and old age, about one-quarter for children's needs (primary education) and less than 10 per cent in order to buy a house or durable goods – the percentages summed to rather more than 100 per cent because some respondents mentioned more than one purpose. By no means all people saved, however, since many – including those 'in good financial condition' – believed they were unable to save. There is evidence, too, that where discretionary savings, as opposed to contractual savings, are concerned, most ordinary individuals simply feel they do not have the knowledge and experience to make fully informed judgements about whether it is better to save or to spend (see, for example, Olander and Seipel, 1970) – the availability of 'expert' advice does not seem to make a great deal of difference.

With regard to the allocation of finance within an overall level of consumption, Olshavsky and Granbois believed that there were again grounds for doubting the existence of any complex decision-making process. Certain categories of personal expenditure were thought to be 'non-discretionary', in the sense that they were essential and could not be avoided. These included food and beverages, housing, clothing and medical care. While these categories of spending do include basic minima required if individuals are to survive, it is stretching matters to describe them all as 'non-discretionary' since we do have considerable discretion over how much we eat, what kind of accommodation we use, and how much we spend on clothing – and even medical care. What could well be true, however, is that much expenditure in the categories listed – with the probable exception of medical care – develops into routinised behaviour, or perhaps is determined by past decisions, as in the case of housing – where choice of house usually entails consequent expenditure, such as the size of rental or mortgage payments and outlays on heating (often more or less fixed after the choice of heating system has been made).

Olshavsky and Granbois also note the effects of social and cultural factors in determining the extent to which certain categories of personal expenditure become 'non-discretionary'. Education, recreation, transportation and household furnishings all contain strong elements associated with socially or culturally determined life styles, and once adopted these tend to be maintained – barring a major shock, such as a sharp drop in income, caused perhaps by unemployment.

Evidence on the allocation of financial resources between the broad categories of spending seems to be rather sparse, but Olshavsky and Granbois quote one survey of 300 Minnesota families, covering three generations (Hill, 1963). It was found that only 7 per cent of grandparents, 21 per cent of parents and 24 per cent of married children reported plans for allocating expenditure across categories, and similar proportions claimed to use procedures for estimating expenses and setting specific amounts aside.

The second heading under which Olshavsky and Granbois examined the roles of external and internal search was that of 'generic allocation', or the allocation of income *within* expenditure categories. Useful evidence in this area has been gathered by Ferber (1973) who from a review of relevant studies found that 20–25 per cent of durable goods and clothing purchases appeared to be 'impulsive', in that a sense of urgency or a special purchase opportunity displaced deliberation and purchase planning in determining buyer behaviour. An even higher proportion of supermarket purchases appear to be based on impulse. Dagnoli (1987) found that over half of all such purchases were unplanned. It was also revealed that 10 per cent of buyers planned to make purchases within broad product categories, but had not decided upon specific brands.

Product innovation affords another example of the extent of pre-purchase deliberation. A review by Rogers and Shoemaker (1971) revealed that twelve out of fourteen studies of information seeking had established that those adopting a new innovation early in its life sought more information about the innovation than late adopters. Considerable evidence also emerged that whereas the early adopters had tended to be more exposed to the influence of the mass media and interpersonal communication channels, the late adopters were subject to a 'diffusion effect', arising from growing social pressures to acquire the new innovation.

Studies of store patronage have also found patterns of activity suggesting that consumers do not make the fullest possible use of the information and buying opportunities available to them. A review by Granbois (1977) revealed that use of non-store sources of goods, such as mail order, telephone order and in-home buying, was distinctly associated with the socio-economic characteristics of shoppers. Furthermore, a significant sub-set of all consumers did not appear to consider sources other than conventional retail outlets. Patronage of shopping areas was also found to vary directly with the variety of shopping on offer, and indirectly with the distance or effort involved in reaching shops. This suggests that while consumers may wish to be able to make comparisons before purchase, there are definite limits to the time and effort they are prepared to put into pre-purchase assessment. A further interesting pointer is that research studies of shopping activity preceding major durable goods purchases have typically found that a high proportion of such purchases are made after only one visit to a store. The implication is that even for high value, complex items purchased infrequently there is still only limited search activity – this is true even of the significant proportion of first time buyers featuring in the studies.

Finally, in the matter of brand purchase, Olshavsky and Granbois (1979) cite evidence to the effect that substantial proportions of buyers consult only one, or even no, sources of information before purchasing major appliances. Several studies are also quoted indicating that large proportions – in some cases over half – of appliance buyers consider only one of the numerous brands available. Information seeking, too, seems to be very restricted among all but a minority of consumers.

CONCLUSIONS

We are now in a position to draw together the various elements of the decision-making problem facing the individual. In Chapters 3 and 4 we saw how individual needs give rise to wants, which are strongly influenced by the social environment in which the individual finds himself, or herself. The individual's goal is to satisfy as many of these wants as possible – although not necessarily at the one time.

There will be no one-to-one correspondence between wants (or attributes, or characteristics) and individual products, since some products may contain more than one satisfier – a fruit for example, may help satisfy both hunger and thirst. If a person is thirsty but not hungry, he or she may, however, still have to purchase the whole fruit, unless the juice is available on its own as a product. Some satisfiers, in effect, will go to waste if there is no one-to-one correspondence between wants and satisfiers – as will frequently be the case.

With the above qualifications, the wants of the individual, represented by a vector $b1, b2, \ldots, bn$, denoted by B, will give rise to the demand for a range of goods to satisfy these wants, represented by the vector $h1, h2, \ldots, hn$, denoted by H, i.e., $B \rightarrow H$. In the real world, however, few individuals are able to satisfy all their wants. In Chapters 5 and 6 I examined the nature of the constraints which generally prevent all wants being satisfied at any one time. Above all, there is the income constraint, since most satisfiers have to be purchased – even if the best things in life are said to be free. With only 24 hours in the day, there is also a time constraint, which in turn has a bearing on the income constraint. Many individuals may be able to earn more if they so desire, by working more hours and taking fewer hours of leisure, but for others this option may not be available, and the only alternative may be to search for a higher paid job. For many, perhaps most, individuals, therefore, the income constraint is insurmountable, at least in the short term, although it would be a mistake – even in the short run – to believe that this is universally the case, since decisions about employment, such as hours, can sometimes be quickly altered.

I also noted earlier in the present chapter that a person's income constraint imposes itself not only in *absolute* terms but in *relative* terms, i.e., in relation to the income(s) of those with whom a person compares himself. Not only, therefore, is an individual i constrained by his money income Wi in the purchase of goods, his ability to purchase goods relative to that of a reference group $r1$ is constrained by the relationship $Wi/\bar{W}r1$, where $\bar{W}r1$ is the mean money income of those members of the reference group $r1$ (i's preferences for goods being influenced by the choices of the members of the reference group).

If not all wants can be satisfied at any given time, how does the individual decide which he will satisfy within his/her income constraint? Here the nature of the decision-making process we examined earlier appears to provide some clues. The satisfying of many wants seems to be a fairly routine business, involving what has been described as 'routinised response behaviour' (RRB), or at most 'limited problem solving' (LPS) or, in our terminology, 'simple decision-making'. Little, if any, information is required in addition to that already stored in the individual's memory, i.e. there is little in the way of external search, and the alternatives available for choice are likely to be relatively few and uncomplicated. The weekly shopping for food and drink seems to fall mainly under this simple decision-making heading, as will outlays on housing (once a commitment to a dwelling has been made at least) and the associated spending on heating, maintenance, etc. In other words, much of the expenditure on life's basic necessities, which must rank highly in any order of spending priorities, will be of a fairly routine, uncomplicated nature for any individual leading a reasonably settled existence.

For the majority of people, therefore, certainly in the more advanced industrial countries, most of the wants associated with simple decision-making may well account for the bulk of an individual's expenditure – with perhaps only periodic exceptions, when large items, such as an automobile, are purchased, and even then the purchase cost may be spread over a lengthy period.

The nature of simple decision-making, and the types of wants which are being satisfied, indicates that in the consumer field many of the purchases made will be repeat purchases. In effect, much personal consumption at any given time will be similar to purchases in the recent past. Habit and routine seem to be quite firmly entrenched features of most people's lives. The economic implications of such behaviour are profound, since they impart a welcome element of stability to economic affairs. In essence, consumption in time t will be a function of consumption in the previous time period and perhaps (with a diminished weighting) of consumption in earlier periods as well. Those familiar with the permanent income hypothesis will recognise the similarities. This is a matter we shall return to when discussing aggregate behaviour.

The other major category of wants we have identified embraces all those wants whose satisfaction entails complex decision-making. The purchase of many of the most expensive satisfiers, such as some consumer durables, would seem to fall within this category, since external information is often helpful to choice, especially as the range of goods on offer is frequently extensive. The *initial* decision on the form of accommodation to be purchased or rented is also likely to be a complex decision – subsequent (simple) decisions being to continue with the purchase or renting. If we think in terms of services rather than goods, decisions about where and when to take annual holidays may often be a complex decision, and one often accounting for a significant proportion of total annual financial outlays. Many of these decisions could be postponed from one year to the next, it seems, since the wants, although they may rate quite highly, are not in the nature of necessities. At any one time, therefore, some of these wants will tend to be satisfied, others not so. Furthermore, since we seem to be dealing with relatively few and large items of expenditure, it is not too fanciful to believe that the individual is able to adopt some form of lexicographic ordering of priorities in respect of this category of wants.

Where lexicographic ordering is not possible, or not used, one of the numerous simplifying decision rules, or heuristics, I explained earlier might be brought to bear. Where heuristics are employed, as seems most likely in decisions involving uncertainty, there seems little point in searching for *the* heuristic, since, given the enormous range of products and services purchased, and the wide and ever changing circumstances surrounding purchases, a variety of heuristics will almost certainly be used, even by the same person. Trying to reduce all decision-making to one form of decision rule would be to distort what happens in practice.

Given the constraints of income and time, only the very wealthy – and perhaps not even they – are likely to be in a position to satisfy all their wants. Not even all wants associated with simple decision-making will be fully satisfied, although, as we noted above, a high proportion – perhaps a majority – of individuals in the more advanced industrial countries may now be in a position to satisfy wants of this nature. Even in these countries, however, many will still not be able to satisfy their most basic wants. We may therefore distinguish between wants which are satisfied (B^s) and those which are not (B^u), i.e., $B^s + B^u = B$.

Economic theory has little or nothing to say about *unsatisfied* wants. It is simply assumed that individuals spend up to the limits of their incomes in a way which maximises their utilities, and there the matter is allowed to rest. Yet to the extent that needs, and the wants associated with these needs, provide a motivating force for action on the part of individuals, unsatisfied wants will influence an individual's future behaviour. In particular, they could be expected to influence an individual's labour force decisions – whether to work, say, if a person has retired, whether to work harder or to work more hours, or whether to change employment. Generally speaking, it seems reasonable to assume that the greater the extent of unsatisfied wants, the greater the motivation to try and do something about it by exercising one or more of the options listed.

Since most people are in the position of having unsatisfied wants, however, and not all are dashing off to work harder or change jobs, it may be the case that some form of threshold effect operates, with action only being taken when B^u exceeds the critical threshold. In general terms, then, individuals undertake employment in order to satisfy their wants; if their initial employment decisions leave a critical level of wants unsatisfied, this will lead to changes in employment designed to satisfy more of the unsatisfied wants. This is another matter I shall return to when I come to discuss aggregate economic behaviour.

Part IV
Socioeconomic Decision-Making

8 Socioeconomic Decision-Making: the Family

We move on now from decision-making by the individual, acting on his, or her, own, to decision-making by individuals acting within groups, sometimes small, but often also large. Much of the earlier analysis of individual behaviour remains crucial to an understanding of how these groups behave. Individual needs remain. Indeed, the principal reason individuals join groups is to enable them to satisfy more fully many of their needs, such as those for safety, belonging, status and self-actualisation. The environmental influences we looked at in Chapter 4 also impinge strongly on group behaviour. The nature of decision-making, however, now changes in a number of important respects. First, instead of there being only one individual's goals, all members of a group are likely to have goals, and certain of these goals may conflict. Some goals may be specific, but others will be of a more general nature. Sometimes, too, there will be joint goals, and responsibility for implementing these will have to be apportioned. There is here scope for differences of opinion, and some system of conflict resolution is therefore central to group behaviour.

I begin my discussion of socioeconomic decision-making by looking once more at the family, since the family is at the centre of many important decisions affecting personal consumption and the labour market. We turn first to family needs and wants, which, as we saw in the case of the individual, play an important part in the formation of the goals which lie at the heart of decision-making. I will also look at the satisfiers of family wants, which once again differ in certain important respects from those relevant to the individual.

FAMILY NEEDS, WANTS AND SATISFIERS

Although the principal basis of family needs is still individual needs, a number of additional factors must be taken into account. In an earlier section, I showed how the needs of a group for food would vary according to the age and sex of members of the group, since nutritional requirements differed according to the stages of each individual life cycle. In the same way, the needs for food of a *family* will differ according to the number, age and sex of the individuals comprising the family. Moreover, individual life cycles ensure that these needs will vary over time.

A further factor affecting family needs is that families benefit from certain economies of scale, as in meeting the need for food. Packaged food is often cheaper when bought in large quantities, and the cost of heat required to cook for, say, four is unlikely to be four times that for one individual. There will also tend to be less wastage per person, since it is possible with a greater number to apportion food more precisely to meet individual needs. Transport provides another good example. It is much cheaper per head to carry four in an automobile than it is to carry one. To take yet another example, membership of clubs and societies is often cheaper per head for a family than it is for one individual. Many further examples of such economies could be cited.

One of the most important factors affecting *family*, as opposed to individual, needs is the family life cycle, which we also examined in Chapter 4. Marriage and the birth of the first child, for example, mark important stages in the family life cycle which affect family needs (and wants) and have repercussions on family spending, and perhaps also labour force decisions. As we saw earlier, the family life cycle has a bearing on the consumption of certain products, such as energy and leisure facilities, which is independent of family income and the ages or social class of family members. The family life cycle, in other words, is an important determinant of family behaviour in its own right. When it comes to explaining changes in family needs, the choice of the most relevant family life cycle variable will depend upon the nature of the particular need in question. Housing needs, for example, are most likely to be determined by marriage itself, by the timing of the birth of the first child, and possibly also the birth of subsequent children and retirement.

As in the case of the individual, however, it is family *wants* rather than family needs which are of greatest concern to economists, since it is the former which have the most direct bearing on behaviour. Here the social influences we looked at in Chapter 4 once again come into play. In the case of the family group we can be more precise about the leaders to whom family members will turn in the search for guidance before taking decisions. They are most likely to be the parents, either singly or jointly – depending, among other things, on the product being purchased, as we shall see below.

When discussing family influence on individual family members in Chapter 4, we also noted that there was strong evidence that family members used their own family as an important reference group. It is from his, or her, family that individuals often adopt their norms of behaviour, with all that implies for their consumption of particular goods and services, working habits, etc. Family members influence each other, individually and collectively, but family influence does not stop there. Families also come into contact, very often close contact, with other families. Inter-family influence is therefore also a potent force not to be ignored.

Pulling together the various factors touched on above, we are now in a position to set down the principal determinants of *family*, as opposed to individual wants. We may express them as follows:

$$FAM_i^x = f(as_{li}, \ldots, as_{4i}, FLC_i^x, as_{li}^x, FAM_j^x) \quad (8.1)$$

where

FAM_i^x is family *i*'s want of *x*;
$as_{1i}, \ldots, as_{4i}$ are the ages and sexes of the four members of family *i*;
FLC_i^x is the life cycle variable of family *i* as it affects want *x*;
as_{li}^x is want of *x* by the family leader in respect of want *x*;
FAM_j^x is family reference group *j*'s want of *x*

As with the individual, the family's goal is to satisfy as many of its wants as possible, within the bounds of any constraints which might apply, such as that of income. Again, as in the case of the individual, there will be a range of satisfiers to match the wants, with the important proviso we made earlier that only if a good embodied one clear attribute which satisfied one particular want would there be a simple one-to-one correspondence between goods, satisfiers and wants. In practice, most goods contain more than one attribute, and matching them to wants in the best way possible is the goal of the decision-making process.

FAMILY DECISION-MAKING

One key feature of families which distinguishes them clearly from the individual decision maker is that there is as a rule more than one decision-making unit within the family. It is not generally the case that only one person makes all decisions on behalf of the family, since that one person would have to fulfil the roles of both parents, and give other family members no say in family decisions.

Family decision-making units

Family decisions may be classed as *autonomous* (by a single member) or *joint* (by two or more members of the family acting in consort). Decisions may be further classified according to whether they are made by an individual on his own behalf, or by the individual on behalf of some or all members of the family. Various permutations are therefore possible, but it seems we can distinguish at least six types of family decision which are likely to be relevant in some situations:

Autonomous Decision-Making

Type 1. On individual's own behalf
Type 2. On behalf of one (other than the decision maker) or more members of the family
Type 3. On behalf of the family as a unit

Joint Decision-Making

Type 4. Individuals acting jointly for their *own* use
Type 5. Joint decisions on behalf of one or more *other* members of the family
Type 6. Decisions on behalf of the family as a unit

Type 1 decisions are likely to be fairly common. The most likely examples are the father or mother purchasing something for his/her own use, such as shaving materials, or a child purchasing for his/her own use. There may also be older children earning incomes of their own, over part or all of which they have autonomy.

An obvious example of a Type 2 decision is a mother or father buying toys or other goods for their children. Type 3 would include the very common case of a mother buying food on behalf of the family for joint consumption.

In the case of joint decision-making, a Type 4 example might be parents purchasing cigarettes for their own use. As an example of Type 5 decisions we might again use the purchase of toys by parents for their children's use, but on this occasion the decision might be made by the parents jointly because it was a more expensive toy, perhaps a home computer or a doll's house. Type 6 might again entail parents acting jointly, this time to purchase such joint family requirements as a home, an automobile, a TV set, or another major consumer durable.

The above examples make it abundantly clear that there is not a family decision-making unit as such, taking all decisions on behalf of the family, but rather a variety of decision-making units taking particular decisions on behalf of some or all family members. This is a complication which economic analysis ignores. Does it really matter? We shall be in a better position to judge when we try to draw our conclusions later. It certainly matters to those concerned with marketing, who want to be able to identify the decision makers, and the products over which they have command, in order to be able to influence them.

Having distinguished a number of decision-making units within the family, and given a few examples of the types of decisions which might be made by each unit, it would obviously be of value if we could go a stage further and try to determine more precisely the nature of the decisions most likely to be taken by each type of decision-making unit. Here we are hampered by the lack of anything approaching a comprehensive theory of family decision behaviour, but research findings do provide some clues to the principal factors at work.

The decision-making unit for different products and product categories

Sheth (1974) has summarised the factors determining whether decisions are taken autonomously or jointly. The first of these was social class, with a number of studies indicating a greater autonomy in buying decisions among upper and lower social classes, and more joint decision-making among middle class families. Sheth also concluded that joint decision-making tended to be greater the greater was the perceived risk of making the wrong buying decision. Where all members of a family might be adversely affected by a wrong decision, there was a tendency to seek support and guidance from each other. The same tended to be true as the importance of the purchase to a family increased – the purchase of houses, automobiles and major durable goods were examples of purchases likely to fall within this category.

A factor working against joint decision-making was time pressure. The increase in the proportion of wives working, and also of children working, frequently reduces the opportunity for joint consideration of decisions. Finally, Sheth noted the importance of role specialisation. In many families individual members assume, or are allotted, specific roles which have an important bearing on whether decisions are taken autonomously or jointly – here we may refer back to my earlier discussion of family influence. Sex roles, in particular, have been the subject of investigation (see Qualls, 1987, for a survey of material in this field).

It will be apparent from the above that not only do the factors listed help determine whether decisions are taken autonomously or jointly, they also have an important bearing on which type of decision-making unit is concerned with the purchases of particular goods and services. In reviewing research evidence on family members' involvement in different categories of economic decisions, Davis (1976) identified three principal categories: frequently purchased goods and services; durable goods; saving-investment decisions. With regard to the first of these, the studies dispelled the conventional wisdom that the world of supermarket purchases was the exclusive domain of the wife. Husbands were often involved in actual purchasing – any trip round a supermarket must surely bear out such findings – although wives clearly predominated. Husbands were aware of brands in many product categories and able to express brand preferences. It seems that although wives do most of the grocery shopping, they do so with an awareness of the products and brands that their families like. The findings therefore lend support to the form in which we expressed equation (8.1) on the determinants of family wants.

In contrast to non-durables, Davis found that purchases of durable goods were often preceded by a progression of interrelated decisions and activities over time. Husbands, wives and children all had an opportunity to become involved at one or more stages in the process. At one extreme, in terms of the length of the decision process, the amount of deliberation and financial importance, was house purchase. There is a strong consensus that house buying is the subject of joint decision-making, even if one or the other parent might have greater influence on particular aspects of the decision.

The purchase of automobiles has been another popular field for family decision-making research. Studies in this field have tended to show that whereas the husband or wife might have a dominant influence on particular aspects of the purchase, such as the wife on colour, in general the influence of the husband is much the greater. However, as we have noted previously, there is some evidence of a trend towards joint decision-making in respect of automobiles. (Cunningham and Green, 1974).

The purchase of home furnishings and a wide variety of other products for home use were discussed in an earlier section, where we noted in particular the studies by Davis and Rigaux (1974) and Bonfield (1978) – Davis (1976) lists a number of other relevant studies. The findings show clear role specialisation, although a tendency toward more joint decision-making was again evident. The one major services item covered by these studies was family vacations. As one might expect, this item was the subject of joint discussion and decision.

Finally, with regard to family saving and investment decisions, the evidence, such as it is, indicates once more a high degree of joint decision-making. Consistent with earlier findings, Ferber and Nicosia (1972) from their collected panel data established that among young married couples as many as four-fifths reported joint decision-making in respect of savings. In the important matter of life insurance, either husbands acting on their own or joint decision-making appear to be most common (e.g. Davis and Rigaux, 1974, Bonfield, 1978).

Conflict resolution

One important feature of families which I have not yet touched upon – which members of a family will be only too well aware of – is the matter of conflict between family members, and how it might best be avoided or resolved. From my discussion so far of family decision-making it will be apparent that conflict might arise at a number of points, and if sufficiently serious might even impede decision-making. Divergence of view might arise, first, over the roles to be played by individual family members. A common example of this *role conflict* nowadays is probably that between husband and working wife over household duties. Other examples might be conflict over the respective roles of each parent in relation to their children, or over the roles of children, especially older children, in relation to the rest of the family.

Even if roles are agreed, there is still the problem of family goals. What should they be, what should be their respective priorities if, as is likely, they cannot all be achieved at once? Goal conflict is potentially so disruptive that it might even lead to the breakdown of the family unit. Effective decision-making requires once again that this problem should be resolved if it arises.

Agreement on goals might still leave a third type of conflict, which we might refer to as *evaluation conflict*. In neo-classical economics there is only one goal for the individual, and only one best means of achieving it; but in the real world, individuals are more often than not faced with alternative means of achieving a given goal, and it is not always apparent – at the outset at least – which it is best to choose. Different family members, for example, have available different information on which to act – internal information, in the sense that parents are older and have more experience of life, but perhaps also external information as well, possible through work.

Using ideas put forward by Thompson and Tuden (1959) in organisation theory, Davis (1976), and in a similar vein Sheth (1974), have suggested that conflict resolution within a group, such as the family, might take two main forms: consensual and accommodative. If decision-making is consensual, there is no disagreement about fundamental motives and goals, although there may well be about evaluation of alternative means of achieving goals. Sheth illustrates the case by an example drawn from the consumer field. Family members might agree about the need for a product or service, but argue about the most appropriate brand. In such cases, *problem solving* is the route to conflict resolution. Davis (1976) suggests that in these instances where different evaluations arise, Simon's (1955) satisficing criteria would appear to predict that a group would engage in problem solving, and continue to search for alternatives until one was found that satisfied the minimum level of expectations in respect of the value(s) perceived to be relevant.

Where group decision makers are unable to agree about goals, the disagreements are of a more fundamental nature, and accommodative strategies are called for. These are described by Davis and by Sheth as *persuasion strategies* and *bargaining strategies*, the distinction between the two not being a sharp one. In the former case, a person is persuaded to do something against his/her better judgement. There may even on occasions be an element of compulsion about it, since there is no give and take between the parties. Under the bargaining strategy, on the other hand, the reluctant member of a family can usually expect something in return for his/her agreement. If father wishes a new automobile and mother a new washing machine, and the family is up against its financial limits, then one of them might have to postpone the purchase until the following year, with compensation being offered and accepted meantime. Such bargaining appears to be quite common in family buying decisions.

Sheth (1974) also introduces a fourth, more drastic, means of conflict resolution within families where disagreement is too fundamental to be resolved by any of the strategies already listed. He refers to it as *politics*, and describes it as applying to situations in which members of a family disagree not only about specific goals, but, more fundamentally, about a whole style of life. The constant conflict is likely to be resolved only by dissolution of the family, or by the formation of coalitions and sub-groups of family members, to try and isolate one or more of the other members, thereby obliging them to concede. At the less serious level, this might be regarded as another form of persuasion, and doubtless sounds quite familiar to those readers with families.

Decision-making within the family

Where decisions are made autonomously within the family, we might use the model of the individual decision maker developed in Part III as the most appropriate guide to family decision-making. There will nevertheless be significant differences between Types 1, 2 and 3 of the autonomous decisions I listed earlier. In Types 2 and 3, especially, the influence of the other members of the family will weigh heavily, since decisions are being taken on their behalf, and we could normally expect them to have some say in the matter – just how much say is likely to vary from one family to another.

The goal of the autonomous decision-making unit within the family will still be to satisfy family wants, as expressed in equation (8.1), to the extent possible within the income and other constraints operating. For the same reasons as I discussed earlier, this will require recourse to decision rules along the lines set out in Chapter 7. Even with the backing of a family, the problems of complexity, lack of information and uncertainty about the future will force individuals to adopt a variety of heuristics.

Where there is joint decision-making, as in Type 4–6 decisions, conflict resolution will generally first be required by one of the means outlined earlier. Unless joint decision-making results in the views of one family member being wholly adopted – as is quite possible – the decisions which emerge will differ from those which would have been taken had any one individual had his/her own way. In other words, joint family decision-making might be likened to an additional (disembodied) member joining the family and having his/her views adopted. As with autonomous decisions, however, other members of the family would still have exerted influence over the decision(s) taken.

In discussing the individual decision maker I distinguished between simple and complex decisions. This distinction applies with equal force in family decision-making, although the unit of decision-making may be joint as well as autonomous, as in the case of shopping expeditions to a supermarket by husband and wife. Much family behaviour is of a fairly routine, repetitive nature, not requiring much thought or effort, and there is every reason to believe, therefore, that, as with the individual, a great deal – perhaps the greater part of family decision-making – is of the simple, rather than the complex, variety. In many families, especially when children are growing up, wants are such that little in the way of discretionary income is available once 'overheads' have been met.

Since the family, like the individual, will generally be unable to satisfy all its wants at once from the resources available, there will remain an unsatisfied residual of wants. These unsatisfied wants, if they are at all significant, are more than likely to have consequences for the next round of decision-making. Labour force decisions, for example, about which family members work – and for how long – would be subject to review in a subsequent round if a family had been markedly unsuccessful in satisfying its wants. Decision-making is a more or less continuous, dynamic feature of family life to which members have to adapt.

CONCLUSIONS

Individual behaviour lies at the heart of family behaviour, and it is to individual motives, in particular the satisfaction of needs, such as security and a sense of belonging, that we must turn if we wish to understand why individuals join families in the first place – and why families remain a popular social unit, even if a changing one and less popular than in the past. Families are also subject to many of the same social influences as individuals, and more besides, since families interact with other families, and have a powerful influence on each other.

Despite the strong presence of individual motivation, however, it could be very misleading to treat families as if they were a single unit for decision-making purposes. I have stressed the importance of role behaviour in families, and how there is in practice a variety of decision-making units within each family, depending upon the type of activity in question. Different family decision-making units are likely to be responsible for the purchases of different products, for example. What is more, roles change with time as opinions on social matters alter. There is, too, a trend toward more joint decision-making. I have also stressed how both individual and *family* life cycles play important parts in *family* behaviour. In sum, the picture which emerges is of a dynamic centre of decision-making, changing over time – it seems helpful to distinguish between the family as a decision-making *centre*, on the one hand, and the family decision-making *units* which actually make decisions within the family, on the other (this is a distinction I shall carry forward when looking at other socioeconomic decision-making centres).

In assessing family wants I did treat the family as one unit, in contrast to decision-making, which I analysed in terms of separate decision-making units. The formation of family wants was, however, expressed in a way which still enabled us to capture differences between individuals within the family. Moreover, many needs may be treated as joint, such as those for most items of food and drink. Decision-making, on the other hand, is a much more specific activity, and the two approaches do not seem inconsistent.

The goal of the family, as with the individual, will be to satisfy as many of its wants as possible within the constraints it faces, such as that of income. The major complication facing groups like the family, however, is that the goals of the individual members may clash with each other, and there may also be differences of opinion over the best means of achieving goals. Where differences do emerge, means must be found of resolving the conflict. The survival of the family as a social institution suggests that for the most part differences are resolved, although the increase in the incidence of divorce and the larger number of broken homes may indicate that decision-making is becoming a less harmonious process.

Where decision-making in families is on an agreed basis, it may not be an undue distortion to treat the different decision-making units within the family as if they were separate individuals, even when decisions are joint. That does not mean, however, that the family *as a whole* can be treated as one individual, with stable preferences. As I noted above, the family is a dynamic centre of activity with the individual and family life cycles and changing roles prominent among the factors contributing to this dynamism.

9 Socioeconomic Decision-Making: Trade Unions

Trade unions have little *direct* effect on expenditure in the economy, since the funds at their disposal are small in relation to total national expenditure. They do, however, have a considerable impact on the wages of the unionised sector of the labour force, as, for example, US studies of the union-non-union wage differential demonstrate – somewhere between 5 and 25 per cent, depending upon the occupation, industry and other characteristics of the worker (Farber, 1986). Trade unions also exercise some control over the supply of labour (as well as its price) and therefore also over employment and unemployment. They are heavily involved, too, in bargaining with employers over a wide range of matters other than pay, such as pensions, physical conditions at the work place, health and safety arrangements, etc. As a last resort, if negotiations fail, they may also institute strikes as a means of bringing pressure to bear on employers. There is therefore a good case for looking at the operations of trade unions before we look at firms, since this will provide us with a better idea of individual goals within the organisational setting of a firm.

Trade unions differ in certain important respects from some of the other decision-making centres examined in the present study. The decision-making process itself is different, in that decisions are often taken – although by no means always – by the use of democratic voting procedures (in this it resembles democratic forms of government, examined in Chapter 11). The ordinary union members, for whose benefit the union primarily exists, generally employ officials to represent them and carry out much of the day-to-day business of the union. This means once again that there are different interests within the decision-making centre. The activities of the trade unions, moreover, are also subject to control by national or local government legislation, often aimed specifically at unions. In some countries, such as the United States, this legislation may go so far as to prevent public service workers from striking, thereby removing the ultimate bargaining weapon.

Despite their separate distinguishing features, there remains the link common to all the socioeconomic decision-making centres, namely, the individual. It is *individuals* who actually make decisions within the union, sometimes autonomously, but in most unions more often jointly. The complex motives of individuals therefore remain the driving force behind all that unions do, even if compromise is required in order to permit individuals to act in consort. I shall therefore once more be drawing on my earlier discussion of individual behaviour.

I also pose my usual question: why should individuals want to join this particular socioeconomic decision-making centre? The most frequent reply from members seems likely to be that it helps them to obtain a higher level of wages than would otherwise be possible – and there is empirical evidence, as I noted above, to support such a view. Income is important insofar as it may be used to purchase a wide range of satisfiers of needs and wants. Membership of a union may, however, also satisfy other needs. It gives a strong sense of belonging, and may offer a feeling of security from job loss, from possible victimisation by an employer, from competition from non-union – or even other union – labour, and so forth. In craft unions, membership may also grant status. Quite a few unions, finally, offer their members a variety of welfare and leisure services, such as hospital or recuperation facilities, games facilities, etc. Over time, as individual prosperity increases, some of these services may be needed less, or become less attractive. The proportion of the labour force unionised has dropped, for example, in the United States, although other factors, such as the decline of certain highly unionised industries, have also been at work, and it is perhaps too early to conclude that the decline is irreversible.

TRADE UNION ORGANISATION

The broad diversity of trade unions makes it difficult to classify them in a precise fashion, but a number of attempts have been made. A common method of classification is to distinguish between craft, general and industrial unions (McCormick, 1969). Craft unions organise workers who have generally acquired skills by serving apprenticeships. General unions (not a feature of the US labour scene) usually place few, if any, restrictions on the provenance of those they recruit, although they tend to find members principally among the semi-skilled and unskilled. Industrial unions, as the term suggests, confine their membership to employees in a particular industry.

For our purposes, a more useful classification of trade unions divides them into closed, open and an intermediate category with both closed and open components (Turner, 1959). Closed unions correspond roughly with the craft unions, whereas open unions more closely resemble the general and industrial unions. The intermediate category covers those closed unions which have expanded to include additional groups of workers which have been kept segregated from the traditional members – sometimes a defensive move.

Turner uses his classification to explain differences in union organisation and government. Closed unions tend to have a small, committed membership actively involved in the running of union affairs and keen to protect wages and conditions of service, especially in relation to other unions. Open unions tend to be characterised by a changing membership, which is therefore less committed to their union and less actively involved in its affairs. In such circumstances, union officials, especially those who are full-time, tend to have a much greater say in the running of the union.

Although brief, and not in any way pretending to be comprehensive, the above is sufficient to draw out the different interest groups within a union. On the one hand there is the membership, which may itself be split into different groups, especially in the general unions, either according to industry or degree of skill. The other principal interest group is the full-time officials, who may have somewhat different goals from the members.

MODELS OF TRADE UNION BEHAVIOUR

In an early debate on the behaviour of trade unions, Dunlop (1944, 1950) and Ross (1948) set out the two principal opposing viewpoints about the nature of trade union behaviour, and many of the comments and criticisms made at that time retain much of their validity. It is therefore worth raking over some of this old ground as a starting point for our discussion.

An early debate

Dunlop's analysis fell within the neo-classical tradition – even although he was well aware of the weaknesses inherent in the traditional assumption that the price of labour was determined by supply and demand, like any commodity. The short-run supply curve of labour was taken to be the outcome of decisions by individuals, based on their relative preferences for income and leisure. The market supply function was derived from the summation of individual preferences. Where a trade union was present, it generally displaced individual decisions, rendering the supply conditions even more obscure.

A difficulty with summing individual supply functions, Dunlop pointed out, was that the household, not the individual, was frequently the relevant decision-making centre. The income of a family, for example, rather than that of any one individual in the family, was more likely to be the crucial factor determining whether or not a particular individual entered the labour market. Furthermore, Dunlop noted that, 'the amount of labour offered for sale at any one price may deviate from that dictated by summing individual preferences because the group acting collectively through the union may have quite different preferences'. For these and other reasons Dunlop therefore rejected any idea of a unique market supply function for labour. Instead, he preferred to think in terms of a 'wage-membership function', showing the total amount of labour that will be attached to the labour organisation at each wage rate – in effect, 'the appraisal by the leadership of the amount of labour that will be allied to the union at each wage rate'.

Dunlop went on to note further that, 'The leadership of the trade union is presumed to know not only the membership function but also the wage-bill employment function, that is, the way in which the total wage bill in this segment of the economy will vary with the amount of labour services employed'. To complicate matters still further, this demand function for labour was subject to change over time.

The final stage in determining the wage level that would be established with the given membership and demand functions, and possible shifts in the functions, now depended upon the maximising goal assumed, and here Dunlop considered a number of possibilities. These included:

1. achieving the largest possible wage bill for union members;
2. if the first objective above should leave some labour unemployed, the union might organise its own unemployment fund or press for a public unemployment or relief programme (the trade union goal would then be revised to obtaining the largest possible wage fund and public unemployment support fund combined);
3. maximising the wage bill of *those members employed*, allowing an out-of-work benefit to those remaining unemployed;
4. securing the largest possible amount of employment;
5. maximising the collective wage 'rents' of those employed, i.e., maximising the surplus income over and above what the members would be able to obtain in a perfectly competitive labour market.

Dunlop's list of possible goals is worth recording in full, because a number of subsequent studies have adopted, or adapted, one or other of the possible goals he identified. Rosen (1970), de Menil (1971) and Calvo (1978), for example, have undertaken studies based on the assumption that a union's goal is to maximise its rent. In recent years, as we shall see below, the emphasis has switched to studies in which the unions attempt to negotiate an 'efficient' contract which achieves the best outcome in terms of both pay and employment. For his own purposes, Dunlop chose the first goal listed – the maximisation of the wage bill – as being, 'The most suitable generalised model of the trade union for analytical purposes . . . '.

In an extensive critique of Dunlop's theory, and of the neo-classical maximising approach in general, Ross (1948) advanced an alternative 'political' model of union behaviour. In his view, the marginal productivity theory of the demand for labour did not offer any significant insight into whether or not a firm would lay off workers as a consequence of, say, a 10 per cent wage increase. The long-run labour supply, moreover, was governed by social customs regarding such matters as family size, rather than by economic forces. Nor was there such a thing as a single price for labour. Ross, in essence, questioned whether all the significant forces affecting wages under collective bargaining could be compressed into a single supply-and-demand explanation.

Ross also maintained that many of the most interesting questions concerning union behaviour could not be answered by any strictly economic analysis – for example, why wage comparisons have little to do with labour market competition, why strikes occur over small differences in pay, and why some wage differentials are ignored while others are attacked. He was also of the view that, ' . . . the most powerful influence linking together separate wage bargains into an interdependent system is the force of equitable comparison' – a view I strongly support in the present study.

It was not that Ross rejected the importance of underlying economic influences, since many clearly do affect a union's bargaining strength, but rather that he envisaged the economic environment as being important to the unions at the second remove: that is, generating political pressures which had to be reckoned with by the union leader. Essentially he was saying that if we are to understand trade union behaviour we have to try and analyse it within a broader context which embraces all the social sciences: ' . . . today it must seriously be doubted whether there is any such thing as purely economic activity, purely political activity, or even purely religious activity'.

In Ross's own model of union behaviour, the central goal of the trade union is 'institutional survival and growth'. To accomplish this purpose, various 'political' pressures have to be reconciled in the bargaining process: 'These pressures are experienced by union leaders in their relationships with the rank and file, the employers, other organisational levels of the union, other unions, and the government.' Ross envisaged union officials identifying their own personal aims with the institutional objectives of the union, and attempting to reconcile the various pressures in a manner which would enable the union goal of survival and growth to be achieved. In the end, '. . . trade union policy is inevitably a leadership function. The reason is not that the leadership has wrested dictatorial power from the rank and file, but that it alone is in possession of the necessary knowledge, experience, and skill to perform the function adequately.'

Ultimately, therefore, the union in Ross's eyes is the leadership of the union, but the leaders are not wholly free agents. They must react in some degree to pressures from their members. Ross foresaw two circumstances, in particular, under which the pressures were likely to become imperatives: the first was where rising inflation or a reduction in pay caused a fall in members' living standards; the other was an invidious comparison with the wages, or wage increases, of other groups of workers. My analysis of needs and wants, and the role of social comparisons, in the present study helps us understand why this should be so.

More recent models of union behaviour

The debate between Dunlop and Ross was inconclusive, and both writers continued to exercise considerable influence in subsequent discussion of union behaviour. There remained considerable dissatisfaction, however, with the state of play as these two writers left it. Those in the neo-classical tradition were especially aware that there was still a failure to integrate union behaviour and wage bargaining fully into the mainstream. A survey article by Johnson (1975) expressed the following view:

> . . . it is worth noting that the problem of modeling trade union behaviour has proved to be virtually intractable. This is because (1) there is no consensus on the goals of union activity (see W.H. Atherton) such as exists with respect to the firm or consumer and (2) the received pure theory of bargaining is devoid of operational content. The absence of a solid theoretical content has handicapped the economic analysis of trade unions . . .

Johnson's statement has proved to be unduly pessimistic. During the 1980s a new strand in the literature emerged which attempted to fill the gap in the theory. An important feature of the new approach (as Mayhew and Turnbull, 1989, have already stressed) is that it abandoned the trade union as the basic unit of analysis, and instead adopted the utility function of the individual union member as a starting point. Union preferences are then supposedly derived from individual preferences. Unfortunately, while showing a greater appreciation of the nature of the problem, the new approach in attempting to solve one difficulty encounters others which it has not yet been successful in overcoming, as we shall see below.

Recent surveys of trade union bargaining behaviour (see, for example, Oswald, 1985, Farber, 1986, and Mayhew and Turnbull, 1989) have identified two principal models: the 'monopoly model' and the 'efficient bargain (or contract) model'. Both are in the neo-classical maximising tradition, although they differ appreciably in other respects. In the monopoly model, in which all employees are represented by one union, and there is only one employer, the union's total utility (U) is given by the function

$$U = U(W, N) \tag{9.1}$$

where, W is the wage rate and N is the level of employment. The union attempts to maximise this function, taking the firm's labour demand function as given. The wage selected is W_m, which is the wage rate yielded by the point of tangency between the union's indifference curve (I_1) and the labour demand schedule (N_d) at point A in Figure 9.1. In effect, the union

Figure 9.1 The efficient bargain (or contract) model

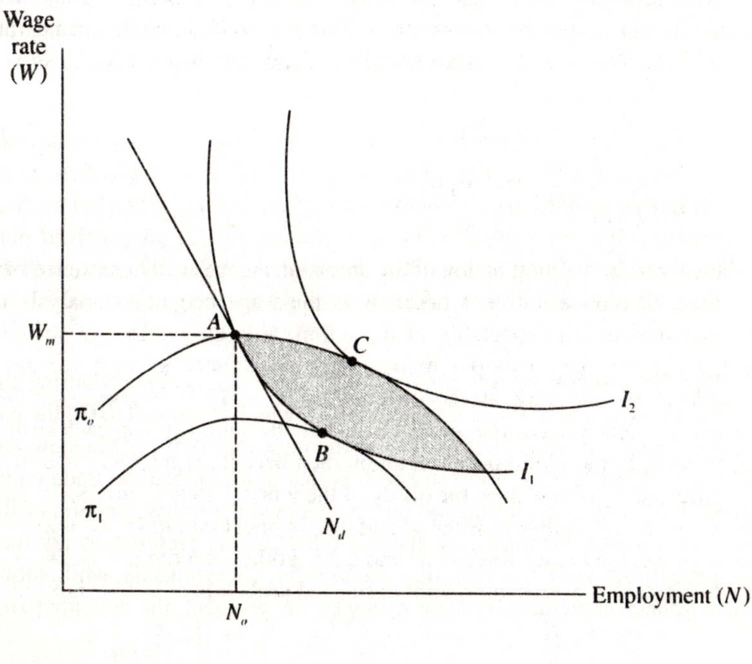

has chosen the wage and the firm has responded by setting the level of employment N_o.

A weakness of the monopoly model is that its outcome is not the most efficient possible if both union and employer are prepared to *bargain* over the outcome. Figure 9.1 shows that a movement down the indifference curve I_1 (which leaves the union's utility unchanged) to point B enables the firm to attain a higher level of profits by moving from the iso-profit curve π_o to the curve π_1. Similarly, a movement along the firm's iso-profit curve π_o to the right of A leaves the firm's profits unchanged while increasing the union's utility – employment is increased, even if the wage falls from W_m, since the union is able to move on to a higher indifference curve I_2, with a maximum utility at point *C*. At other points within the shaded area, both union and employer will benefit. However, efficient contracts, or bargaining outcomes, are those given by the locus of points of tangency between indifference curves and the iso-profit curves (including points *B* and *C*). The foregoing discussion is sufficient to make the key point: only bargaining over *both* wage and employment permits an efficient outcome.

A variety of objective utility maximising functions have been used to test the models outlined above, although the basic approach remains the same. Two of these functions, which take much the same form, are usually referred to as the 'utilitarian' and 'expected utility' functions. They have been used in studies by, for example, Farber (1978), Carruth and Oswald (1983) and Brown and Ashenfelter (1986), and may be expressed as:

$$U = Nu(w) + (M - N)\, u\,(b) \tag{9.2}$$

$$U = \frac{Nu(w)}{M} + \frac{(M - N)\, u\,(b)}{M} \tag{9.3}$$

where, *U* is the utility function of the union, *u*(.) is the utility function of the median, or representative, worker, w is the wage rate negotiated by the union, *M* is total membership of the union, *N* is the number of workers employed and *b* is unemployment pay or an alternative wage for those unable to obtain work at the contract wage *w*. If *M* is fixed, the two functions clearly have the same form, but the rationale for each differs somewhat. In the utilitarian case, union members are regarded as identical, and the goal is to maximise the utility of the union, which is simply the sum of its members' utility at wage *w* and employment pay *b*. In the expected utility case, the labour force is *M* and each worker in a random draw has a probability *N*/*M* of obtaining utility *u*(*w*) and probability (*N*–*M*)/*M* of utility

$u(b)$. The two cases shown in equations (9.2) and (9.3) may be expressed in a more general form as:

$$U = \alpha u(w)N + (1-\alpha)u(b)(M-N) \qquad (9.4)$$

where, $0 \leq \alpha \leq 1$
and α is the relative weight, or influence, of the employed and unemployed union members on the union's policy.

Another general form of the union's objective utility function which has been used quite extensively (see, for example, Dertouzos and Pencavel, 1981, MaCurdy and Pencavel, 1986, and Pencavel, 1984) is a modified version of the so-called Stone-Geary utility function. The function may be expressed as:

$$U = \alpha\,(w-w^{*})^{\mu}(N-N^{*})^{\mu-1} \qquad (9.5)$$

where, w^{*} and N^{*} may be interpreted as the minimum wage and employment levels that the union is prepared to accept, and the values of μ and $\mu-1$ indicate the relative importance of wages and employment in the union's utility function. Advantages of the Stone-Geary function are its tractability and flexibility. On the debit side, there is not even any pretence that it is derived from the preferences of individual workers via a union's 'political' process (Farber, 1986).

Following a review of the evidence from the testing of the above functions – much of it at the industry level for a few carefully chosen trade unions, such as the United Mine Workers and the International Typographical Union in the United States, and National Union of Mineworkers in the UK – Farber attempted to assess whether any *general* conclusions could be drawn from the results. He concluded that optimists would argue that the evidence showed trade unions to be sensitive to the employment consequences of their wage policies, and that they attached considerable importance to employment relative to wages – the precise relative weighting varying according to context. A pessimist, Farber maintained, would, on the other hand, argue that such strong conclusions were unwarranted for at least two reasons: first, because the studies were undertaken in a form which implied that the union could impose whatever settlement it wished on the parties; secondly, while workers might have similar preferences in different contexts, the structural, institutional and 'political' characteristics governing collective bargaining were sufficiently variable to ensure that the union objective functions would differ considerably across contexts. The latter criticisms form part of a much broader critique of the neo-classical approach to trade union behaviour to which we now turn.

Issues raised by the models

In a Utilitarian world there is no need to distinguish one individual from another, and no difficulty arises therefore in summing the individual utilities of a group of people. This approach is carried over into the recent neo-classical models of union behaviour, with the assumption (not always explicit) that union members are homogeneous. Such an assumption flies in the face of all the evidence. In Chapters 3 and 4 I assembled a good deal of material to show that needs, and therefore wants, will vary according to the age and sex of individuals, and within a family group according to the stage of the family life cycle. Individuals are also subject to widely varying social influences which help bring about marked differences in preferences. The only conclusion one can draw is that the Utilitarian person (we do not know whether it is male or female) lives in a social vacuum, completely untouched by the surrounding world. What conclusions of a practical nature, one might wonder, can be drawn from analysis of the behaviour of such an individual.

Recognising this serious flaw in the analysis, some writers have attempted to introduce a measure of heterogeneity. Farber (1978), for example, uses the device of a median-aged member – chiefly to minimise the risk that union leaders might be among those losing their jobs. Seniority has also been introduced (Grossman, 1983) as a criterion by which dismissal might be ordered. Such devices, however, do not in any way overcome the basic faults in the Utilitarian approach. A trade union is a group of individuals, including not only ordinary members but also union leaders, and all have goals of their own. A better means of specifying and reconciling these goals must be found.

A further criticism which has been made of the Utilitarian approach is that union membership is generally taken as being exogenously determined – tantamount to the assumption of a pre-entry closed shop, and therefore seriously limiting the application of such models (Mayhew and Turnbull, 1989). Oswald (1985) has maintained that, while the assumption of exogeneity may not matter for some purposes, if we are to have a *general* theory of the trade union we must be able to explain union size. Some not wholly successful attempts have been made to tackle the issue. Assuming free entry into the union, and using his seniority rule, Grossman (1983) is able to demonstrate that in certain circumstances unemployment may ensue. Oswald (1985) notes, however, that the questions of why it is rational for a union to operate a seniority system, and why the parties should be willing to agree to the Pareto-inefficient equilibria of his model, are left unexplained. The assumption of free entry may also be more appropriate in the US than in European countries. In other models, more employment may be generated than under competitive conditions (e.g. Kidd and Oswald, 1983). Attempts at explaining membership therefore still leave a good many unanswered questions.

The above issues are certainly not unimportant, but the nub of the problem with the newer approaches to trade union behaviour, as with all neo-classical economics, is the failure to face up to the full implications of the problems of uncertainty, complexity and the lack of full information. Situations of risk, with assessable probabilities, may be catered for, but not those of true uncertainty, where such probabilities are incalculable. The problems are well illustrated by the nature of bargaining between union and employer. There is, to start with, a situation of asymmetric information, in that the employer is better placed to assess the employment implications of different wage rates, although even the employer will be obliged to take employment decisions in a climate of uncertainty, since future sales, production and prices will depend upon factors some of which will lie outside his control, like the world economic climate.

In such circumstances, unions are faced not with simple, repetitive decisions, but with complex ones. Only if a union were on occasions prepared to play safe by accepting a very low pay award could it be reasonably certain of averting redundancies for its members – and even then there could be no certainty. How then, in such circumstances, do unions conduct their affairs? I will turn now to look for some answers in the decision-making processes of trade unions.

DECISION-MAKING BY TRADE UNIONS

Within a trade union the two principal parties which can be identified are the union members and the union officials. Individuals within each of these groups will have their own personal goals, and before we can talk about a 'union goal' we must first examine the likely goals of the two parties, and discuss how these might be reconciled. In order to understand the motivating factors at work I will have to draw upon my earlier discussion of individual motivation in Chapter 3. In essence, both union officials and members will be motivated to satisfy their needs and wants to the greatest extent possible. Their wants will, in turn, be greatly influenced by the social influences surrounding them, with social comparisons being an important vehicle for the transmission of these influences. Union members and officials will also attach considerable importance to equitable treatment in their dealings with employers, since equity, as we saw in Chapter 3, is also one of the principal motivating forces.

In an organisational setting, such as that within a firm, considerations of equity become especially important, since not only are individuals often working in close proximity to each other, and therefore able to compare inputs and outcomes at first hand, but they have fairly well-defined reference groups in the form of similar workers, either in other parts of the same organisation or in other firms. Furthermore, considerations of equity embrace not just the question of pay (a general, and for most people the predominant, means of satisfying needs and wants) but also the important matter of status, intertwined with a sense of belonging to a certain group of employees. Considerations of equity will therefore be important in the formulation of individual goals within the firm. We may restate Adams's (1963, 1965) conditions for equity as one of the chief goals of employees in a firm:

$$\Sigma Op/\Sigma Ip = \Sigma Oa/\Sigma Ia$$

The employee, or in Adams's terms Person, will aim to ensure that the ratio of the weighted sum of his inputs (ΣIp) in relation to the weighted sum of his outcomes (ΣOp) matches the corresponding ratio for Other (any person with whom Person compares himself when both he and Other are in an exchange relationship with a third person, such as an employer, or with third parties who are considered by Person to be comparable, such as employers in a particular industry or geographic location).

The outcomes of Person, as noted in Chapter 3, will comprise both a pecuniary element (which we denote by Ox) and a non-pecuniary element (Oy). Within a firm the pecuniary element for all employees will ultimately be constrained by the organisational goal for that firm, which is the need to earn a normal return on its assets. If there is a failure to agree between employer and employee, some means of conflict resolution to reconcile goals will be required.

Since wages are likely to comprise much the largest component of the pecuniary element of an employee's outcomes, we can be even more specific about an employee's goals in this most important and sensitive area of an organisation's activities – the analysis which follows draws heavily on the discussion in Baxter (1988). Included in Person's outcomes will be a level of pay considered to be equitable (Wp^*) both in relation to Person's other outcomes and his inputs, and in relation to the inputs and outcomes of Other. Should Person's actual wage (Wp) differ from the equitable wage, Person will be motivated to try and rectify the situation. If $Wp < Wp^*$, Person has the options of trying to raise Wp, raise his other outcomes, reduce his inputs, or achieve a combination of all these. The evidence available also suggests that if $Wp > Wp^*$ Person will again be motivated, by one means or another, to restore a more equitable balance.

The above argument has been conducted in terms of the relationship between only two individuals, but the argument may be generalised to cover an individual's (or a group's) pay comparisons with one or more reference groups used for the purpose of pay comparisons. In this broader context the employee's pay goal may be expressed as:

$$Wi = Wi^* = k\bar{W}rl \qquad (9.6)$$

where, Wi is the actual wage of individual i, Wi^* is i's perception of his equitable wage and $k\bar{W}rl$ is the equitable wage expressed as a proportion of the mean wage of reference group rl.

Assuming individual i had been successful in obtaining his equitable wage, his objective then would be to maintain that position over time. This would require a forward looking stance by i, since he would have to try and anticipate, and match, any wage increase obtained by rl. If we now regard equation (9.6) as only one element in i's overall pay goal, we might express the second element as:

$$\dot{W}i^e = \dot{\bar{W}}^e rl \qquad (9.7)$$

where $\dot{\bar{W}}^e rl$ is the expected rate of change of rl's wage and $\dot{W}i^e$ is the matching rate of change desired by i for his own wage – if i is in the habit of using more than one reference group, then the target growth of i's wage would be determined by the reference group likely to obtain the most rapid growth in wages (a familiar situation in pay bargaining).

Since a tendency for prices to rise faster than i's wage would cause a reduction in his *real* wage, and therefore in his ability to satisfy his needs and wants, a third element in his pay goal is likely to be:

$$\dot{W}i^e = \dot{P}^e \qquad (9.8)$$

where $\dot{P}^e$ the expected rate of change of prices and $\dot{W}i^e$ is the rate of change of i's wage required to maintain its real value. An alternative strategy would be to seek compensation for past price increases, but such a strategy could lead to appreciable, even if temporary, reductions in real income during periods of accelerating inflation.

Finally, since there has been a well-established tendency (in most Western advanced industrial countries, at least) for employees' pay to outstrip the rise in prices, thereby enabling real wages and living standards to increase, it would not be at all surprising to find employees including a target growth of real wages as a final element in their pay goal – indeed there is empirical evidence to support such a view (see Baxter, 1988). This aspect of the pay goal might be represented as:

$$\dot{W}i^e = \dot{P}^e + \alpha \tag{9.9}$$

where α is a constant representing the target growth of real wages.

Drawing together the various elements of the pay goal outlined above, we could now present a unified pay goal for i. The value of $\dot{W}i^e$ will depend upon whichever of the independent variables in equations (9.7) to (9.9) has the greatest value. A simple example would be the case in which $Wi = W^*i = k\bar{W}rl$ at the outset, and $(\dot{P}^e + \alpha) > \dot{\bar{W}}rl > \dot{P}^e$.

The unified pay goal would then be that depicted in equation (9.9).

Where $Wi < W^*i$ a measure of catch-up would be required and $\dot{W}i^e$ would have to be greater than that indicated in equation (9.9) – again a not unfamiliar situation, where a group of employees has fallen behind in the pay league, as in the public sector in the UK during prolonged periods of incomes policy.

Faced with i's pay goal, the employer will no doubt wish to negotiate. The latter will, for example, almost certainly want to bring into consideration other elements of wage cost, such as pensions and fringe benefits. The ultimate constraint on the firm in its bargaining, as we stressed earlier, will be the need to earn a normal return on its assets. If that goal appears to be threatened, the resistance of the employer can be expected to stiffen appreciably. Even before it is reached, an employer may be forced to make workers redundant if he feels obliged to make concessions on pay which increase the cost of labour unduly, for example in relation to alternative means of production which use more capital relative to labour.

Until now we have viewed the union member's goals in terms of pecuniary outcomes, principally pay, but continued employment must also be an important consideration. A member's need for security, after all, depends not just on a high level of pay but on that pay continuing. The problem is that the links between pay and employment are not direct and transparent to all. Even an employer cannot say precisely what the consequences of a given pay award will be for the firm's employment, since that requires a forward look, and no one can predict with certainty the level of sales, prices and profits in the future. Any suggestion, therefore, of a smooth marginal trade-off between pay and employment is misleading.

There is certainly no evidence of widespread bargaining over pay and employment in tandem – indeed in the light of all the uncertainties noted above it would be surprising if there were. There may be examples of declining industries, or industries/occupations with declining employment arising from technological change, where employment guarantees have been negotiated, but, as Farber (1986) has remarked in the case of the United States, it is difficult to think of industries with stable or growing employment where such guarantees have been negotiated.

Confirmation of the above view appears to be provided by a survey of the bargaining strategies of the 60 largest trade unions in both the US and the UK by Oswald (1987). He found that only a small minority of unions in both countries said they normally negotiated over the number of jobs as well as over wages and conditions – a more common practice was negotiation over hours of work and manning decisions, agreement on which was often written into labour contracts. Similarly, when asked if employment was set unilaterally by the employer, the great majority replied in the affirmative. In a further, more extensive, study, Clark and Oswald (1989) carried out a survey of British trade union leaders' views about the bargaining priorities of their unions. Despite the possible weaknesses in such an approach, the response rate was very high, with 57 of the 83 Trade Unions Congress (TUC) affiliated unions (accounting for 90 per cent of the combined membership) providing usable responses. They showed that by a margin of two to one British unions gave top priority to wages over employment. A total of 25 unions said they usually negotiated over the total number of workers employed as well as over wages, but when also asked if the level of employment was usually decided by the employer, 49 (accounting for 86 per cent of the combined membership) replied in the affirmative.

In circumstances where any pay rise, or a pay rise of a particular order, might cause unemployment, or where an employer threatens unemployment, what sorts of consideration might be uppermost in the minds of union members? Here conflicts of interest between members might come into play. Those who felt least threatened by redundancy might be all in favour of pressing ahead regardless in pursuit of a large pay rise. Those not too far from retirement, or those happy to leave the firm, might favour *negotiated* redundancy (perhaps even compulsory redundancy if there were legal requirements for firms to offer reasonable compensation). Precisely what the outcomes of such conflicts of interest will be is again very difficult, if not impossible, to predict. Such variables as the age distribution of union members, or the nature of any legal requirements, might provide some clues to the likely outcome, but whether the effects would be sufficiently regular to permit prediction must be doubted. More empirical research in this area is required.

In the face of all the uncertainties, it is not surprising that union members concentrate most on pay, where there is likely to be the best chance of consensus, permitting the use of simple decision rules of the sort expressed in equations (9.6) to (9.9) above. The problem of uncertainties is not wholly overcome, of course, since predicting inflation, for example, is a hazardous business; but choices are clear and more easily understood. There is a good deal of evidence, furthermore, that the sorts of considerations expressed in the equations are in fact those which most exercise the minds of union members (see Baxter, 1988).

What of the trade union officials? Farber (1986) has noted that, 'A major problem with the analysis of union behaviour where the leadership has some freedom to pursue its own goals (malfeasance) is that very little is known about what these goals might be or how they might be analysed in a systematic fashion'. I would suggest that the analysis of individual needs and wants, the social comparison process, and the effects which social influences have on wants, along the lines outlined in the present study, would provide at least some clues to the factors likely to determine the goals of union leaders. As individuals, there is no reason why the factors motivating their behaviour should differ greatly from those motivating union members, although the relative weightings might vary somewhat. The prime consideration for a union official, as Ross (1948) mentioned, must be the continued survival of the union, since without the union the official has no job, and loses all pay and security. Other motivating forces which might well rank highly are the desires for power and status – although here again concrete evidence seems to be lacking.

The continued existence of a union depends in turn on keeping union members adequately satisfied. The pay goals expressed in equations (9.6) to (9.9) will therefore weigh heavily in officials' priorities. The more democratic the union, the greater the weighting one might expect. In unions with less democratic structures, the more importance we might expect to find attached to sheer size, with the union's resources perhaps being directed more to recruitment, takeovers of other unions, etc., than to the welfare of existing union members.

Despite the wide diversity of trade unions, and possibly some divergence of interests between trade union members and officials, we feel that equations (9.6) to (9.9) are sufficiently representative of the interests of all the parties to be adopted as the union goals in negotiations with employers. As indicated earlier, all the goals could in certain circumstances be reduced to that expressed in equation (9.9), which could then in effect represent the organisational goal. I shall therefore carry it forward to the next chapter, in which I discuss the behaviour of firms.

10 Socioeconomic Decision-Making: Firms

In Chapter 7 of the present study I examined behaviour by an individual acting as a decision-making unit. In Chapter 8 I then turned to the family, a small group of individuals acting as a formal decision-making centre, but only loosely structured. Even within such a small grouping, however, decision-making became a much more complex process. Responsibility for making and implementing decisions was often jointly exercised, or responsibility for different activities alloted to different individuals. A logical progression from the decision-making of the family would have been to go on and examine decision-making in those (often small) non-profit making organisations whose spending also forms part of consumers' expenditure. A characteristic of these organisations is that they tend to be more formally structured than families, with elected or appointed officials, and often with formal rules governing their activities. We would nonetheless find many of the features already highlighted in our discussions of the individual and the family, or about to be highlighted in the present and subsequent chapters. I will therefore proceed now to an examination of decision-making within the firm, one of the most important units of analysis in economics.

The common link between the various decision-making units, or centres (there may be more than one decision-making unit within a decision-making centre, such as the family) is the individual. In particular, individual motivation, based principally on the satisfaction of individual needs and wants, is a potent force in all decision-making. Where individuals are acting in consort, there may, however, be differences of view about the relative priorities to be accorded the satisfaction of the different needs and wants, and some means of reaching agreement on common goals is therefore required.

Given the variety of tasks to be performed, individuals tend to be allotted or to adopt roles within the decision-making centre. Once again there is the possibility of conflict, perhaps over the precise definition of roles, or between roles. A means of resolving conflict therefore becomes a central requirement of group behaviour.

In the face of the complexity of many decisions, the frequent unavailability of relevant information and the uncertainty surrounding much decision-making, the adoption of simplifying rules is another common feature of decision-making by groups as well as individuals.

Firms have all the common features noted above, but in addition have certain distinguishing characteristics. They tend to be much more formally organised, with structures which identify the principal interest groups: shareholders (where there is an equity interest), managers and employees. Shareholders form a distinct additional interest group, whose interests are formally represented, but who may have little or no direct say in decision-making, other than possibly at the highest tier of authority, the Board of Directors. Even there, their influence on their representatives may be more apparent than real.

In the case of firms it is also meaningful to talk in terms of organisational goals, which are distinct from, but not wholly divorced from, the goals of individuals associated with firms, be they employees, managers or shareholders. Such goals, as we shall see, are founded principally upon the constraints within which firms have to operate if they are to survive in the longer-term. These constraints, in turn, are in some measure a reflection of the interests of the individuals upon whom firms are dependent for their continued existence. Since organisational goals are not easy to define precisely, and may conflict, or appear to conflict, with the goals of individuals or sub-groups within an organisation, goal conflict is frequently another characteristic of firms.

The more formal structure of firms also leads to a greater formalisation of roles, without however managing to avoid conflict over the precise definition of these roles. Within larger groupings like firms, there is also likely to be greater scope for conflict between sub-groups, and therefore yet a further requirement for conflict resolution.

A final feature of firms' activities which I wish to stress is that the problems faced by most firms tend to be even more complex than those faced by individuals on their own, or by the smaller, less formal, groups like the family. The greater complexity of problems also increases the information requirements of firms when attempting to choose between alternative courses of action. The greater range of relevant variables in decision-making means, furthermore, that uncertainty is usually even more pronounced a problem than it is with individuals or families – even more so if the firm operates internationally. Even although firms have greater resources at their disposal, financial and otherwise, to help them with decision-making, they are really no better placed than the other decision-making centres I have discussed to select the 'best' from the alternative courses of action available. Just like individuals and trade unions, therefore, we continue to see the need for simplifying decision rules.

While I have mentioned that decision-making in firms differs in certain significant respects from that of either the individual or the family, I have nevertheless stressed the strong common links between the various decision-making centres – the strongest being that they are all composed of individuals. The question might therefore be asked – as it was in the case of the family and the trade union – why do individuals join and make use of the institution of the firm? For a time economists were not very concerned about such questions. The emphasis was on the analysis of inputs to firms and the subsequent outputs, with what happened in between judged not to be of great importance (that 'black box' again, as Sawyer, 1989, has remarked). Coase (1937), however, developed what has come to be known as the 'transaction cost' view of the firm. In essence, a firm will undertake those activities which it can carry out more cheaply and effectively itself, rather than relying on the market (including individuals or other firms) to do the work for it. Williamson (1975) has suggested a number of reasons favouring internal production rather than reliance on the markets. First, individuals' capacity to receive, store and process information is limited (what Simon called 'bounded rationality') and therefore so too is their ability to make full use of the market. The passage of time and, associated with it, uncertainty about economic events, and the sheer complexity of decision-making, also favour internal production as a means of trying to reduce such difficulties.

Other writers (Alchian and Demsetz, 1972) have suggested that the reasons for the existence of firms lie in the nature of the production process, which generally requires that resources be combined in order to produce something. This creates problems which cannot be resolved through a market process. First, how to determine the reward appropriate to the productive contribution of every resource input; second, how to monitor the productive effort by every resource input, which might otherwise be disposed to shirk.

More recent work by Aoki (1984) harks back to the problem that not all resources used within the firm will have prices uniquely determined by external markets. In his view there is therefore room for bargaining, and this is best modelled as a co-operative game, the players of which are the shareholders and the workers (managers being reduced to the role of technocratic mediators).

In many respects, the economic analysis explaining the existence of firms dovetails quite closely with the reasons which might be advanced by psychologists or sociologists. The principal goal of individuals is to satisfy their needs, and many needs are satisfied by the production of goods and services. Individuals may either undertake the production themselves or do so jointly with others in return for a share of the output (either in kind or as financial remuneration). Joint production, as we saw, offers a greater measure of security, because it helps cope with the problem of uncertainty, and it also offers help in dealing with the obstacles of complexity and bounded rationality.

In addition to these benefits provided by firms, however, there are other benefits derived from joint working of which we are becoming increasingly aware – some of these benefits became clear as many more were deprived of work during the 1970s and 1980s. For many people, organised work in firms provides an important sense of belonging and companionship. It is these features of work, it seems, which attract a good many women back to work after rearing young children. In Baxter (1988) it was noted that 11 per cent of a representative sample of part-time workers gave as their *principal* reason for working that it enabled them to enjoy the company of others – much higher percentages included it on their list of main reasons for working. If we consider the other needs of individuals, strong cases could also be made out for regarding working for firms as an important means of achieving status, of self-actualisation, and, of course, of acquiring power – even if firms are by no means exclusive satisfiers of these needs.

GOALS OF THE FIRM AND ITS EMPLOYEES

Many different approaches have been adopted to the question of firms' goals, and it is helpful to summarise these before proceeding further.

Alternative approaches to the question of goals

In the standard neo-classical theory of the firm, no distinction is made between an organisation and a single entrepreneur. The organisation is always a private firm (public corporations are not meant to exist, and if they do, are regarded in the same light as monopolists or oligopolists) and its goals are simply the same as those of the entrepreneur. Such a view of affairs might have been acceptable in the 18th or early 19th centuries, but it is much more difficult to sustain today. Numerically, the number of small firms far exceeds that of the large joint stock companies, but it is the larger firms which make the running in such important areas as investment, research and development and exporting.

Simon (1976) has claimed that, where we are dealing with organisations, we must either explain organisational behaviour in terms of the goals of the *individual* members of the organisation, or we must postulate the existence of one or more organisational goals, over and above the goals of individuals. In what follows I shall marry these two approaches to organisational goals. I shall assert that organisational goals certainly do exist, but that they must, on the other hand, take account of the goals of individual members of the organisation if they are to be achieved.

In Chapter 6 I explained the constraints within which firms are obliged to operate. If firms are to survive in the long run they must be able to achieve an acceptable return on their assets, otherwise existing shareholders might take their funds away to invest in more profitable enterprises, and new shareholders prove difficult to attract. Even if shareholders were not alert to the poor financial performance of a firm they owned, and in theory ultimately controlled, financial predators seeking to purchase assets on the cheap would sooner or later be attracted and bid for the assets. The practice is now especially common in the US and the UK, although less so in other industrial countries, partly because of institutional impediments to company takeovers – such as large shareholdings by commercial banks, as in Germany, or legislation used to prevent unfriendly takeovers, as in Switzerland.

Even if we accept the idea of a 'normal return' goal for firms (not to be confused, of course, with the 'normal profits' of the firm in perfect competition) it is another matter to define more precisely what we mean by normal return. The economist's idea of opportunity cost is, however, useful in this context. The ultimate constraint on the firm is that, if shareholders can obtain a better financial reward from putting their funds into alternative investments, they will be tempted so to do. In practice, of course, the return on investment is not uniform throughout economies – even less so between economies – since financial markets do not work smoothly and efficiently. Nor is there any reason why the normal return should be synonymous with profit maximising, since all institutions may be working at less than the maximum. There is also the matter of the differences in risks attaching to investments, with riskier projects requiring higher rewards. 'Normal return' will therefore allow for the degree of risk involved, and will vary from one industry or use of funds to another. Finally, some divergence from normal return will be acceptable, especially in the short run, owing to the cost and inconvenience of moving funds. Inertia on the part of shareholders also seems to be quite a common failing.

The normal return of the firm as enunciated above is the minimum goal which will be satisfactory to shareholders, who form one of the principal interest groups in the firm. The other principal interest group within the firm is employees – management included, if they too are employed, although for some purposes management may see themselves more as the representatives of the shareholding interest. They have their own motives, as we noted earlier, for participating in firms, and therefore goals of their own. A number of the theories of the firm which have been advanced as alternatives to the standard neo-classical model have dealt at some length with the issue of employee goals (see Baxter, 1988). Cyert and March (1963) saw an organisation's goal(s) emerging from a process of bargaining between the interested parties (from which the largely passive stockholders were excluded) over 'side payments', which were said to cover not just money but the benefits to personnel of a non-financial nature. This bargaining process, it was held, goes on more or less continuously, but is given a certain stability by the fact that it operates within certain constraints, among which are the organisation's budget, limits to the discretion accorded to individuals within the organisation, and organisational precedents.

The above process, Cyert and March argued, leads to the adoption of five major goals within the firm, relating to production, inventories, sales, market share and profits. All these goals would clearly be subservient to the principal goal which we have set for firms of a normal return on assets, but Cyert and March make the important point that within organisations their five major goals are likely to be the concerns of different people, some of whom may rate one goal higher than another. There will therefore be conflict – and perhaps even inconsistencies – between the goals set, with conflict perhaps never being fully resolved.

Two other theories of the firm which have attempted to take account of personal goals in arriving at overall goals for the firm are those of Williamson (1964) and Marris (1964), although both placed rather less emphasis on relationships within the firm than did Cyert and March. Williamson – citing support from economists and organisation theorists – lists the 'immediate determinants' of individual behaviour within firms as: salary, security, status, power, prestige, professional excellence and social service (the last-mentioned he subsequently eliminated on the grounds that the scope for such behaviour was probably not great in the business firm).

Williamson went on to compare the various determinants of behaviour with Maslow's hierachy of needs, noting that security might be said to correspond with Maslow's safety and love needs, that dominance (under which heading he grouped status, power and prestige) accorded with the need for esteem, and that professional excellence might be regarded as a form of Maslow's 'self-actualisation'. Only salary did not fit neatly into the hierachy, but as I pointed out in Baxter (1988), salary might be regarded as a general means of satisfying a variety of needs requiring financial outlays. Williamson also cautioned that his list of motives might not be exhaustive

– one obvious omission, which I highlighted during my discussion of personal motives, is the desire for equitable treatment (of which I shall have more to say below).

In formulating his model of the firm, Marris (1964) also faced up to the question of personal motivation. His theory is explicitly managerial, largely ignoring the motives of other employees, and this could be considered a significant weakness, since manual, clerical and other employees also influence firms' goals. Marris's theory is also concerned with the long run and a firm's choice of a sustainable growth path, and in this respect shows similarities with my own approach.

Marris distinguishes three main approaches to motivation: the psychological, the sociological and the economic. The three approaches are used to segment discussion, but they turn out to have much in common, and lead to much the same conclusion. Under the psychological heading Marris includes the drive for achievement among managers and the tendency for their aspiration levels to rise as their objectives are achieved. He sympathises with Katona's (1951) view that managers do not see the firm as a mere apparatus for satisfying their own wants; they may even go so far as to see the prosperity and success of the firm as an actual proxy for their wants.

On the sociological side, the evidence cited by Marris again points to the business executive being 'many-sided and multi-motivated'. It is, however, the discussion of the 'economic' motives which is in some respects most interesting. Drawing mainly on the work of R.A. Gordon (1961), Marris concludes that managers desire not just 'narrow' economic gain, but also power, status, the opportunity for creative satisfaction and for group belonging and security. The list is one which could quite easily have been fitted into a categorisation of needs, and could therefore equally well have featured under the psychological and sociological headings.

The 'narrow' economic rewards to managers take three main forms: bonuses, stock options and basic compensation. Marris concludes from his analysis that it is the growth of the firm which is most important in determining these, as well as most of the other goals – non-economic as well as economic – such as the desires for achievement, status and power. Managers do not, however, throw caution entirely to the winds. They also have a desire for security, as was noted, and will wish to avoid possible takeover of their firms. Managers are, therefore, constrained to maintain the valuation ratio of their firms – defined as the ratio of the market value of the firm to its book value. Given all the above considerations, managers are led to set as their primary goal the maximisation of the rate of growth of their firms, subject to the constraint imposed by the security motive.

Although Marris's managers are concerned to avoid a takeover of their firms, and therefore to maintain maximum growth and the valuation ratio, it is not at all clear that they would be successful on the basis of these goals. If the goal of the firm is not to be the maximisation goal assumed in the neo-classical model, then it seems that shareholders, and investors generally, will be concerned not just with the growth of the firm, but with how well it performs relative to other firms, and how the return on their funds compares with the alternatives available elsewhere. There are plenty of examples of firms which have given high priority to growth only to find themselves running into financial difficulties at the first signs of economic recession – maximum growth generally entails heavy borrowing, for one thing. While Marris seems right to stress the value of growth in meeting managers' and other employees' aspirations, the overriding goal must be long-term survival, and that will require firms to provide their shareholders with an adequate return on the assets provided.

Other writers who have stressed the importance of personal motivation and goals, explicitly or implicitly, include Leibenstein (1976), Baumol (1967), Katona (1951), Scitovsky (1976) and Galbraith (1969). Each develops a distinctive approach, but as in the case of the other models examined above, there are common threads running through them all. In particular, it is acknowledged that personal needs continue to influence individual behaviour within organisations, and that organisational goals must therefore accommodate them to some degree.

Individual goals within a firm

Before going on to look at the goals of the firm, we must have a brief look at the goals of a firm's employees, since these may either be taken into account by the firm in setting its own goals, or they will have to be reconciled at some later stage with the goals of the firm. Our discussion in Chapter 9 indicates that the organisational goal of a trade union is overwhelmingly concerned with increasing the pay of union members – and, within that goal, of achieving equity in relation to reference groups, or individuals. The employment level as a consideration comes some considerable way behind. To the extent that there is bargaining over employment, it is more likely to be concerned with hours of work and/or crew size and manning decisions. In declining industries, or industries suffering from a sudden, severe worsening of trading conditions, employment considerations may weigh more heavily, but this is not the norm.

Not all factors motivating individuals are covered by trade union negotiations, of course. Oswald's (1987) survey revealed that, in the UK at least, no unions negotiated to reduce work effort, yet stress is a common problem in the workplace, and many individuals must be motivated to try and reduce it in the interests of their health – others may simply want an easier life (*want*, perhaps, rather than *need*). Power and status are other possible motivating forces for employees (as well as for trade union officials, as we noted earlier) and they may also want various amenities as part of their working conditions. Trying to quantify, or specify precisely, the consequences of all such factors for the operations of a firm is a very difficult task, and not all the consequences may have a significant impact on the operations, or profits, of a firm. In the case of firms covered by trade unions, therefore, we shall assume the trade union goal is that expressed in equation (9.9) – with the important proviso that the equation must also incorporate those goals expressed in equations (9.6) to (9.8).

What of non-union employees, who after all account for the bulk of the labour force in the United States and over one-half of that in the UK and some other countries? Since we draw on the same motive sources for *all* individuals, there is no reason to expect non-union members' goals to differ significantly from those of union members. The difference between the two sets of employees seems to rest essentially on whether or not the union is viewed as an effective *means* of achieving goals – and in some industries or firms there may also, of course, be employer resistance to union representation. For our purposes, therefore, we view equation (9.9) as expressing not only the goal of the union (or unions, if there is more than one) within a firm, but of all employees.

Subsidiary goals of the firm

We saw earlier that Cyert and March listed five major goals of the firm, covering production, inventories, sales, market share and profits. Since in our analysis a firm has the one overriding goal of earning a normal return on its assets, all but the last of Cyert and March's five goals might be better described as 'subsidiary goals', since they are no more than means to an end rather than ends in themselves – although to the extent that sheer size might be relevant to a felt need for status, for example, production, sales and market share could in themselves be regarded as ends rather than means. Even then, however, the requirement to earn a normal return would remain of paramount importance for the firm. The key question is: how might firms go about setting these subsidiary goals in order to ensure that they do not conflict with the firm's overriding goal? This takes us once more into the realms of decision-making, which I shall return to later in the chapter, but I need at least to make some preliminary observations at this stage.

The first point to note is that, since we are ultimately concerned in our model with aggregate behaviour, and therefore total expenditure in an economy, I also wish to include business fixed investment among the subsidiary goals of the firm. It is a major component of demand, and has an important bearing on the long-term health of a firm and its ability to meet both other subsidiary goals and the principal goal of a normal return.

The overriding goal of earning a normal return provides the firm with reasonably specific sub-goals, although in a constant climate of uncertainty the firm must stand ready to alter the mix of sub-goals as market conditions dictate. At any given time, a certain combination of sales and price (and therefore revenue) and costs will yield the desired normal return. In order to support the desired level of sales, certain levels of production (and therefore investment) and inventories, and probably also advertising, will be necessary. Most firms, however, might be expected to aim at a return somewhat in excess of the normal return, if only to compensate for periods when, due to unforeseen circumstances, the normal return is not achieved.

Simple although the above scenario appears in outline, trying to calculate in practice precisely what a firm's mix of subsidiary goals should be is a horrendously complex matter. Standard economic theory 'solves' the problem by prescribing how the profit maximising goal should be achieved, either on the assumption of a perfectly competitive market and the availability of full information about alternatives, or on the assumption of pure monopoly. When it comes to other market structures, however, more akin to those likely to be encountered in real life, such as oligopoly, uncertainty dominates decision-making, and predicting the outcome is only made possible by introducing supplementary hypotheses which prescribe firms' behaviour.

How then can firms proceed? The answer is that, despite the array of modern decision-making aids, such as computers, decisions are ultimately based on fairly simple decision-making rules which are comprehensible to individuals, reasonably flexible and take account of circumstances as they are, rather than as we might like them to be in an ideal world. The outcome is unlikely to be profit maximising behaviour, but firms will nevertheless be subject to market disciplines of a sort, depending upon how competitive market structures are in practice – and in this matter governments will have an important say.

I shall return to the question of the subsidiary goals of the firm below, when I examine decision-making within firms.

ORGANISATIONAL INFLUENCES ON FIRMS' BEHAVIOUR

In their study of organisational buying behaviour, Webster and Wind (1972) categorised the principal influences on organisations as: individual, environmental, organisational and interpersonal. To date we have considered the influences on the firm – especially on its goals – of individual motivation, in particular the desires to satisfy needs and wants, and to be treated equitably. In the matter of environmental influences, it is the constraint exercised by the requirement to earn a normal return which dictates the overriding goal of the firm. I will now turn to consider the influences of organisational and interpersonal factors. I find these difficult to separate, since the structure of an organisation has such a powerful influence on interpersonal relations. The causal links may sometimes run in the reverse direction, too, with interpersonal relations *within* a given organisational structure important in determining an organisation's behaviour, but organisation and interpersonal relations seem so closely intertwined that I shall consider them together in what follows.

The individual decision-maker within the firm

Economics skirts round the problems of organisational behaviour by assuming that the firm always acts as a unit. The implicit assumption appears to be that firms are represented by an entrepreneur who takes all the decisions of any consequence. Such an assumption might have been acceptable during the early stages of the development of economics, but in modern times there are just too many exceptions to the rule to make it any longer tenable. In the modern firm, many individuals participate in decision-making, and they often act *jointly*. Nevertheless small firms and individual entrepreneurs remain a very important force, even in advanced industrial economies, and within such firms decisions may still largely be left in the hands of only one or two people, often acting with a good deal of autonomy. Even outside the field of economics, therefore, analysis has sometimes been conducted in terms of one chief purchaser or buying agent acting on behalf of the firm.

When a buying agent within a firm does have a good deal of autonomy in making purchases, which factors are likely to have the greatest influence on him, or her? Most decisions will tend to be relatively simple ones, entailing straight repurchases or only slightly modified repurchases. But in more complex decisions there will be greater scope for the individual's own views to enter the calculations. There may even be room for personal motivation to play its part. Where, for example, a firm purchases automobiles for its more senior employees, a conflict may arise between the buyer's own desire for a vehicle to enhance his personal status, and the requirements of the firm for a vehicle that is no more than functional and adequate for the task. The firm's costs and profits will be affected by the outcome.

Even fairly autonomous decision makers within a firm, however, are unlikely to take decisions as if they were wholly divorced from their working environment. Before taking a decision about which automobile to purchase in the example given above, the buyer might consult other senior executives, some of whom, like the firm's accountant, could attach greater weight to the consequences for the firm's profits of the different models on offer. Any engineers in the firm might see the decision from yet another perspective. In other words, the 'autonomous' buyer will still be subjected to influences from other sources, both within and without the firm. There is in many respects a parallel with the individual decision maker of Chapter 7, in so far as personal motivation may still have an effect on individual behaviour; but there are now additional influences at work. For the most part these may well predominate, the more so if the purchasing agent is acting on behalf of a publicly quoted firm whose shares are available on the open market.

Taking purchasing decisions on one's own is a fairly exposed job, in that it is more difficult to pass the buck if things go wrong. It is interesting, therefore, that in a survey of studies concerned with the factors influencing individual purchasing managers, Johnston and Spekman (1987) found that habit, caution and a tendency towards risk reduction and certainty were all factors which had been highlighted. This may be why much decision-making within firms is now done jointly. Although the individual buyer in the firm is certainly not without importance, the attention of researchers has switched mainly to joint decision-making, with the buying centre (and within that, the actual decision-making unit) seen as the key vehicle for decisions within firms. We now turn therefore to look at joint decision-making in firms.

Joint decision-making within firms

The buying centre

Cyert, Simon and Trow (1956) were among the first to argue that decisions in organisations are frequently made by more than one person, and that it is therefore insufficient simply to attribute all of a firm's actions to any one individual. The most appropriate unit of analysis in the view of many researchers in this field is the *buying centre.* This is not a unit whose boundaries are easily defined, partly because they are not fixed, but rather change over time. It seems helpful, however, to think of buying as a *process*, with a number of stages in that process. Robinson, Faris and Wind (1967) suggested as many as eight stages in the buying process, although some might be omitted, depending upon whether the purchase was a straight rebuy of a known product, a modified rebuy or a new buy. Others have suggested fewer stages.

Hill and Hillier (1977), after considering the various stages which had been proposed for the buying process, advocated four, each constituting a focal point of buying activity. The first, the *precipitation stage*, arises when the need for the purchase has been identified and authority is given to proceed to purchase. The second is the *product-specification* stage, at which the characteristics of the product required are defined. In the third stage, the *supplier-selection stage*, the agreed product characteristics required are matched with the goods on offer by suppliers, and the supplier most closely meeting the requirements is chosen. Finally, at the *commitment stage*, not only is an order placed but an attempt is made to ensure that the firm's expectations are met or exceeded, in order that a favourable repeat-purchase situation can be established.

Since each of the four stages is associated with at least one major decision, Hill and Hillier (1977) refer to each stage in the buying process as a *decision area*. They go on to show that the location within an organisation of the individuals involved in each decision area can be fixed in terms of two coordinates which identify the focal points of buying activity: the *lateral loci*, representing the functional area, and the *vertical loci*, representing the managerial hierachy.

In a survey of the empirical evidence available, Hill and Hillier (1977) found, as one might have expected, that engineers of various sorts were dominant influences in the purchase of plant and equipment. Design and development engineers had an important say in purchases in the chemical and allied industries, and in paper, printing and publishing industries. Production engineers were the greatest influence in purchases of plant for the food, drink and tobacco industries. Engineers were also found to be involved in purchases of materials and component parts.

Other evidence pointed to groups of specialists being involved at each stage in the industrial buying process, with the purchasing department only entering the process in the later stages. 'Management' (presumably general, more senior management) was closely involved with experts at most stages of decisions. The more the purchase deviated from a straight replacement situation, the more people tended to be involved from the different functional areas, particularly engineering and purchasing. Greatest involvement therefore took place in the case of a new buy or first time purchase. In sum, the degree of involvement of the various functional areas at each stage was very much dictated by the nature of the purchase and familiarity with it.

Studies of the levels of management involved in each decision area (the vertical loci) indicate that it is very often senior management, usually the Board of Directors, which makes the final decision about whether or not to buy, but the decisions about what should be bought, and from whom, are often made by middle or low level management. Combining the lateral and vertical loci, the picture which emerges is of a dynamic and complex decision-making procedure, one which varies at each stage of purchase, with the number making the final decision on whether or not to purchase much fewer than the sum of all those who have at one stage or another had some say in the decision.

The different roles in the buying centre

Another way of looking at buying centres is to consider not just who is involved at each stage of the decision process but the *role* that each person plays. This helps cast useful additional light on the ways in which buying centres function. The role of a person within an organisation serves to determine the behaviour of that individual, including his or her behaviour in the purchasing process. The role may be official or unofficial, but it gives rise to expectations about the activities of a person in relation to others in the organisation, as well as to expectations which the person has about his, or her, own behaviour towards others.

Several classifications of roles have been suggested (see, for example, Webster and Wind, 1972). Hill and Hillier (1977) boil down the proposals which have been made into five units operating within the buying centre: the user; information; decision-making; buyer; and control units. These they felt could be further contracted to only three units, each concerned with a primary function. The first was the information unit, comprising those who provided background or specialist information relevant to a decision. The second was the decision-making unit, consisting of those who actively participated in decision-making at the final stages. The third was the control unit, which again had an informatory role, but this time concerning the constraints within which the organisation had to function, ranging from product decisions to purchasing policies to the constraints of national economic policy.

The Hill and Hilliard way of looking at roles within a firm dovetails closely with the approach I have adopted in the present study. For our purposes, the decision-making unit is of central importance, since it actually makes the decisions which have economic and other consequences. It is the organisational equivalent of the individual decision maker – although I did note earlier that some, generally small, organisations may also operate with autonomous decision makers. The control unit, on the other hand, would ensure that the firm operated within the bounds of the constraints facing the firm; above all that it observed the organisational goal of achieving a normal return on its operations. Such a unit would also be charged with the responsibility of ensuring that the firm's sub-goals, concerning production, sales, pricing, etc., were in conformity with the overall organisational goal. Finally, the activities of the information unit are reasonably self-explanatory, but we would include here not only the information collected for internal use, but also the information imparted to outsiders about the firm's activities. In other words, we would include in the unit the advertising role to which so much importance is attached nowadays.

One difficulty with role behaviour is that conflict may arise, both between those involved in the decision-making process about the precise definition of their roles, and between those with decision-making roles and those not included in decision-making. Once again, therefore, as in the case of goals, the need is likely to arise for some form of conflict resolution, and I will address this matter below.

CONFLICT RESOLUTION

Types of conflict

With firms we introduce the potential for conflict at the level of the organisation, in addition to possible conflict at the individual and group levels. We therefore have the possibility of conflict in a variety of permutations, the most common of which seem likely to be:

1. *conflict between individuals*, perhaps between two employees, or an employee and a manager;
2. *conflict between an individual and a group*, such as a group of fellow employees;
3. *conflict between groups within an organisation*, often between different departments, or perhaps between different trade unions;
4. *conflict between a group and the organisation*, very often between a

trade union, or other group representing employees, and the organisation (represented by management);

5. *conflict between organisations* which goes beyond mere competition, and might include, for example, conflicts which require recourse to law.

The list is obviously not exhaustive, but the dangers of conflict will be all too evident. Conflict need not, of course, always be wholly destructive. If controlled and channelled, good may well emerge from it in the form of new ideas or new solutions to, perhaps old, problems. Indeed, many commentators now regard conflict within an organisation as the rule rather than the exception, and take the view that organisations ought therefore to accept this fact of life and try to devise means of resolving conflict which turn it to constructive rather than destructive purposes.

In addition to the question of *who* conflict is between, there is also the question of *what* conflict is about. Within organisations there is, first, a good deal of scope for disagreement over goals. Individual employees, as I have already stressed, have their own goals, based upon their personal needs. An individual's desire for increased financial reward, for the trappings of status in his job (in the form perhaps of too many secretarial or other support staff) or for self-actualisation (for example, doing a job thoroughly, rather than just adequately) may often conflict with the organisational goal, discussed earlier, of earning a normal return on assets. Groups within organisations may also have sub-goals which are difficult to reconcile with the goals of other groups within the organisation, or with the overall organisational goal. A common source of friction is the need to reconcile production and sales goals, and these must in turn be consistent with the organisational goal.

Closely associated with goals are the *values* adhered to by individuals, since it is values which determine the priorities given to alternative goals. Employees, for example, may value a reasonably relaxed, democratic management style, with devolution of responsibility. An autocratic employer, on the other hand, may wish to centralise responsibility, in the belief that this will produce greater efficiency. The high value placed by employees on equitable treatment may also be something which managers sometimes find difficult to understand or tolerate.

Differing *perceptions* may be a further source of conflict. What we perceive may sometimes have little foundation in reality. People may even perceive the very same situation in very different lights. Management, for example, may think that employees are well off when not only pay but also working conditions, welfare provision, leisure facilities, pensions and so forth, are taken into account. If, however, employees' perceptions are determined principally by pay, which might be relatively modest in comparison with other workers, then the organisation's employees could perceive their situation very differently from management.

Finally, as we saw in the case of families, conflict may arise over the *roles* people play, or feel they ought to play. The ways people behave may not accord with the way others expect them to behave, given their formal positions within an organisation. A manager, for example, might attempt to extend his influence beyond his normal domain. It is precisely in order to avoid such conflicts that some organisations feel it necessary to draw up detailed job descriptions.

Models of conflict and means of resolving conflict

A number of writers have attempted to construct models of conflict. Thomas (1976) has divided these into *process* models and *structural* models. The former attempt to understand the phenomenon of conflict better by studying the internal dynamics of cases of conflict. Events within each case are identified and the effects of each event upon succeeding events traced. Conflict is seen here as very much a continuing process. In structural models, on the other hand, the emphasis is on studying how underlying conditions shape events. The objective is to identify the parameters which influence conflict behaviour, and to specify the form of that influence. Examples of relevant parameters are social pressures, personal predispositions, established negotiating procedures and organisational rules. The term 'structural' is used to describe such models because the parameters are held to be slow to change.

Enough has been said, it is hoped, to indicate that the two types of model are complementary rather than contradictory. The emphasis in each is rather different, with process models concerned more with dynamic situations and the structural models more with situations which are relatively static, yet require change in order to resolve conflicts.

An interesting feature of the structural models identified by Thomas (1976) is the importance of rules and procedures as a means of resolving conflict. I shall be looking below at the use of decision rules by firms as an aid to decision-making, but decision rules may also fulfil the important function of specifying which alternative, or course of action, is to be selected or avoided when issues arise. Rules may be devised, for example, to govern the sensitive relations between production and sales within a firm, perhaps specifying minimum and maximum periods between the placing of an order and the production of goods to meet the order. In such a case, both parties in effect yield some of their authority and freedom of action in the overriding interests of the firm. Such rules may be set out formally or agreed informally. Recourse to such rules ought to help prevent friction arising, but also help to dissolve it if it does.

Rules may, however, give rise to a number of drawbacks, especially if insisted upon in an unduly rigid manner. In the opinion of Thomas, rules may even discourage problem solving in certain cases: 'Essentially, as the rule becomes stronger, the merits of a particular case and the degree to which both parties' concerns are satisfied becomes less relevant.' Rules may also tend to promote 'black and white thinking', with answers to problems seen only in terms of right or wrong, correct or incorrect. There is a danger, too, that rules may proliferate, as has frequently become the case, for example, in rules governing relations between management and trade unions.

Other writers who have stressed the use of decision rules as a means of resolving conflict include Cyert and March (1963). They agreed in favour of what they called 'acceptable-level decision rules'. In other words, their decision rules did not require that local optimisation in a series of independent decision centres would result in overall optimisation. Rather they required only that local decisions satisfying local demands made by a series of independent decision centres resulted in a joint decision which satisfied all demands. Such rules clearly need not lead to optimisation for the firm as a whole.

Although classifications of methods of resolving conflict in organisations differ somewhat in detail, there is a good deal of common ground. In his model of industrial buyer behaviour, Sheth (1973) listed the same four means of conflict resolution as he later advanced in respect of the family (Sheth, 1974): problem solving, persuasion, bargaining and politicking (all of which I touched on earlier when discussing the family in Chapter 8). In addition to problem solving and compromise (which included both persuasion and bargaining) Stoner and Wankel (1986) cited dominance and suppression as one of the three most used methods of conflict resolution. The latter, however, represses conflict rather than resolving it, creating a win-lose situation in which the loser, forced to give way to higher authority or a greater power, may end up disappointed and hostile.

Cyert and March (1963) also suggest some interesting variations on the customary proposals for conflict resolution. In addition to the acceptable-level decision rules noted above, they suggest 'local rationality' and 'sequential attention to goals'. The former is effectively an attempt to break down decision problems into sub-problems tackled by sub-units within organisations. By tackling, say, only one problem in relation to only one goal, *complex* interrelated problems may be reduced to *simple* problems, thereby reducing the scope for conflict. A difficulty with such an approach, however, is that unless sub-problems are closely linked with the organisational goal, it would be only too easy to lose sight of what the organisation was trying to do. Avoiding conflict at a lower level of goals might simply open up conflict between levels of goals. Consistency in the Cyert and March approach is facilitated by their insistence on the need at the same time for acceptable-level decision rules and sequential attention to goals. With respect to the last-mentioned, Cyert and March take the view that organisations resolve conflict among goals in part by attending to different goals *at different times*. While this might be a recipe for conflict resolution at any point in time, however, it is doubtful if it would ensure the consistency required, and could even lead to greater conflict in the longer term as the inconsistencies became apparent.

One important point which does emerge from the Cyert and March analysis, however, is the closeness of the links between conflict resolution, on the one hand, and decision-making rules on the other. Clear, agreed and widely accepted decision rules not only help tackle such problems as uncertainty and complexity, they may also help reduce conflict, thereby further facilitating attainment of the overall organisational goal. I now turn to examine at greater length the use of decision-making rules by firms.

DECISION-MAKING WITHIN FIRMS

The heading of this section is very deliberate in its wording. We often talk of decision-making *by* firms, but of course no such entity as a 'firm' takes decisions. The relevant decisions are taken by *individuals* within firms, acting on behalf of the firm. This point cannot be overemphasised, since individuals, whether acting on their own behalf or on behalf of a firm, have their own personal goals, which may on occasions be at odds with the goals of their firm. Individuals working within firms are also still subject to the same human limitations which Simon (1957) so cogently expressed in his term 'bounded rationality'. Indeed the limitations apply with even greater force. The resources – human, financial, mechanical, informational, computational, etc. – available to support decision makers within firms are generally greater (often much greater) than for the individual acting on his own, but so long as humans ultimately have to make the decisions there is little prospect of 'rational behaviour' in the sense of the neo-classical economic model.

Moreover, as was stressed at the outset of the present chapter, the complexity and uncertainty surrounding decisions within firms are even greater than in the case of the individual acting on his own behalf, or within the family environment. Information requirements are also likely to be much greater, and the potential for conflict arises in forms not seen in the other decision-making centres discussed so far. All this strongly suggests that decision makers within firms must also be obliged to resort to decision-making rules as the only practical way forward. I now therefore want to examine the forms which these decision rules might take.

The use of decision-making rules within firms

I have stressed at several points in the present chapter that the overriding goal of the firm – since it is the overriding constraint under which it must operate – is to earn a normal return on its assets. This does not mean that a firm must *always* be earning a normal return on its assets, since there will be occasions, as during economic recessions, when this might be impossible. But there are pressures on firms nowadays from financial markets – particularly strong, it seems, in the relatively open economies of the US and the UK – to ensure that for the most part the goal is achieved, otherwise the firm may not survive, in its existing form at least. Given the organisational goal, the important question then is, how can it be translated, in practice, into specific policies, or sub-goals, which will guide the actions of the firm's employees? It is to this question that we now turn.

If we multiply the value of a firm's assets, at current prices, by the normal rate of return demanded (which we denote by r_n) we will obtain an indication of the total profits which the firm ought to be earning. We should be clear, of course, that we are not dealing at any stage with precise data upon which we can place one hundred per cent reliance. Valuing a firm's assets is beset with many theoretical and practical problems, and there is ample room for disagreement.

Similarly, different views are likely to emerge over the approporiate value of r_n, since there is no single, obviously right approach to determining what the value should be – hence the variety of models promoted in the field of corporate finance. Moreover, the value of r_n selected will generally be based, in part at least, on the rather hazardous assumption that the past and the present provide a reasonably reliable guide to the future, as is the case, for example, with the Capital Asset Pricing model and the Arbitrage Pricing Theory model, both of which are popular in the area of corporate finance. There is no obviously correct approach, however, only a plausible variety of alternatives from which to choose. The difficulties facing the firm – or, more accurately, the decision-making individuals within the firm – are familiar ones: complexity, lack of full information and true uncertainty about the future course of events. In such circumstances, firms are forced in practice to fall back on simplifying decision rules, adopting one particular method of determining r_n, without knowing for certain that it is the 'right' one. Determining the normal rate of return expected is, in any case, only part of the firm's problem. It must then translate this overriding goal into a variety of sub-goals within the organisation.

Pricing behaviour and the sales goal

Given a profit goal, the firm will, on the basis of its costs, also be able to determine its pricing policy and calculate a goal for sales. Different combinations of sales volume and price would yield the same desired total revenue which, once costs were deducted, would leave the level of profit for which the firm was aiming. The firm's pricing decision would not be wholly market determined. There is a great deal of evidence that firms use a variety of decision rules when setting prices. They cannot entirely ignore the market, however, and we would therefore expect the firm's costs, market forces and its pricing decision rules all to play some part in price determination. For present purposes I will follow Cyert and March (1963) and others in assuming an oligopolistic market, since that resembles the type of market structure within which a great many firms operate.

The above seems quite straightforward, but a number of questions may be raised. Which costs are we talking about, for example, since these may be calculated in a number of ways, and what form might the decision rules take? Furthermore, what actions might a firm take if its sales target is not met? We can answer these and other possible questions by examining price behaviour by firms.

In the perfect competition model of standard economic theory, individual firms are assumed to have complete knowledge of the cost and revenue functions facing all firms in the market, and there is no difficulty in calculating the levels at which prices should be set in order to maximise profits. Similarly, in other market structures firms have at their disposal full knowledge of at least their own cost and revenue functions. Although many firms now allocate considerable resources to the collection of cost and revenue data, the assumption of complete knowledge on the part of firms is, quite simply, misplaced if one is thinking of applying such assumptions to real world situations. In practice, firms can at best hope for approximations to the perfect knowledge assumed, and most have no alternative but to resort to relatively simple decision rules.

Quite a number of decision rules base prices on a firm's costs, since information on costs is generally the most readily available. One of the most common methods is mark-up pricing, with prices being set as a certain percentage mark-up over costs. The mark-up is generally on variable costs, since the allocation of overhead costs to individual products is often not possible with a reasonable degree of precision. Mark-up pricing is especially popular in the service industries, such as retailing, where the mark-up is frequently based on the invoiced cost of a product. In a test of their behavioural theory of the firm, Cyert and March (1963) carried out an empirical study of mark-up pricing in one department of a large retail department store. They found that their mark-up rule of thumb was able to predict correctly, down to the last cent, the prices charged in 188 cases out of a sample of 197. In a later test of the model, Baumol and Stewart (1971) concluded that, although the model did not perform as accurately as Cyert and March maintained, it still predicted an impressive 70 per cent of prices correctly, and therefore appeared to be an accurate reflection of firms' behaviour.

A further form of pricing based on costs which is very popular, more so this time in manufacturing industry, is full-cost pricing. Once again, as Sawyer (1979) has observed, this behaviour, like mark-up pricing, may be described, in Simon's terminology, as 'satisficing' rather than maximising, since the firm aims at a satisfactory rather than an optimal outcome. The notion of full-cost pricing first emerged from a study by Hall and Hitch (1939) of business behaviour. They found firms' prices to be based on full average cost (including an allowance for profit). Full average cost was said to be calculated in the following manner: 'prime (or 'direct') cost per unit is taken as the base, a percentage addition is made to cover overheads (or 'oncost' or 'indirect' cost), and a further conventional addition (frequently 10 per cent) is made for profit'. A difficulty with this definition, of course, is that costs so calculated will vary according to the level of output, since the overheads are fixed, and will be spread over varying outputs. Two ways round this problem have been suggested. There is evidence, first of all, that in the short-run cost curves are often horizontal over the range of output within which firms normally operate. With average costs constant, the level of output would be immaterial – from the cost point of view, at least. A second approach has been to maintain that costs are calculated in relation to a 'normal' level of output, i.e., the level of output at which the firm would customarily operate, not the levels of output associated with, for example, booms or slumps. This would mean once again that prices remained fairly stable.

It has been pointed out (see, for example, Sawyer, 1979) that under certain assumptions the profit maximising economic model could result in firms behaving in a fashion closely resembling full-cost pricing. Profit maximising yields a price equal to (marginal cost)/(*1–1/e*), where *e* is the price elasticity of demand (the percentage change in quantity demanded of a good in relation to a given percentage change in the price of the good). If we also assume that *e* here incorporates the firm's beliefs about the reactions of its rivals to a price change, then if the firm perceives the elasticity of demand as likely to remain unchanged over time (a not unrealistic assumption, in the short term at least) price will follow marginal cost. Under conditions in which cost curves remain unchanged over a wide range of output (for which there is empirical evidence, as I remarked above) average and marginal costs would be equal, and price would then follow average cost. Firms would be behaving as if they followed a full-cost pricing rule. We should note, however, that while not implausible, the profit maximising model does require *supplementary* assumptions before it can produce the desired result – frequently a feature of work based on the standard economic model, as I have previously noted.

A final pricing decision rule worth examining, since it is closely allied to mark-up and full-cost pricing, and also links up with the normal return profit goal I outlined earlier, is target pricing to achieve a target rate of return on investment. Price is fixed as a percentage mark-up on costs according to the formula:

$$\text{percentage mark-up on costs} = \text{target return on investment} \times \text{average capital employed/cost of sales}$$

Costs are again calculated according to a 'normal' level of output, and the target return on investment can be determined on the basis of the asset pricing model we set out earlier, or in some alternative manner. The formula also provides us with the *sales goal* which must be set, given the capital employed and the target return on capital. It equals costs plus the profits which have to be earned to meet the target return.

Target pricing has also proved to be a common practice in firms. A study for the Brookings Institution by Kaplan *et al.* (1958) found that it was the most common pricing decision rule used by large firms in the United States. However, the evidence does not all point in the one direction. Maxcy and Silberston (1959), in their work on the British motor industry, brought out the fact, for example, that different firms had very different profit margins, even although their cars sold at comparable prices – and this must be true of many industries. Such a finding obviously casts doubts on any rigid adherence to the full-cost principle. It is interesting, too, that in their behavioural model of the firm, Cyert and March (1963) felt obliged to allow for the possible influence of a firms's competitors on its pricing policy. Market structure and the degree of competition must, in other words, also be taken into account by a firm when operating decision rules, and so too must changes in market demand conditions.

Despite possible objections, there is sufficient evidence, for example in the studies by Balkin (1956), Hague (1949), Howe (1962), Barback (1964) and Silberston (1970), to support the view that mark-up pricing, which enters all the forms of pricing behaviour outlined above, is a decision rule commonly used by firms. Silberston (1970) concluded after his review of the British studies that:

> . . . full cost can be given a mark of beta query plus, but no more than this, since there are so many marginalist and behavioural qualifications. It seems clear that the *procedure* of calculating prices very often starts with an average-cost type of calculation, but the qualifications that arise are concerned with the next stages of the process, including the exact method by which full costs are calculated.

Silberston went on to point out that the studies he covered concentrated mainly on home-market prices, and that there was abundant evidence that in export pricing marginal calculations figured much more prominently.

My own conclusion is that while mark-up pricing, or a variant of it, may not be universally used by firms, its use is nevertheless sufficiently widespread to force economists to take serious note of it, and its implications. Even if it were to be claimed that what firms do bears a closer *resemblance* to marginalist, or profit maximising, behaviour, that is not at all the same as saying that firms *always* maximise their profits. The overriding fact is that complexity, uncertainty and lack of full information make it impossible to achieve profit maximisation – and probably anything approaching it – even for the most sophisticated firm. At some crucial stage in the decision-making process firms will resort to simplifying rules, even if these rules may on occasions be rather more sophisticated than the ones I have highlighted here.

Before moving on we must consider what actions are open to the firms if its mark-up pricing policy does not enable, initially at least, its sales and profitability goals to be achieved. I have already stressed the dynamic nature of the firm's activities, and, following Cyert and March (1963), would also stress the importance of learning to the manner in which firms will react to such problems. Mark-ups are not rigidly fixed. Basing their judgements on experience gained, firms will react to changes in market conditions, including changes in competitors' pricing behaviour, as well as to changes in costs. Greater marketing effort, including advertising, is one means of trying to avoid reductions in profit margins. Here again, given the difficulties of assessing the effectiveness of advertising expenditure, simplifying decision rules may often be adopted, such as spending a fixed proportion of sales revenue on promotion.

Production, investment and inventory goals

Given the profit and sales goals, and the pricing strategy essential to attaining these, a firm must try to ensure that its production and inventory goals are also consistent with its principal objectives. Production will generally be set at a rate which enables sales demand to be satisfied without undue delays, with inventories acting as a buffer when the two do not match. Sales may fluctuate, depending upon seasonal and other factors, but firms will usually wish to try and even out production rather than follow sales closely (assuming that were possible) since such a policy would be less likely to cause production bottlenecks, due to labour or other shortages. The appropriate level of inventories may once again be fixed according to relatively simple rules, based upon past experience. The stock-output ratio is one yardstick frequently adopted and monitored by firms. In the case of wholesale or retail firms, the equivalent of a certain number of days' sales may be kept in stock.

So far as fixed capital investment is concerned, sophisticated tools of analysis are increasingly being used by firms in an effort to cope with the (doubtless increasingly) complex world in which they have to operate. A study by Moore and Reichert (1983) of comparable surveys of the Fortune 500 industrial firms in the US established that use of time-adjusted capital budgeting techniques (i.e., net present value (NPV) or internal rate of return (IRR) techniques) increased from as little as 9 per cent of firms in 1955 to 47 per cent in 1965, and to 86 per cent in 1981. The single most commonly used capital budgeting technique in 1981 was, however, the payback period (80 per cent of the 298 firms responding to the authors' own survey used it frequently, only 6 per cent never), with 87 per cent of firms using either payback or an average rate of return calculation. A further interesting finding, by Haka *et al.* (1985), has been that, even after controlling for risk, size and industry effects, there is no improvement in financial performance by those firms using the more sophisticated capital budgeting techniques, such as NPV, IRR or the use of a profitability index.

A general problem with capital budgeting techniques is that, since they are forward looking, the estimated values obtained are usually themselves based on subsidiary estimates, whether of future sales volume, the prices of goods when sold, future levels of risk, or whatever. Whereas it may be possible, drawing on past experience, to attach probabilities to some of these estimates, and their likely variation, we should constantly remind ourselves that, no matter how sophisticated the techniques, the estimates obtained are only as good as the quality of the data employed – the old computing adage of 'garbage in, garbage out' applies with equal force to capital budgeting calculations. For many investment projects the prospects will be so uncertain that decisions have to be taken under conditions of what we have described as 'true uncertainty' – in certain countries, for example, political uncertainty is such that very short payback periods are used, as at present in Hong Kong. It may well be for this reason that so many large enterprises, despite having the ability to use the more sophisticated techniques, still employ the more 'naive' methods – many firms, of course, employ a variety of techniques, sophisticated and naive, in order to compare the results.

The adoption of a short, fixed time horizon in assessing capital investment makes it easier to relate investment to changes in output, and it is not surprising, therefore, that many studies have revealed a close relationship between output and investment. As a general rule of thumb, capital-output ratios appear to provide a fairly reliable guide to firms' investment decisions. Evidence for this can be found in numerous studies. A good example is the extensive study of non-residential fixed investment by Clark (1979), covering a period of twenty-five years. He concluded that, 'output is clearly the primary determinant of nonresidential fixed investment'. Similar conclusions were reached in another extensive review of the theories and evidence by Junankar (1972), covering both the UK and the US. He found that:

> . . . demand factors as represented by the accelerator are more important than relative prices in determining investment. The implications for policy seem to be that changes in rates of interest and other elements in the cost of capital (e.g. tax rates) would, after a long lag, lead to a change in investment, while changes in aggregate demand would be a quicker and more potent way of affecting investment.

Not all would agree with these findings, of course. Bernanke (1983), drawing attention to the conjunction of unusually high real interest rates and weak investment spending during much of the 1980s, re-examined the determinants of US non-residential investment over the years 1947–79, and found that, 'the importance of capital costs for investment comes through strongly'.

Once again, although the evidence appears on the surface to conflict, the differences may be more of emphasis and timing than of real substance. There is sufficient evidence, none the less, in support of the view that non-residential investment is closely related to output to suggest that many firms in laying their investment plans have regard to their actual and anticipated levels of output – Clark (1979) found *levels* of output rather than *changes* in output to be the better explanatory variable. Many businessmen, in other words, appear to work to relatively simple capital-output decision rules in determining their investment requirements.

The employer's pay goal

We now have not only one overriding 'organisational goal' for the firm of earning a normal return on its assets, but also a number of subsidiary goals essential to the attainment of the overriding goal. There is one other subsidiary goal which I feel ought to be added to the list already drawn up. We examined in Chapter 9 the likely shape of employee's notions of equity. Since equitable treatment is an important concern of employees, only foolish employers would ignore it entirely, although theories of the firm seldom treat this aspect of firms' behaviour at any length – if at all. Even if the managements of firms do not have any real interest in equity, they do have an interest in the cost of employees' pay, which accounts for a considerable proportion of total costs in most firms. In order simply to control costs, they must therefore have a policy for pay. It is not just costs that matter, however: firms must also be able to attract the labour they require, and must to this end maintain competitive rates of pay. Given its central importance, I would therefore add a *pay goal* to the other subsidiary goals of the firm already listed.

The pay goal of a firm must take account of the need to offer rates of pay which are sufficiently attractive, relative to the pay of employees doing comparable work in other firms, to enable the firm to keep its existing employees and attract any additional ones it needs. In the aggregate (since we are dealing with aggregates within the firm) the firm's pay goal may be expressed in the following form:

$$\text{firm's pay goal} = \bar{W}_f = k\bar{W}_r \qquad (10.1)$$

where, $\bar{W}_f$ is the average rate of pay of a group of workers in the firm, $\bar{W}_r$ is the average rate of pay of a comparable group of workers in another firm, treated as a reference group, and k is a constant. Similar expressions could be used for other groups of workers in the firm.

Equation (10.1) brings into play the behavioural aspects of pay determination. It brings into play, in other words, the key elements of social comparisons and equity considerations, which seldom feature in standard economic models, despite all the evidence of their paramount importance (for a discussion of much of the evidence see Baxter, 1988). Firms have an interest in bringing such behavioural influences into their calculations because of their need to attract and retain staff. It is not being claimed, of course, that these are the sole considerations of the firm – the firm's productivity, market situation and desire to earn at the very least a normal return on its assets will all be relevant considerations – only that they should not be left out of account.

Even if both the firm and its employee(s) treat pay comparisons and equity as important considerations in their pay goals, this does not, of course, guarantee accord between them. Pay is only one element in the outcomes (in Adams's terminology) of employees. There are other aspects of financial remuneration, such as pensions, possibly the availability of overtime work, etc., and there are also non-financial outcomes which it may be quite impossible to translate into financial terms, such as working conditions, the availability of leisure facilities, etc. Employees' and employers' *perceptions* of the value to employees of all non-pay outcomes may therefore differ appreciably, and, of course, there is also the possibility of differences in assessment of employee inputs. Further differences may emerge over the compensation which should be accorded employees to offset inflation, and over what constitutes a reasonable growth in real incomes over time. If, therefore, we compare equations (10.1) and (9.6), an employer's estimate of the appropriate value of k may differ from that of employees; and there may, too, be differences of view over the appropriate values of $\dot{P}^e$ and α in equation (9.9). If both parties stick to their positions, some means of conflict resolution will be required.

Bargaining is the most common means of conflict resolution between employers and employees over matters of pay, with gains and concessions usual on each side before agreement is reached. In terms of Sheth's (1973) four means of conflict resolution in industrial organisations, persuasion would also have a role. The problem solving approach, in which more information is sought and considered jointly by the parties in conflict, is one which probably ought to be adopted more frequently. It would enable, for example, such matters as the competitive situation of the firm, productivity, the organisational goal, etc. to be considered, and, it is to be hoped, facilitate the emergence of a consensus. At the other extreme, politicking may be the fall-back position of the employer, with attempts perhaps even made to destroy trade unions or otherwise undermine the bargaining strength of employees. The precise outcome(s) of all these forces seems virtually impossible to predict – unless overwhelming priority is given to one aspect of outcomes, such as pay – but if conflict is to be resolved the outcomes do not seem very likely to depart too far from the principal goals of employer and employees.

CONCLUSIONS

At the very least, we must assume that the goal of those who own and run a firm is the survival of that firm. This implies that the firm must earn at least a normal return on its assets (in the long run, if not always in the short run) otherwise it will fail to attract the funds essential for future investment, and/or suffer a withdrawal of shareholders' existing funds – this is likely to be true even if markets do not work with maximum efficiency, although the consequences of failure may take longer to emerge in such markets. From the overriding goal of earning a normal return, a set of subsidiary goals emerge for sales, profits, output and inventories.

The behavioural theory of the firm sees firms' goals not just from the point of view of employers, however. Employees (including managers, if they are not also the owners) also have their own goals, and no firm which hopes to achieve its overriding goal can ignore these. Employee goals will take a variety of forms, often with financial consequences for the firm, but not necessarily always so, since simply belonging to a social (as well as economic) unit – and even work itself – are important satisfiers of human needs. Many employees' needs can be encapsulated in their pay, especially their *relative* pay, since pay gives them command over many satisfiers of needs. Moreover, relative pay is an important element in the social comparison process, and is central to notions of equity, as outlined, for example, in the theory of Adams. Employers must therefore respond to employees' pay goals with their own goal for employees' pay. Since pay is such an important component of total costs, I would rank pay goals along with the other subsidiary goals of the firm in respect of sales, profits, output and inventories.

In order to help achieve firms' goals, employees have to fulfil roles within their firms. These roles are partly determined by the main functional areas of the firms – production, sales, finance, etc. – and are frequently a source of conflict. Added to possible conflicts between the firm's goals, and between the goals of employers and employees, conflict resolution becomes one of the principal requirements if firms are to meet their overriding goal. We looked at possible ways of resolving conflict, but I do not see conflicts within firms ever being fully resolved, since the general environment within which firms operate is constantly changing, and even as old conflicts are being settled new ones are evolving.

Conflict resolution is, however, only one factor in the complex web of problems facing firms. At the heart of these problems, as I have continually stressed, lies the insurmountable obstacle of uncertainty. Firms do not, and cannot, have at their disposal all the information required for the sort of maximising behaviour envisaged in standard economic theory. No matter how sophisticated the techniques and aids employed, not all economic behaviour can be based on assessments of probabilities. The requisite information in many instances simply does not exist. In such circumstances, frequent resort to simplifying decision rules is inescapable. There is a good deal of empirical evidence to indicate that this is precisely what happens in practice. Some of these rules may now be quite sophisticated, but they are simplifying rules nonetheless, and therefore inimical to maximising behaviour. What is more, different firms use different decision rules. Can they all be right?

The strong emphasis on decision rules rather than maximising behaviour might be criticised by some on the grounds that it displaces 'rational' behaviour from its economic throne, and that implies chaos. We have repeatedly seen at each stage in our examination of decision-making, however, how much personal behaviour is of a repetitive, routine nature. There is no reason to think that decision-making within firms is, for the most part, any different. Complexity and uncertainty there certainly is, but there is also reasonable stability, emanating from the fact that people learn from their past experiences, and are therefore able to reduce much decision-making to routine, repetitive behaviour.

11 Socioeconomic Decision-Making: Government

Philosophers, political scientists and others have long argued about the reasons for the existence of government, and its appropriate role. Economists generally have concerned themselves solely with those aspects of government activity which seemed to impinge most directly on economic affairs, and for this reason have underestimated people's *need* for government. To put the matter more precisely, I shall be arguing in the present chapter that the satisfaction of certain human needs can best be met (perhaps can only be met) with the aid of a benevolent government. Appreciation of this *need* for government helps provide a better explanation of the functions which governments have acquired in the more industrialised economies, and the economic consequences which have ensued. In order to place my approach in context, I will start with a brief look at the principal approaches to government.

DIFFERING VIEWS OF THE ROLE OF GOVERNMENT AND THE STATE

Most theories of government have tended to be classified as 'mechanistic' or 'organic' (After, 1972). The former approach is closely associated with the liberal democratic tradition evident in most of the advanced industrial economies. It sees government as a means of resolving conflict between competing interests in society (individual and group), thereby facilitating decision-making to the benefit of all. Governments in effect mediate between a variety of socially determined 'inputs', including customs and beliefs (normative characteristics), classes and interests (structural characteristics), preferences and perceptions (behavioural characteristics). The corresponding 'outputs' are the policy decisions taken by government. All activity takes place within a legal framework whose legitimacy is based upon equity. Government is also seen as a contrivance, rather than something that grows organically.

The organic approach, on the other hand, sees government evolving along with society – from lower to higher forms, in the writings of Plato and Aristotle. Government strives to direct society to higher ends. This approach proved attractive to Hegel and Marx, who developed their own particular models, but it has also attracted more liberal minded proponents. The community tends to take precedence over the individual, who lies at the heart of the mechanistic approach. The goals of government may be elevated into ethical precepts – with all the dangers that such may entail. Government now becomes the input, with changes in the social system the outputs.

Economists, as we have noted, have generally adopted a very restricted approach to government and the role of the State. The explanation, it seems, can be traced back to the influence of Adam Smith, and his powerful argument that the pursuit of individual self-interest, guided by the workings of the 'invisible hand', produces not only the best economic outcome for the individual but also for society as a whole. In such a scheme of things, the role for government is clearly minimal – although none the less vital. Smith was only too well aware that the motive of self-interest was enlisted in the cause of general welfare only under definite institutional arrangements (Blaug, 1985). Government had definite functions to perform, but these were limited to the safeguarding of property rights, the provision of national defence and the maintenance of certain public works. So far as the social side-effects of economic developments were concerned, individuals might pursue their self-interest, 'but it was self-interest shot through with social values' (O'Brien, 1976). A harmony existed between social and self-interest.

Neo-classical economics has attempted to define more precisely the conditions under which State interference in the operations of free markets would be admissible. In the neo-classical model individuals still pursue their self-interest by attempting to maximise their 'utility', but they may be hampered in their efforts by the failure of markets to always perform as pure theory would suggest. Market failure is thus the key precondition for government intervention. At the aggregated level of the economy, the aim is to maximise a 'social welfare function', with social interest viewed as also representing the interests of individuals, each of whom is given equal weighting in the utility calculus. Unfortunately, the summation of individual welfare in order to arrive at social welfare entails interpersonal comparisons of utility – against which Arrow (1951, 1967) and others have levelled some deadly shafts – and the availability of information about personal preferences, and their appropriate weighting, which governments simply do not possess in practice. Even identifying market failure might therefore be a problem.

Nevertheless, there are felt to be clear instances of market failure requiring government intervention. One important instance is in the provision of so-called 'public goods' – goods which are provided most efficiently when consumed jointly by individuals, and for which all ought to help pay, in order to avoid the 'free rider' problem. The most commonly cited examples are national defence, the maintenance of law and order and the provision of lighthouses. At one time even some large countries were heavily dependent upon mercenaries for their defence, but most countries now consider such forces inadequate for the task. This means that governments, rather than markets, must provide, since the decisions of the many individuals making up the market would not necessarily add up to a coherent, or adequate, defence policy. Linked to the free rider problem there is too the difficulty of 'excludability' – some individuals might refuse to contribute financially to jointly consumed services, yet they would still benefit from them, since it is impossible to exclude them from some benefits, such as defence.

'Externalities' provide a further example of possible market failure. Here pollution of water or air, perhaps by a manufacturer, is commonly cited. Unless government steps in to make sure 'the polluter pays', some individuals or firms would not bear the full cost of their activities, and these costs would therefore have to be borne by others. Looked at from the point of view of society as a whole, some activities might even have costs which outweighed their benefits, and should therefore cease. If, however, producers do not pay the full costs, they might still find production worthwhile.

Yet another important example of market failure is the existence of imperfect competition, due, for example, to the existence of monopolies or restrictive practices – possibly on the part of labour as well as employers. The consequence will be inefficiencies, perhaps because prices and profits are too high, and output lower than would be the case in a more competitive market.

Following the publication of Keynes's *General Theory* in 1936, the predominant view was that governments also had a role to play in stabilising national economies. This view was widely held until around the early 1970s, but since then has become decidedly less prevalent. Keynes's argument, in a nutshell, was that, contrary to the classical view, markets did not always automatically clear; and, in the absence of offsetting government action to raise the level of demand, economies could operate well below their full capacity, even over long periods of time. It was largely as a consequence of Keynes's work, it seems, that a broad consensus emerged about the principal goals of government economic policy – although precisely how these goals emerged is not entirely clear. The goals are often stated to be: full employment (now variously defined), economic growth, price stability (also variously defined) and balance of payments equilibrium. Although perhaps less uniformly held, there also appeared to be a view that governments had to be concerned with the distribution of income – of which I shall have more to say later.

A new emphasis on 'monetarism' within the neo-classical school cast serious doubts on the beneficial effects of government intervention, especially following the poor economic performance of most economies during the 1970s. Friedman (1968) and others favoured a stable long-term growth of the money supply as the best means of stabilising an economy. Keynesian 'fine tuning' tended to fall out of favour, although in practice governments continued to intervene in their economies – even varying the rate of growth of the money supply, although not always intentionally, since defining and controlling the money supply proved much more difficult than anticipated.

The questioning of the need for, or the advisability of, government intervention received added impetus from the emergence of what is now commonly referred to as the 'new classical' school of thought, with its emphasis on rational expectations and equilibrium economics. The basic conclusion with regard to economic policy is that systematic changes in policy variables have no effects on real variables. For the most part, government policy is ineffective, and therefore pointless. By no means all economists accept such conclusions, of course, but they do now seem to have gained a powerful hold in some quarters. We may, however, simply have reached one extremity in the swing of the pendulum of economic thought, and in time will return to a more balanced view of the role of government.

So far I have outlined a number of instances of market failure which are concerned with efficiency, or, more precisely, with reasons why markets may not in practice yield efficient outcomes, and may therefore benefit from government intervention. But governments are not concerned solely with efficiency. It was noted earlier that the legitimacy of government rests ultimately on the feeling of the governed that they are, within bounds, receiving equitable treatment. This does not mean that all subjects must have the same income or wealth, but rather that there should be a reasonable consensus about what disparities in income and wealth are tolerable, and that all citizens should be equal before the law. I shall return to this matter of equity below.

A BEHAVIOURAL VIEW OF THE ROLE OF GOVERNMENT AND THE STATE

Market failure is a powerful argument for government intervention in an economy, but it cannot on its own explain the full nature and scale of government activity, or its growth over time. The reasons for the existence of government intervention go much deeper. In essence they can be traced back to a common source: that of personal motivation, which lies at the heart of individual behaviour, including that in collectives, such as the family, the firm, the trade union, and even nations.

I have argued throughout this study that human needs and wants, and the desire to satisfy them, are the predominant motivating force governing individual behaviour. In the more advanced industrial societies, the great bulk of the populations have command over sufficient financial resources to provide themselves with what might loosely be described as 'basic needs' – although in Baxter (1988) I noted that there is no generally accepted definition of 'basic needs', since at their most basic these amount to the means of mere survival, and anything less basic immediately runs into problems of definition owing to an inescapable subjective element of judgement. Despite difficulties of definition, however, basic needs would certainly cover the need for food and drink, clothing and shelter (the physiological needs for survival), and individuals who doubted their own abilities always to provide themselves with these basic necessities could be expected to look for alternative means of provision.

Over the years, people have been prepared to submit themselves to different forms of central authority – increasingly in the form of democratically elected governments – in return for an understanding (not necessarily explicit) that the authority would do its best to help meet their basic needs if circumstances required it. Even those normally having access to resources substantially in excess of basic needs might also be expected to feel it advisable to have a central authority to turn to in emergencies. In effect, one of the principal reasons for government is that it should stand ready to act as provider of last resort for those unable to meet their basic needs. This provision is evident, as we shall see below, in the substantial social security transfers made from governments to individuals in the form of, for example, unemployment benefit and income support – in less well-off countries, such provision may only be in kind, and then perhaps only *in extremis*, after natural disasters have struck.

Closely allied to a government's function as provider of last resort is government's role in meeting individuals' safety needs. In the narrow and most obvious sense, governments, as we noted earlier, are the best means of providing an adequate defence force, principally to meet external threats. Domestically, individuals also tend to look to governments to provide a police force and a legal system to ensure the maintenance of law and order. Nowadays, however, individuals' 'safety' can be viewed within a broader context in which governments also provide a safety net to help prevent individuals from suffering undue consequences arising from personal misfortune. National health services might be regarded as a form of safety net provision – although to the extent that such provision is cost effective it could also be justified on transactions cost grounds. In countries where average incomes are high, there may be a tendency for individuals to have recourse to private medical care, but such care may not cover the most expensive illnesses, such as those requiring brain surgery or those giving rise to prolonged, debilitating illnesses. Government health provision might, of course, now be classified by some as a 'basic need', and in many respects it is, although in the sense that it is not necessarily a continuous need, like that for food and drink, but usually more sporadic – true generally too of defence and law and order – I have chosen to include it under the 'safety' umbrella.

The desire for government to act as provider of last resort, and to cater for safety needs, are needs which individuals share and from which they benefit in common – even if some individuals benefit more than others. Individuals may also have competing interests, however – certainly in a narrow sense – in particular in matters concerning the distribution of goods and services produced by society. There is no reason to think that, left to market forces, the distribution of such goods would occur in anything like an equitable fashion – indeed, the evidence suggests rather the reverse, that gross disparities in distribution are the likely outcome of the free play of markets.

In discussing individual motivation, we have seen how the desire for equitable treatment is one of the most powerful motivating forces. As was noted in Baxter (1988), equity operates at different levels of aggregation in society. At the level of society as a whole, what is often referred to as 'social justice' is most relevant – rather than, say, equity in exchange relationships. At this most aggregated of levels we would therefore expect the desire for equity to be reflected somehow in the functions of government.

The difficulty with the notion of social justice, as I noted earlier in Baxter (1988), is that there is no generally accepted definition of what the term means – in theory, let alone in practice. Fortunately, the inability to define a concept precisely need not impose a complete bar on its use – although it obviously places limitations on such use. Rawls in his *Theory of Justice* (1971) probably still comes closest to providing answers to the questions raised, even if his work has generated a minor boom in critical assessments – as well as much critical acclaim. Rawls's work is discussed at greater length in Baxter (1988). Here it is sufficient to note that his work is basically egalitarian. This attitude is spelled out in his 'difference principle', or 'maximin rule', which, it should be noted, applies only to 'primary goods', excluding liberty, which is accorded the highest priority in Rawls's lexicographic ordering of 'goods', and is not therefore tradeable for an improvement in economic welfare – at least once a certain level of wealth has been attained.

The operation of Rawls's maximin rule requires that the distribution of goods should be such as to yield the maximum expectations for the least advantaged. As critics have been quick to point out, this maximin rule could be used to justify extreme disparities in income and wealth, provided only that the expectations of the least fortunate were thereby raised in some slight degree. Rawls's riposte is that his conception of justice must be viewed as a whole, and that his principles of equal liberty and open positions would prevent extreme situations of the sort referred to ever arising.

Like Rawls, Buchanan (1986) has sympathy with the view that the rules of social justice should be set before play begins, but in order not to stray too far from his purposes his approach is in fact much more restricted. He poses the question: 'Could my claims, my current holdings, have emerged as an outcome of a game carried out under tolerably fair rules?' After discussion, he concludes that rules of fairness would seem to suggest the need for imposing handicaps, in order to achieve something approaching equality in starting positions. The problem is, who is to do the handicapping? The dilemma is resolved by the selection of *institutional rules* that place quasi-permanent constraints on the behaviour of governments and private parties. Buchanan's conclusions are that: 'Some system of taxation of asset transfers would almost certainly emerge from any agreement on a set of fair rules'; and, 'A second institution that seems justified on basic fairness criteria, and still within the objective of equalising starting positions, is publicly or governmentally financed education.' Buchanan acknowledged that, despite these provisions, inequalities would remain, and he went on to introduce additional rules – 'equal treatment of equals' and the right to secede from a polity – in a further attempt to mitigate inequalities in individuals' starting positions.

Buchanan and others, like Atkinson (1972), have gone to some lengths to devise acceptable criteria for social justice, but the arguments do not really go back to first principles, and in the end we are left, in essence, with decision rules for social justice. For the time being, at least, we are faced with a form of bounded rationality in the field of social justice, and, as in other fields of decision-making touched upon in the present study, the consequence is that we are obliged to resort to simplified decision rules as a guide to action. Often, as in the case of the writers referred to here, the arguments are persuasive and well marshalled, but the outcome is a series of decision rules – even if expressed in a form which any reasonable men and women might be expected to accept. Upon one thing most writers in the field of social justice do seem agreed: the distribution of income and wealth cannot be left solely to the dictates of market forces. We would therefore expect something of this widely held view to be reflected in the activities of governments.

Finally, I have until now discussed the role of government on the assumption that government exists for the benefit of the governed. In democratic societies, at least, governments are notionally accountable to the governed; but my earlier discussions of trade unions and firms help make it clear that in any organisation where one collection of individuals acts on behalf of another, those supposedly in control and those supposedly subject to control may have different goals. So far I have discussed the likely goals of the governed, but what of the goals of those doing the governing on their behalf, namely, the politicians and public officials?

Since politicians and government officials are also human beings, it is reasonable to assume that they are motivated by the same desires as those which motivate the governed. We can therefore expect satisfaction of needs and wants and notions of equity to be strong influences on their behaviour. In the case of politicians and officials, however, there may be scope to indulge in a form of need satisfaction not open to the governed. Maslow, Alderfer, Herzberg and other writers on motivation whose work we looked at earlier, stressed the need for esteem (self-esteem and the esteem of others) as a potent motivator. One of the most obvious ways for politicians and officials to raise their level of esteem is to increase the *size* (and perhaps with it the *scope*) of the empires over which they hold sway. They may also be tempted for the same reason to indulge in expenditures associated more with show than substance.

Closely linked with the desire for esteem may be a desire for power, since, generally speaking, the greater the budgets over which politicians and officials have authority, the greater their discretionary power. In short, politicians and public officials may have strong motivation to increase the size and scope of the government sector in an economy, taking it beyond the level required to meet the goals of the governed which we identified earlier.

I shall look at the scale and nature of government activity, and how it has changed over time; but before doing so we must first examine the means of conflict resolution in government, since it is by now apparent that the goals of the governors and the governed may indeed conflict.

CONFLICT RESOLUTION AT GOVERNMENT LEVEL

We have now identified the principal interest groups relevant to the size and scope of government activity, namely, voters, politicians and public officials. Voters are likely to have differing political philosophies and different views about how economic affairs should be conducted by governments. In democratic societies, politicians will reflect, in some degree at least, these differences of viewpoint. We are therefore faced once again with the questions which have arisen in the case of each socioeconomic decision-making centre: who actually make the important decisions, how are they made, and how are conflicts between the different decision-making units within the centres resolved?

Economists writing on the topic of government have resorted to a variety of devices to avoid the problem of differing decision-making units within government. Downs (1957), an influential writer in the field, concentrated solely on political parties, which he treated as analogous to entrepreneurs in a profit-seeking economy, i.e., he assumed that in order to attain their private ends, or goals, parties formulated whatever policies would gain them most votes. He also assumed that voters behaved 'rationally', which in political terms meant that they voted for the party they believed would provide more benefits than any other.

Buchanan and Tullock (1962), two other prominent writers in what has become known as the theory of public choice, have attempted a broader approach than Downs. Early in their analysis they introduced a key question: should they consider the collective as the decision-making unit, and therefore scale or order collective choices against some social (organisational) goal or set of goals; or, should they consider the individual participant in collective choice as the only real decision maker. They opted for the latter, and true to the neo-classical tradition, assumed that the individual was able to rank all the alternatives of *collective* as well as of individual choice, and that this ranking was transitive.

The choice between individual and collective action, in the analysis of Buchanan and Tullock, rests on the relative cost of organising decisions. If an activity is to be collectivised, the most efficient decision-making rule will be selected, i.e., the one which minimises the expected interdependence costs – which is the same as saying that an individual will act in order to maximise expected utility from social interdependence.

The problem of uncertainty surrounding decision-making is acknowledged, although, unsurprisingly, not satisfactorily resolved. Their argument is that, since collective choice is a continuous process, it does not matter that each decision is unique, since it represents only one link in a long chain of social action over time. Uncertainty is thereby reduced in importance. This does not, however, satisfactorily dispose of the issue. As I have noted before at the individual level – and the point appears to carry even more weight at the level of government, since even more variables come into play – true uncertainty prevails in much decision-making, since the information on which to base calculations of probabilities is simply not available. In such circumstances it is irrelevant whether or not a decision is one of a linked series of decisions.

By regarding political choice as a sequence of events over time, and by concentrating their attention on voting behaviour in a direct democracy, Buchanan and Tullock were able to treat voting behaviour as akin to participation in a market. They maintained that, 'The individual may effectively, but imperfectly, "sell" his vote on a particular issue, securing in return the votes of other individuals on issues of more direct interest'. This 'logrolling' process they felt also provided a general model for other kinds of voting rules, including those for representative democracy. Such argument is not, however, entirely convincing. Where there is a large number of voters and a large number of issues, as is the case in most important government elections, opportunities for trading votes in the manner suggested are much more limited than is implied. Logrolling is sometimes a feature of agreement among *politicians* (and therefore indirectly, it might be argued, voters) as in apportioning budgets, but such behaviour cannot cover *all* issues, otherwise agreement would never be reached. Any suggestion that this might amount to maximising behaviour therefore seems misplaced.

Rather than trying to reduce voting behaviour to no more than a replica of market behaviour, we regard the voting process as a very imperfect, but nevertheless acceptable, form of conflict resolution between voters. Some forms of voting rule, such as proportional representation, appear to reflect voters' choices more closely than others – the 'first past the post' system used in the United Kingdom, for example, enabled a minority of voters to elect majority governments throughout the 1980s. But whichever voting system is used, the links between a voter's choice and particular policy outcomes is often tenuous. Voters may well find that, if the party they have supported is in a minority, none of their main policy choices will be implemented. Voters really are frequently obliged to cast their votes under conditions of complexity, lack of full information and uncertainty. In these circumstances we would expect them to behave much as they do when making any choice under such conditions: they resort to simplifying decision rules – a matter I shall return to in a later chapter.

In a democratic system, some, possibly many, voters may fail over long periods to see their cherished policy outcomes realised. So long, however, as the State continues to meet the principal needs of voters – those we identified earlier – and is reasonably equitable in its treatment of the populace, then the great majority of voters may continue to support even a very imperfect democratic system. What we tend to find in many democracies nowadays is the emergence of a broad political consensus which is content to see government acting as provider of last resort, and undertaking safety functions, with argument only over the limits of such provision. Similarly, there tends to be a fairly broad consensus on the desirability of government being 'equitable', with argument once more only over how far the principle should be taken in practice.

I move on now to consider the second group of key decision makers in government: the politicians. Like the voters, they will have goals of their own. If they wish to remain in politics, one of their principal goals will be to ensure their re-election at voting time – or to secure their election if they are out of power. Since it is generally political parties which form governments and determine policies, it is principally on these bodies that we must focus our attention. A good deal of work, usually in the neoclassical tradition, has attempted to analyse how parties will behave when faced by utility maximising voters with differing views on policy matters – a good survey of this work is provided in Mueller (1989). In the representative democracies found in most industrialised countries, the two-party model, first presented by Hotelling (1929) and later by Downs (1957) depicts political opinion as lying along a single liberal-conservative (left-right) dimension, with each voter assumed to have a preferred position within the spectrum for a candidate or party. The further a party is from the preferred position, the less attractive it is to the voter.

In the simplest case, the preferred positions of voters can be represented by a frequency distribution which is both symmetric and unimodal. In order to garner as many votes as possible, the two parties are obliged to move towards the position on the spectrum favoured by the *median voter* – for a fuller analysis see Mueller (1989). Problems arise, however, if the unrealistic assumptions made in the two-party model are relaxed. Not all those eligible to vote may vote, in which case the median outcome would not be the optimum. Asymmetric or multinational distributions of preferences can drive parties towards the mode rather than the median. Moreover, a majority rule equilibrium is in general assured only when there is a single issue, and therefore a single dimension. Where there are numerous issues, and a party is faced with a problem of devising a multi-dimensional platform, the analysis breaks down. Only if the various issues can be reduced to *the* issue of the moment, can the problem be overcome.

It will be apparent from the above that in a two-party system with a variety of policy issues, the preferences of many voters need not be closely reflected in the policies of the parties from which they must choose. Choice is limited, and voters are in effect handing over widespread powers to the winning party, even if only for a maximum time period. In a multi-party system, choice is greater, and there is a better chance of being able to vote for a party which corresponds more closely with a voter's preferences. One of the attractions of the proportional representation system in use in many countries is that it offers just this sort of improved choice. On the other hand, there is a variety of proportional representation systems, and criticism of those versions which try to reflect as accurately as possible the wishes of the electors, as in Israel, is that they may in practice give disproportionate power to very small parties, if they happen to end up holding the balance of power between party coalitions. In such a case, the policies of a coalition may be heavily distorted in the desire to form a majority government which includes one or more of the small parties – in which case the preferences of many voters for the policies of the larger parties may be thwarted, to some extent at least. The fact of the matter is that once voters have cast their votes, they lose power over the outcomes decided by the politicians. Only the threat of retribution at a future poll may ensure that politicians do not stray too far from their mandates. What does seem certain is that neither voters nor politicians can decide upon their actions in a manner which guarantees that they are able to maximise their utilities, or for that matter any other measure of welfare.

Democratic political systems do therefore provide a means of resolving conflict at the level of government, but only in the last analysis by voters agreeing to pass decision-making authority over to politicians for limited periods. Politicians do not have *carte blanche* in deciding how to use that power, since they will wish to be re-elected, and must therefore heed the wishes of voters (or at least the wishes of a sufficient number of voters to be re-elected) but they nevertheless have a measure of freedom of action, especially since economic and other circumstances can usually be expected to change after an election. They may use their freedom of action to pursue other personal goals. Our study of personal motivation suggests that, in addition to wishing to be re-elected, they will wish to increase their real incomes as a means of satisfying more of their wants. They may well also be motivated by the desires for esteem and power. Since all these aspects of motivation are often linked to the size and scope of the activities over which politicians have authority, they may well lead the politicians to encourage the growth of government.

I will turn, finally, to the third major interest group in government: the public officials, or bureaucrats. Together politicians and officials have an important influence on the supply side of government, in contrast to the demand for government. Studies of the workings of bureaucracy have identified a variety of possible goals for bureaucrats, some of which might be held in common with politicians. In addition to a desire for an increase in salary, financial bonuses and other forms of pecuniary reward, writers have also focused attention on a number of additional, or perhaps on occasions substitute, non-pecuniary rewards. In the case of large corporations, Williamson (1964) thought these were most likely to take the form of on-the-job consumption and excessive staffing. Fisher and Hall (1969) stressed the desire for security, and Leibenstein (1966) and Comanor and Leibenstein (1969) brought together a broad range of non-pecuniary goals under the broad heading of 'x-inefficiency'. Mueller (1989) has also drawn attention to the manner in which the desire for power may motivate those in authority, and how the basis of this power often lies in uncertainty and the possession of information. He also cites risk aversion as a possible bureaucratic goal. Niskanen (1971) in the first systematic study within a public choice framework, summed up the possible goals of a bureaucrat as: salary, perquisites of the office, public reputation, power, patronage, output of the bureau, ease of making changes, and ease in managing the bureau. All but the last two, he went on to assert, were positively and monotonically related to the size of the budget.

The link between the personal goals of administrators and the size and growth of organisations is one which Marris (1964) and others noted in the case of firms. Bureaucrats in both the public and the private sectors, it seems, are driven by much the same motivating forces. Firm evidence that bureaucrats are able to increase spending beyond an 'optimum' level is, however, not easy to obtain, as one might expect. A series of studies of the manner in which school budgets are determined in Oregon, USA, where the procedures are unusually open to public scrutiny, are sometimes quoted as evidence of the forces at work – for a review see Mueller (1989). These studies, however, generally make use of the concept of the median voter, and the conclusions are therefore dependent upon the particular assumptions noted earlier.

Drawing together the different strands of the discussion above, we may conclude that representative democracy is a useful means of helping resolve some of the conflicts which may arise between the three principal parties to government, but it is far from being a perfect vehicle for this purpose. It does not overcome the problem of interpersonal comparisons if there are losers as well as gainers, as is frequently the case when governments decide to act. In practice, there is no calculus enabling us to devise policies which maximise the sum of total welfare. Most of the governed probably benefit from government, but that is by no means the same as saying that matters could not be improved upon. No practical means has yet been devised of ensuring that politicians always carry out the wishes of voters. Closer control would probably require more frequent elections and voting on all measures of any consequence. Even then, the actions of government would not exactly match the wishes of voters. Furthermore, voters only account for one part, even if generally the majority, of a population. Studies of government seldom consider the interests of *non-voters* – those below voting age (or, in some countries, those of the female sex). There is no reason to believe that voters can always be relied upon to take the best possible care of the interests of those who do not have the vote. Will those without children, for example, necessarily vote to pay more in tax to ensure sufficient is spent on schools, or child care in general? Can we even assume that all parents are adequately concerned with the best interests of their children, assuming they know them?

Not only are voters unable to control politicians, but politicians and voters are unable to exercise close control over public officials. Since politicians are subject to changes in voting behaviour more than officials, politicians tend to be more transitory. This often leaves officials with more influence and discretion over policy matters than ought to be the case in a democracy. Nor can all their activities be continually monitored – even hiring more bureaucrats to do the monitoring will not achieve full accountability.

What we end up with in representative democracy is a rather messy compromise which generally enables government to work to the benefit of nearly all, but still leaves politicians and public officials with sufficient freedom of action to pursue personal goals in ways which are not always in the best interests of voters (or non-voters). Only by assuming severe constraints on the actions of individuals, as is the case with standard economic models of government, can such a system be expected to give rise to maximising behaviour on the part of all concerned.

We now go on to examine the scale and nature of government activity, and how it has changed over time. This will enable us to assess just how well it fits the pattern we would expect on the basis of the behavioural influences outlined above.

THE SCALE AND NATURE OF GOVERNMENT ACTIVITY

One of the most noticeable features of the economies of many countries during this century, and in some cases even earlier, has been the steady increase in the importance of the government sector. Mueller (1989) has shown, for example, how total government expenditure in the United States, expressed as a percentage of the gross national product, increased from 10 per cent in 1929 to 23 per cent in 1949, and to 35 per cent in 1987. Recent statistics for the OECD countries (Table 11.1) show just how all-

Table 11.1 General government expenditure, revenue and net lending relative to GDP at current prices

	per cent			
	Expenditure		*Revenue*	
	1960	*1982*	*1960*	*1982*
Australia	22.1	36.3	25.4	34.2
Austria	32.1	50.3	31.0	46.7
Belgium	30.3	56.6	27.5	45.4
Canada	28.9	45.8	26.0	39.0
Denmark	24.8	60.7	27.3	50.7
Finland	26.7	41.3	30.0	39.7
France	34.6	50.7	34.9	46.9
Germany (West)	32.5	49.4	35.1	45.3
Greece	17.4[1]	37.0[1]	21.1	31.3
Iceland (1960–80)	28.2	34.4	36.4	36.0
Ireland (1960–81)	28.0	57.1	24.8	42.3
Italy	30.1	53.7	28.8	41.5
Japan	18.3	34.2	20.7	30.2
Luxembourg (1960–80)	30.5	54.3	32.5	51.5
Netherlands	33.7	63.7	33.9	55.8
Norway	29.9	48.8	33.1	52.8
Portugal (1960–81)	17.0	42.7	17.6	33.2
Spain (1964–81)	18.8	34.1	18.8	30.6
Sweden	31.1	67.3	32.0	59.7
Switzerland	17.2[1]	30.0[1]	23.3	33.2
Turkey (1962)	18.0	*	19.1	*
United Kingdom	32.6	47.4	30.3	43.7
United States	27.6	37.6	27.3	32.0
Mean (unweighted)	26.3	47.0	27.7	41.9
Coefficient of Variation	0.24	0.22	0.21	0.21

[1] Current disbursement only.
* Not available.

Source: P. Saunders and F. Klau, *The Role of the Public Sector: Causes and Consequences of the Growth of Government* (Paris: OECD, 1985).

embracing this trend has been, irrespective of the dominant political or economic philosophy in each country. There must, it seems, have been powerful underlying forces at work.

A study of OECD countries by Saunders and Klau (1985) has provided a breakdown of the growth of public spending during the 1970s by major category. The study distinguishes four principal forms of expenditure: public goods (defence, general public services); merit goods (education, health, housing, community and social services); income maintenance (pensions, sickness benefits, family allowances and unemployment compensation); economic services (mainly capital transactions, subsidies). Public debt interest was also listed separately. For the nine countries for which data were available (including the US, UK, France, West Germany and Japan) broadly similar trends emerged. The expansion of government expenditure (as a proportion of GDP) generally occurred in the supply of merit goods and in income maintenance support. Expenditure on public goods, on the other hand, remained fairly stable, while the share of GDP spent on economic services declined on average.

Further analysis revealed that within the merit goods category the fastest growing component was health expenditure, followed by education. In the case of income maintenance, much of the increase was due to greater pension provisions, especially in the case of Japan. Unemployment compensation also rose markedly (a development which continued during the 1980s) as the number out of work increased. Finally, there was a general rise over the period in public debt interest payments relative to GDP, reflecting both a tendency for public debt to increase more rapidly than GDP and a higher level of interest rates.

Comparisons of government spending with corresponding spending in the private sector revealed a number of other interesting developments. Movements in the price deflators for government consumption (corresponding roughly to the current provision of public goods, merit goods and economic services) and private consumption showed that the 'relative price effect' averaged just over 2½ per cent during the 1960s, but fell below 1 per cent in the 1970s. Owing to the difficulties of calculating productivity changes in the public sector, such figures, as the OECD study notes, ought to be treated with caution, but the faster rise in prices in the public sector is one important reason why public expenditure, in nominal terms, has risen faster than GDP. The lower relative price effect in the 1970s was partly the consequence, it seems, of the slowdown in productivity growth in the private sector after the large oil price rise in 1973.

Comparisons of trends in public and private expenditure also showed some slight decline in the general government share of total gross fixed investment, in constant price terms – expressed in current prices, the share altered little. The share of government transfers in household receipts (before tax) confirms a trend noted above. Over the 1960s and 1970s, the share rose from 9 per cent to around 15 per cent, an increase of two-thirds. Total government payments, including wages and salaries, also increased sharply as employment in the public sector rose during the period.

Decomposing the expenditures on education, health and income maintenance into components reflecting demographic changes, extensions of programme coverage and increases in service or benefit levels produced other interesting findings in the OECD study. Between 1960 and 1975, higher real benefits accounted on average for about two-thirds of the overall increases in real expenditure on both education and health. The remaining one-third could be traced to demographic pressures (more students and more patients) and extensions in coverage. After 1975, demographic pressures eased due to the effects of lower birth rates; but more importantly, the general tendency for real benefits to increase largely came to a halt, as the harsher economic climate following the oil price rises took its toll.

The general picture which emerges, then, is of a growing role for government within the economies of the industrial countries. Up until the mid-1970s, this growing role had little to do with the security aspects of people's lives (or, in economic terminology, with the provision of public goods, such as defence and law and order) or with the role of government as provider of last resort. The trend appears to have been more the consequence of developing notions of equity, and its demands in a modern, advanced society. The large increase in transfer payments has been concerned with extending income maintenance benefits beyond the levels of 'basic' provision, relating them instead more closely to the general level of incomes in society. The emphasis on equitable provision, in other words, has shifted from *absolute* levels to *relative* levels of income – not a surprising development in a society in which, as I said earlier, social comparisons are important. There are signs now, however, that the limits of this trend may have been reached in some countries or localities (perhaps temporarily) and that the notions of equity by no means extend to equal, or even near equal, incomes.

Notions of equity also now seem to embrace reasonable provision of education and health services for all, and the provision of certain social services, especially for the most vulnerable members of society, such as the young, elderly and disabled. There may in addition be a growing recognition that modern industrial societies require healthy, well educated work forces if they are to be economically competitive.

The above comments need to be qualified in certain respects with regard to developments during the 1980s. For a period NATO countries agreed to increase expenditure on defence by 3 per cent a year in real terms – although not all member countries achieved the target – and rapidly rising unemployment caused heavier demands on government as provider of last resort. These developments appear, however, to be temporary – at least it is to be hoped so.

Finally, what are sometimes referred to as 'proximate' determinants of government spending seem to have been important, especially during certain periods. Demographic changes, which are important because of their consequences for the sum of personal needs, have been quite substantial in the period since the end of the Second World War. The relative price effect has also varied in importance, as we saw earlier, but it has always had the consequence of causing many categories of government spending to rise faster than GDP – and this effect is likely to continue. Looking more to the future, there is every reason to expect that externalities will provide much of the impetus behind government spending, as nations attempt to cope with the side effects of economic growth on our planet.

The principal developments noted above in government activities are entirely consistent with the goals of voters, politicians and bureaucrats, as I outlined them earlier. Voters will be inclined to favour improvements in, or extensions to, benefits, especially if they are on relatively low incomes, and paying relatively little in tax. Politicians will also be tempted to sanction greater benefit payments as a means of pleasing voters and increasing the size and scope of activities over which they preside. Bureaucrats, too, could be expected to favour a growth of transfer payments from government as a means of furthering their own importance and increasing their financial and other rewards. Only if voters eventually call a halt, is the general trend towards growing government likely to peter out, or perhaps even be reversed.

DECISION-MAKING IN GOVERNMENT

Government as an entity may be viewed as one large decision-making centre within which there is a large number of decision-making units, some of much greater importance – from an economic point of view – than others. The first decision-making unit of significance we shall look at is the electorate – that part of it which actually votes. In a democracy it clearly has some influence on government behaviour. In a neo-classical model these individuals will be rational, and concerned to act in a way which maximises their utility. Unfortunately, faced often by two, and possible more, political parties offering a wide diversity of policies from which a voter might ideally like to select some from each party, there is not in practice complete freedom of choice. Compromise will almost certainly have to be made in order to try and select one party (or candidate, if voters are inclined to vote for candidate rather than party).

The voter's dilemma is greater still, however. Voting is decidedly not like purchasing a good or service, since in casting his vote the voter is even more uncertain of its consequences for the final outcome – especially in multi-party political systems in which alliances usually have to be made between parties in order to form a government. Moreover, since the voter is only able to express his choice at lengthy intervals, politicians have a measure of flexibility in how closely they adhere to any promises about policies – the 'read my lips' promise of US President Bush not to increase taxes is a notable example. Party programmes, too, are unlikely to touch on all matters of concern to voters. The voter is therefore typically faced with a complex decision for which he does not by any means have all the information he requires, and for which the outcome may be said to be truly *uncertain* in the sense in which we have defined that term.

How, then, does the voter decide? The individual behaves as he, or she, does in any other comparable circumstance, such as the purchase of certain complex goods. Simplifying decision rules are used. The voter might decide, for example, to adopt either the conjunctive or disjunctive non-compensatory decision rules examined in Chapter 7. Or a lexicographic ordering of parties' policies might be preferred. Doubtless some voters will favour one type of rule, while some will favour others. Determining which form of decision-making rule is most commonly used is a matter for empirical investigation.

The decision-making problems facing politicians are just as perplexing as those facing voters. Any idea of a social welfare function has to be jettisoned, for the reasons I outlined earlier. The theory of public choice, while it has helped clarify the issues, does not render a maximising outcome any more attainable. The problems, quite simply, are much more complex than the approach can handle – in theory and in practice. In trying to determine how best to appeal to voters and secure sufficient support for re-election, the politicians, too, are therefore forced to fall back on simple heuristics. We have seen some striking examples of this in the United States and the United Kingdom in recent years. Faced with a multiplicity of pressures for greater Federal spending – with increased defence requirements very much to the fore during the 1980s – at the same time as budget deficits were threatening to have serious detrimental effects on the economy, Congress passed the Gramm-Rudman–Hollings Act in 1985, with the aim of producing a balanced budget by 1991. The Act, which was quite clearly a decision rule for budget policy, and was described as such in the 1990 Economic Report of the President, set down target deficits which were to be reduced each year until budget balance was achieved.

In the United Kingdom, the use of policy decision-making rules has been most evident in the Medium Term Financial Strategy (MTFS) introduced by a Conservative Government in 1979. Initially the MTFS included two goals: to move towards a balanced budget over the medium term and to maintain a steadily reducing target range for the growth of money supply (initially defined as sterling M3, but later replaced by M0). When the budget moved into substantial surplus rather than balance, a further rule was introduced: that a downward trend should be maintained over the medium term in the ratio of general government expenditure to GDP (*Financial Statement and Budget Report*, 1989).

An interesting feature of the rules outlined above (and there are many others, such as those in the environmental field, to which I drew attention in Chapter 5) is that there was no attempt to justify the rules on the grounds that they would somehow maximise welfare for the total population. Indeed, no such justification exists. It has never been demonstrated that a balanced budget must always in practice guarantee maximum utility, nor that the same end will be achieved by a particular rate of growth of the money supply, nor a particular ratio of government spending to GDP. Such rules are merely espoused for convenience. Decision makers in government are no better placed than any other individuals making decisions, despite the much greater resources at their disposal. Furthermore, the decisions faced may be more complex than elsewhere, since even more variables come into play. Bounded rationality, lack of full information and true uncertainty are just as serious constraints on government as they are elsewhere in the economy. What it boils down to is that, faced with the impossible task of determining and allocating government expenditure in a maximising fashion, governments too resort to simplifying decision rules – rules which may seem to point in the right direction, although even that is by no means always certain.

If we were to accept that full employment, rapid economic growth, low inflation and balance of payments equilibrium, coupled with an 'equitable' distribution of income, were all essential ingredients of maximum social welfare, we would have still more cause to doubt that government policies were always for the best. Given the difficulties of reconciling and attaining all these different objectives at the same time, governments in practice again often simplify matters by deciding to give priority to one or other of the goals at particular times. During the 1950s and 1960s, the achievement of faster economic growth was generally the principal objective of policy in the US and the UK, sometimes at the expense of the balance of payments. By the standards of today, inflation and unemployment were not serious problems – although there was concern that unemployment in the US was high relative to that of other major industrial countries. During the 1980s, in contrast, control of inflation was accorded highest priority in most countries, and, in Western Europe at least, unemployment was allowed to rise to exceptionally high levels not seen since the 1920s and 1930s. Despite the resources at their disposal, complexity, lack of information and uncertainty contrived to defeat even the efforts of governments to manage their affairs in anything approaching an optimum manner.

Even with greater expertise in policy matters, bureaucrats are not better placed than the politicians they serve to ensure maximising behaviour on the part of government. Indeed, more often than not it will be the bureaucrats who have devised the simplifying decision-making rules of the type referred to earlier. Fortunately, much government decision-making is of a routine, repetitive nature, in common with that of the individual decision makers. It is this feature of government spending which lends it so much stability, even during periods of severe economic recession. Nevertheless, many important decisions at government level are of great complexity. Full information is not always available, and a state of true uncertainty is therefore common. It is this very state of uncertainty that gives bureaucrats a certain latitude in their decision-making. Since there is often no clear cut answer to many problems, mistakes are less obvious, and underperformance may be disguised. It is not too difficult in such circumstances for officials to introduce an element of their personal goals into decisions. A growth in government spending to the benefit of a bureaucrat may be dressed up primarily as an outcome beneficial to the voters – and perhaps even as being beneficial to the politicians. In practice, politicians and bureaucrats must often collude, since their interests have much in common.

The overriding impression of government remains one of a system in which no one is very clear about what ought to be done, since there is not at present – and perhaps never will be – any means of determining which actions will do most to promote the welfare of a whole population. Decisions must nevertheless be taken, and decision makers in government therefore oblige by resorting to simplifying rules which, for the greater part, enable welfare to be improved, even if not in any optimum sense.

CONCLUSIONS

It would take a great deal more space than I have available to deal with all the major aspects of government, but certain features have emerged once again which I have found to be common to all the socioeconomic decision-making centres studied. First, there is no such decision-making entity as government. There is, rather, a variety of decision-making units functioning within government. Second, these different decision-making units have their own goals, even if they sometimes do share certain common interests. The existence of different goals means, as always, that some method must be found of resolving the conflicts which arise. In democratic political systems this is achieved in part through a system of voting, the degree of influence voters are able to exercise over politicians varying according to the voting system in use.

The behavioural foundations of economics are indispensable in helping explain why government exists, and why its activities have assumed particular forms. Government has often been imposed by autocratic rulers thirsting for power, but the gradual spread of democratic government shows that individuals, given a free choice, will usually opt for that form of government. They must therefore feel that it is in their interests so to do. The explanation, I maintain, is that it helps satisfy some of the important individual needs which have been identified. Most obviously, government helps satisfy the need for security by providing more effective forces for defence and law and order than individuals can hope to provide via the market. Economists have identified such goods as 'public goods', and so they are, but the preference for such goods in the first place stems from the felt need for security.

The level of provision required for defence and the maintenance of law and order is not something that can easily be gauged, and the growing sophistication of weapons means that defence in particular can absorb very large and increasing funds. But unless potential enemies are increasing their budgets, there is no reason why defence should absorb a *growing share* of resources. Nor, unless something is seriously wrong with society, should law and order require ever increasing budgets.

Nor would the activities of government as provider of last resort, standing ready to meet the basic needs of citizens when called upon, necessarily lead to forever increasing size of government. Where populations were expanding, the extent of provision would, of course, also increase, other things being equal. But population growth is slowing in most industrial countries. The main impetus to growing spending in this area has come, as we saw, from a variety of income maintenance schemes. Rising unemployment, especially in Western Europe, has been a principal cause of these greater demands. It must be hoped that this unwelcome development will in time be reversed, although the signs are that it may take longer than anticipated. Meantime the unemployment problems of Eastern Europe have been added to those of the West.

It is not just the total number of the population, and within that the total unemployed, which bears on government assistance in meeting basic needs. The changing age composition of the populations of most industrial countries means that, while there are fewer young people to care for, there are many more elderly, a great number of whom have inadequate incomes, and who increasingly require medical assistance as life expectancy continues to lengthen.

For a variety of reasons, therefore, the role of government as provider of last resort has tended to be a major factor underlying the growth of government. I ought not to leave this field of government activity, however, without remarking finally on what has been one of the most important factors of all in the area of basic needs, namely, that there has been a tendency to re-define such needs. It was noted in Baxter (1988) that at their most basic the term 'basic needs' would cover no more than the means for mere survival. We have long since moved beyond that definition, however, and Stewart (1985), for example, has distinguished two main interpretations now commonly used: first, the more conservative, which is that every human being ought to be able to enjoy these goods and services which enable him, or her, to 'live a decent life'; secondly, the 'full-life objective', which may also include provision for social, cultural and recreational activities.

Such definitions are obviously open to widely varying interpretations, but for present purposes the main point is that in all the major industrial countries basic needs have been re-defined in ways requiring more government spending. The provider of last resort is no longer expected to meet just the means of mere survival, but something more comfortable, even if most would not wish to find themselves in the shoes of those dependent solely on the basic provision.

The changing view of the role of government as provider of last resort appears to be clearly associated with changing notions of what is equitable in increasingly wealthy societies. Theories of justice, as we have seen, have not yet proved of great practical assistance when it comes to assessing policies. Yet decisions have to be taken, and one central plank of equity now seems to have emerged: individuals mostly feel that equity demands not just the provision of some absolute level of benefits, but rather a level of benefits which reflects the general standard of living in society. This has meant not just some catching up in the levels of real social benefits, but also *continued growth* as real incomes have risen. In some countries, at least, the catch-up phase may now have been completed, and in one or two countries, notably the US and the UK, there may even have been a feeling that this phase has gone too far, and needs to be reversed to some degree.

Changing views on equity also appear to have played a part in the greater role which many governments have assumed in the provision of certain services, especially those for education, health and a range of social services. The first two of these – and perhaps even the third – might also be supported, of course, on purely economic grounds. Japan, for example, and some of the newly industrialised economies, like Korea and Taiwan, obviously regard well-educated populations as crucial to their continued economic success. The desire for more equitable arrangements nevertheless appears to have been a powerful driving force. The call for 'equality of opportunity' has a strong appeal. The effects on government spending have been compounded by the relative price effects we noted earlier.

The above remarks have principally concerned the wishes of voters.

When we turn to politicians and bureaucrats we find that personal motivation is again to the fore. The desires for continued office, for esteem, status and power all tend to work in the direction of more, rather than less, government. Only the electorates in democratic societies can check these tendencies, and there is now evidence in some countries, such as the US and the UK, that they are inclined to do just that. Whether these tendencies amount to more than just passing phases remains to be seen. Electorates are greatly hampered by the fact that they are only able to express their preferences to any great effect at infrequent intervals.

Sufficient has been said, it is hoped, to demonstrate that individual motivation, in the shape of a desire to satisfy important needs, together with a desire for greater equity, have been, and will continue to be, at the very heart of government. They have influenced the nature of government activities and changes in the relative importance of these activities. They also help explain the continued growth of government. They do not, of course, on their own explain all government actions, but they certainly serve to take us beyond what are often presented as purely 'economic' explanations of government.

Decision-making in government exhibits certain characteristics which we have encountered repeatedly when examining other socioeconomic decision-making centres, and also decision-making by the individual acting on his, or her, own behalf. Much decision-making is complex, undertaken in conditions of less than full information, and subject to true uncertainty. There is plenty of evidence that in these circumstances individuals (because it is always individuals who in the end make decisions) resort to decision-making rules to guide their actions. The rules generally are not arbitrary. It is likely that in most instances there is a desire to improve social welfare; but in practice no one is in a position to say precisely how that might best be achieved. The rules are often no more than informed guesses about the most appropriate policies, and will on occasions almost certainly be sadly mistaken. The maximising individual of the standard economic model is a far cry from reality.

When discussing aggregate behaviour in Chapter 12, I shall draw on the above discussion in attempting to specify more precisely the independent variables helping explain government expenditure.

Part V
Aggregate Behaviour and Conclusions

12 Aggregate Behaviour

In economics it is maintained that there is no difficulty, in principle, in aggregating across individuals or across firms: the combined demand curve for two (or more) individuals is simply the sum of the two individual demand curves; similarly for two or more firms. Not all economists feel entirely happy about such procedures – even if they believe that such a thing as a smooth, continuous demand curve exists – since many do recognise that individuals acting independently of each other need not behave in exactly the same way as individuals acting jointly, as a group. I stressed in earlier chapters that people in groups influence each other; and there may be a variety of decision-making units within the groups. Moreover, the responsibilities of the decision-making units in a group may change over time – over the family life cycle, for example.

We can demonstrate some of these points by reference to our earlier discussion of individual behaviour. In equation (4.4) we expressed the demand for a good x by individual i (subject to the usual income constraint) in the form:

$$b_i^x = b(a_i, s_i, E_i^x lm, R_i^x) \quad (4.4)$$

If we now tried to aggregate the demand for x by combining several individuals, each with different opinion leaders and reference groups, some of the explanatory variables could well lose their force, since a reference group, for example, might be relevant to only one individual and not to the others. If the individuals act *jointly*, pooling their incomes, the greater income will be likely to yield them wider choice, and their preferences might well change. Alternatively, the group might allow one individual in the group to take decisions on behalf of the group. In that case, the individual's preferences could determine the group's purchases, or some composite preferences might emerge. Other permutations are possible, and do not need to be spelled out in order to make the point.

Whereas we cannot simply sum across individuals in order to determine the aggregate demand by these individuals for a good, we do nevertheless have a variety of measures of aggregate behaviour. Where the actions of individuals and socioeconomic decision-making centres are associated with expenditures on goods and services, money provides a common unit of measurement which permits the sum of all outcomes (revealed preferences, if you like) to be calculated. Corresponding to these expenditures there will also be, of course, associated incomes. Similarly, we can, given the relevant data, calculate the volume of output by firms during a given period. The social and psychological variables I highlighted in my earlier analysis can, in other words, be linked to the customary macroeconomic aggregates of expenditure, income and output with which economists are familiar – the former will appear, in effect, as additional explanatory variables in behavioural equations (as expectational variables do now, for example).

The socio-psychological variables will not affect all the equations in a macro model. Some equations will be merely accounting identities; others might be based on relationships between objective factors, such as changes in the money supply and the availability of credit; while in some the socio-psychological influences may be too small to matter. Our procedure, therefore, will simply be to identify those behavioural equations of a macro model in which we believe, on the basis of our earlier analysis, socio-psychological variables are likely to have significant effects.

While it is not necessary for the purposes of the present study to set out formally a complete macro model of the economy, I should say a word about the theoretical underpinnings of the type of model I would expect to be used. It will be apparent from the general tenor of my study that a neo-classical type model would be inappropriate. The belief that 'economic man' is somehow typical of real-life men and women just does not appear to be borne out by the facts. Nor does the real world of large-scale, persistent unemployment, monopolistic practices and degradation of the environment suggest that efficient, market-clearing mechanisms are at work which will automatically ensure the best possible outcomes. My analysis is therefore more in keeping with the broadly Keynesian view of the world, in which markets function imperfectly, in which true uncertainty is commonplace, and in which there is an important role for government in helping check or remove market distortions, and ensure that equity as well as purely commercial considerations govern economic affairs.

In the discussion which follows, I will consider the roles of the behavioural variables at the macro level under the conventional headings of goods markets, labour markets and money markets. Since we are dealing with individuals and socioeconomic decision-making units in the aggregate, some of the variables which are of key importance at the micro level may now no longer be so at the macro level, perhaps because certain effects on individuals cancel each other out when combined, or because they no longer operate in large groupings.

THE GOODS MARKETS

If we think in national income and expenditure terms, by adding together the expenditure of households, firms, government and the external sector, and making the appropriate factor cost adjustments, we can obtain an estimate of the gross domestic product. Since I treat exports as exogenously determined (*Xa* in Figure 2.1), I will concentrate on the other three sectors, starting with households, which I consider under the general heading of 'consumers'.

Consumers

While at the micro level there is a great deal of evidence (as we saw in Chapter 4) that, in economic terminology, consumers' preferences are interdependent, i.e., that a consumer's purchasing behaviour is strongly influenced by the purchasing behaviour of others (contrary to neo-classical theory), trying to capture such social influences at the macro level is problematic. There is unlikely to be one opinion leader for the purchase of all goods, for example: nor is there likely to be one reference group common to all individuals, or groups of individuals. It would seem, therefore, that we have no alternative but to drop these explanatory variables at the macro level. Are there, nevertheless, relevant variables from our earlier discussion of personal characteristics and decision-making whose effects we might still be able to test at the macro level?

If we consider, first, individual motivation, and the desire to satisfy personal needs, changes in the total number of individuals in a population is obviously of importance, since that would affect total consumption. Any changes in the age-sex composition of a given population would also affect the total needs of that population, and therefore the relationship between C and Y, and ought consequently to feature among explanatory variables in a consumption function.

A number of *family* life cycle variables might also prove to be significant at the macro level. A tendency for young people to marry later could be expected, for example, to alter spending and saving decisions, since it is the arrival of children which places heavy spending demands on households, perhaps even requiring a move to a new home. Later marriage may also lead to a reduction in the average size of families, since the number of child-bearing years will be reduced. Given the close link with needs, and the high cost of bringing up children, the latter development could again be expected to have effects on family spending and saving decisions.

The introduction of what are often referred to as 'demographic' variables may not appear a novel departure, since these are often introduced into consumer studies. The fundamental difference on this occasion, however, is that there is both theoretical and empirical justification for their introduction, whereas in neo-classical models (as Ferber, 1973, noted) they are introduced on an ad hoc basis, simply because they seem too obviously important to be left out, and because they generally improve the explanation of consumer behaviour.

When we examined decision-making by consumers, we concluded that in the cases of both the individual and socioeconomic groups there was a need to distinguish between routine, habitual decision-making on the one hand and complex decision-making on the other, especially where the latter was subject to true uncertainty. Only detailed budget studies are likely to be able to determine the relative importance of the different types of decision-making with any precision, but it does seem possible, even at the macro level, to distinguish types of spending which will be largely, if not entirely, routine. Much expenditure on food, for example, is of this nature. So, too, will be most spending on heating, lighting and accommodation. These together account for a sizeable proportion of most budgets, especially of lower income budgets. For such items, the most appropriate form of the consumption function would appear to be:

$$C_t^h = c(C_{t-1}^h, POP, POP^{30-55}, Y_{dt}) \qquad (12.1)$$

where all the consumption variables are expressed in real terms, and C_t^h is consumption of habitual items in the current time period t, C_{t-1}^h is the corresponding consumption in the previous time period, *POP* is the total number in the population, POP^{30-55} is the *proportion* of the population aged 30–55 (a variable designed to catch any effects from changes in the age distribution) and Y_{dt} is total consumer disposable income in the current time period. Since habits take time to form, consumption in periods earlier than t–1 also seem likely to be relevant, but probably less so with the passage of time, and it might therefore be accorded declining weight the further back in time it goes. The customary income constraint would also apply.

In the case of non-habitual purchases, with uncertainty a dominant factor, the effects of decision rules could be identified only if they were a sufficiently common practice to show up at the macro level. This is an important area where further research is required. Since, however, the more complex decisions facing consumers will often relate to durable goods, especially the more expensive ones, it seems likely that the consumption function for non-habitual purchases will include such variables as interest rates and the availability of credit, in addition to the customary disposable income variable. Purchases of such goods are also subject to changes in consumer attitudes and expectations. We noted in Chapter 6 how anticipatory variables are now commonly used in forecasting changes in consumer behaviour, although further research is also required into precisely how the changes in attitudes and expectations are themselves brought about.

Finally, although I have at various points in my study stressed the importance of *relative* income to consumer (and wage) behaviour, representing this influence at the macro level poses the difficult problem of trying to find a suitable proxy variable. Tests of Duesenberry's relative income hypothesis have usually focused on the influence on current consumption of the highest level of income previously reached. Insofar as income and consumption generally increase year on year in real terms, this effect could very well be caught, in part at least, by our equation (12.1). Any short-term fall in income, for example, would still leave C_t^h dependent upon previous levels of habitual consumption. In other words, consumption would not instantly, and fully, adjust to the drop in income.

To sum up, a behavioural approach would suggest that macroeconomic models should distinguish between habitual/routine behaviour by consumers, on the one hand, and more complex decision-making on the other. Within both categories – but perhaps more so in the case of routine behaviour – needs-related 'demographic' variables ought to prove significant. Anticipatory variables, of the kind suggested by Katona and others, seem likely to be of greatest importance in respect of goods purchases entailing complex decision-making, since these are generally of a less essential, less basic kind. Short-term changes in attitudes and expectations mean that goods purchases associated with complex decision-making will tend to be much more volatile than purchases of a routine, habitual nature.

Firms

In my earlier discussion of decision-making by firms, I noted the evidence that firms have increasingly been using sophisticated capital budgeting techniques in evaluating alternative investment proposals. The single most popular method of appraisal, however, still appears to be the simple payback period, and other 'naive' forms of assessment are also very popular. Moreover, these findings relate to the larger, and one would hope more aware, firms, with the resources to make use of the most complex techniques. Many firms almost certainly adopt a variety of techniques and compare the findings. A crucial implication, from our point of view, is that the use of the more complex techniques does not yield any better results than the simpler naive methods – and indeed the evidence available bears this out. In the smaller, less well resourced, firms, use of the naive methods seems likely to be even more common, and these firms, since they are much more numerous, account for an appreciable share of total business fixed investment.

The nub of the problem for businessmen is that trying to assess the future course of events is such a complex exercise, for which they possess only limited information, that for the most part they must take decisions under conditions of true uncertainty. Sophisticated techniques can often help in assessing the consequences of alternative outcomes, and perhaps narrow the likely margins of error, but they cannot wholly overcome the problems of true uncertainty. Some capital investment decisions may be reducible to reasonably precise calculations of probabilities, but many will continue to defy such an approach.

Despite the predominant uncertainty surrounding capital investment appraisal, some of the decisions will be more in the nature of the simple, habitual decisions often taken by consumers. Where it is a question of capital widening rather than capital deepening, for example, with a firm simply adding the same, or similar, machines to its existing stock of machines – or simply replacing worn out machines with like machines, rather than introducing machines incorporating new technology – much uncertainty will be removed. The machines' performance will be known, and the firm will already be familiar with the market for the output.

Whether dealing with simple or complex capital investment decisions, there are grounds for believing that investment will be related closely to output. Even in complex cases, the simplified procedures often used to overcome the problems of uncertainty mean that time horizons will tend to be short, and probably fixed somewhat arbitrarily – rapid technological development also ensures that much capital equipment has a relatively short life. The shorter the time horizon, the closer the link between investment in any given time period and the accompanying output. In my view, therefore, behavioural factors suggest that an accelerator-type model is most appropriate to represent the relationship between investment and output at the macro level. In the simplest case, ignoring replacement investment and assuming a constant capital-output ratio (v), with instant adjustment of net investment (I) to changes in output (Y), we would have:

$$I = v(Y_t - Y_{t-1}) \quad (12.2)$$

The form of this relationship can also be given a forward look, with net investment being some fraction of the difference between *expected* output and actual output.

With regard to the price setting behaviour of firms, I have placed the emphasis on firms' costs as the primary determinant, while recognising that supply and demand factors must also play a role. Firms' behaviour is again determined by the information most readily available to them, rather than the more complex calculations requiring full information, which are essential if they are always to be maximising their profits. In most industries over one-half of total costs are accounted for by labour costs (principally wages and salaries, but also including pension contributions by employers and any required social security contributions, etc.). Changes in unit labour costs and the costs of raw materials supplied to industry will therefore account for the bulk of firms' costs. In countries heavily dependent on imported goods and raw materials, the price of imports will also be important. The price of firms' output (P_f), which will in turn heavily influence the general price level, we therefore show as:

$$P_f = \emptyset(CST)_f \qquad (12.3)$$

Where, ø is a constant, and $(CST)_f$ is the total unit cost of firms' output. I maintain, in other words, that costs are a more important direct determinant of firms' prices than other variables, such as the money supply. The precise form of the link between costs and prices can only be determined by empirical investigation. It may well prove to be more complex than the simple relationship shown in equation (12.3).

Government

Government activity in economic models is treated as exogenous, although, as we saw in Chapter 11, in democratic societies it can be expected to respond in some measure to the needs and wants of voters, and to a desire for equitable treatment. These form one of the principal strands of government activity which we try to reflect at the macro level: the other is the usual dichotomy between, on the one hand, routine/habitual decision-making and, on the other, the simplifying decision rules required to cope with complex decision-making, frequently under conditions of true uncertainty.

Routine/habitual decision-making covers extensive areas of government activity. In functional terms, much habitual decision-making relates to income maintenance and the provision of so-called 'merit' goods. The former covers such major items of spending as unemployment benefit, pensions, sickness benefit and family allowances. The intention generally is that these should enable individuals and families to meet their 'basic' needs. In some countries, however, the real level of these benefits has been raised over time, suggesting that equity considerations have become more important, and that it is not just the absolute incomes of those assisted but their incomes *relative* to those of the population at large which are considered important. Once higher levels are reached, there seems to be a tendency to maintain relative standards, although occasionally the process may be put into reverse – for example, a Conservative government in the United Kingdom decided during the 1980s that increases in State pensions should be linked to changes in retail prices rather than average earnings.

Income maintenance expenditure, while usually included under the heading of what is referred to as 'automatic stabilisers', is therefore still subject to occasional discretionary changes in policy. In general, however, we can it seems expect income maintenance payments to rise in line with nominal incomes in the economy. Allowance ought to be made, however, for any major changes in the number of people of pensionable age (POP^p), the number unemployed (POP^u) and the number of children qualifying for family allowances (POP^f), since these are potentially major changes which would *automatically* affect total expenditure on income maintenance. In the absence of discretionary changes in policy, we could then represent government expenditure on income maintenance (G^y) as:

$$G^y = f(GDP, POP^p, POP^u, POP^f) \qquad (12.4)$$

Expenditure on 'merit' goods – usually defined to include education, health, housing and community and social services – also tends to be on a large scale, and very largely committed. For that reason it is also generally thought of as an automatic stabiliser. Once again, when the appropriate levels of spending have been determined by policy decisions, expenditure tends to rise in line with nominal GDP – subject as always to any subsequent discretionary policy changes. The needs aspect is reflected in changes in the numbers benefiting – for example the number of schoolchildren. Changes in the total population are also relevant to the demands for housing, health and social services. Finally, we must allow for a relative price effect (RP) to take account of the fact that the prices of merit goods tend to rise faster than the prices of goods and services in the economy as a whole. In the absence of discretionary changes in policy, we could represent government expenditure on merit goods (G^m) by:

$$G^m = f(GDP, RP, POP, POP^e) \tag{12.5}$$

where *POP* and POP^e represent the total population and the population in full-time education, respectively (the latter perhaps weighted according to the relative numbers in school and higher education). There are already signs in some countries that the growing proportion of elderly in many populations is beginning to affect spending on health and social services, so that it may also be necessary to reflect this development.

The provision of public goods is yet another functional area of government expenditure which might be described as 'habitual'. Few quarrel with the view that defence and the upholding of law and order are appropriate areas of government activity. The provision of public goods, like most government services, is very labour intensive, and the wages and salaries of those employed in providing the services will have to reflect rising living standards, although there is no intrinsic reason why economic growth should entail a requirement for more servicemen or more policemen. Overall, expenditure on public goods in most countries has tended to remain fairly stable as a proportion of GDP, or even to decline slightly, adding to the automatic stabiliser effects I have already noted above. I must include the usual caveat about discretionary changes in government policy, however. In the case of defence, for example, it is possible that many countries will benefit in the next few years from a 'peace dividend', following the easing of tensions between East and West. This is in marked contrast to the situation in the early 1980s when NATO countries decided to raise their defence spending by 3 per cent a year in real terms. Finally, as with expenditure on merit goods, there is a relative price effect to take into account. In the light of the above, we can, once more in the absence of discretionary changes in policy, represent government expenditure on public goods (G^p) as:

$$G^p = f(GDP, RP) \tag{12.6}$$

In addition to the three functional areas of government spending referred to above, the OECD study by Saunders and Klau (1985) identified 'economic services' as a fourth area of activity. This covered capital transactions, including spending on infrastructure projects such as roads. It also included subsidies. In order to obtain a full measure of the impact of the public sector on the economy we would have to include, in addition, spending by nationalised industries and public corporations, although these are generally treated as 'off-budget' items financed by borrowing, often under government guarantee.

In the period covered by the OECD study, from the early 1960s to the early 1980s, expenditure on economic services declined as a share of GDP, although experience varied markedly between countries. The study did not, unfortunately, consider short-term cyclical variations in government spending, but economic services comprise the functions most likely to be influenced by cyclical movements in the economy. Even if 'fine tuning' an economy is now out of favour, it is difficult for governments not to respond to cyclical changes. When an economy is in recession, political pressures mount for governments to 'do something', and when an economy is booming and inflation posing a threat, governments are under external as well as internal pressures to impose constraints. Discretionary changes in government policies are, however, very much in the nature of complex decision-making, since the appropriate timing, choice of policy instruments and extent of intervention are matters surrounded by great uncertainty. Broadly speaking, it does not seem uncharacteristic to describe much discretionary activity by governments – even nowadays – as 'counter cyclical'.

I turn, finally, to debt interest. Most of this item reflects decisions made in the past, and is therefore inescapable, and a further form of routine/habitual spending. Current discretionary measures may, however, give rise to reductions or increases in the levels of debt outstanding, and to variations in the rate of interest paid – although interest rates are not wholly within the preserve of governments in open economies. One approach might be to treat repayments of capital as routine spending and interest payments as in some measure counter-cyclical.

It will be apparent from the above, it is hoped, that while explaining and forecasting government expenditure is a complex business, the underlying behavioural influences do lend a very large measure of stability to government spending. It is interesting that the OECD study referred to earlier found that the best single predictor of government size at the end of the 1970s was its size at the beginning of the 1960s, 'pointing to the importance of country-specific cultural, social and historical factors not amenable to quantification.' At the very least, therefore, the habitual-complex decision-making dichotomy ought to be reflected in a macro-model of the economy.

The habitual spending of government ($G^{HAB} = G^y + G^m + G^p$) we have represented in equations (12.4) to (12.6). Government expenditure primarily associated with discretionary, complex decision-making (G^{com}) – primarily economic services and interest payments on debt, but perhaps also including at least part of the spending on nationalised industries and public corporations – we treat as essentially counter-cyclical in its consequences, and therefore represent as follows:

$$G^{com} = f(1/GDP) \tag{12.7}$$

Government expenditure associated with complex decision-making will, in other words, tend to rise as GDP falls, and vice versa – perhaps with a time lag.

Far from being exogenous, government expenditure decisions are very much a reflection of personal needs and environmental influences – social, and increasingly physical, as well as economic. This gives government expenditure a great deal of stability. Even in countries such as the United Kingdom, which have attempted far reaching reappraisals of the role of government, the consequences have been fairly marginal. The influences at work are very deep-rooted.

LABOUR MARKETS

In standard neo-classical economics, labour markets are treated very much like goods markets. The price of labour, given by the wage rate, brings supply and demand into balance, although the proponents of the neo-classical view have been obliged to admit that the process works neither as quickly nor as smoothly as claimed. I shall be looking at two major areas of labour market activity in a macro context: wage behaviour and the supply of labour.

Wage behaviour

My earlier analysis in Chapter 9 concluded that, at the micro level, a number of key considerations determine the pay goals of individuals and groups (including trade unions) in the work situation. In order to satisfy their needs and wants, their primary interest is in maintaining their real pay, and, if at all possible, increasing it. Closely associated with the needs aspect is the process of social comparison. Employees are intensely interested in what others are being paid, and are constantly comparing their pay with that of others. In particular, they wish to ensure they receive equitable treatment. In Adams's (1963, 1965) terms, they wish to ensure that their outcomes relative to their inputs match those for comparable individuals or groups. I summarised an individual's pay goal (and the pay goal for any group could be summarised in the same fashion) in equation (9.9), on certain simplifying assumptions, as:

$$\dot{W}i^e = \dot{P}^e + \alpha \tag{9.9}$$

The simplifying assumptions were that $Wi = W^{*}i = k\dot{W}^{e}r1$, and that $(\dot{P}^{e} + \alpha) > \dot{W}^{e}r1 > \dot{P}^{e}$. In other words, we started off from a situation in which equity for Person, defined in relation to the wage of a reference group ($Wr1$), prevailed, and the expected change in wage payments to the reference group was greater than the expected rate of inflation. The only other influence on Person's wage was then his/her target rate of growth in his/her real wage (α).

At the macro level, again on the assumption that, broadly speaking, equity was felt to prevail in the existing wage structure, price expectations and the target growth of real wages would be the key explanatory variables. There is in fact evidence to support the notion of a target real wage (see Baxter, 1988), although quite how such a target is formulated is not clear. Expectations, it seems, are likely to be linked to past experience. A feature of pay increases in industrial countries since the Second World War has been the steady increase in real wages, with money wages outstripping inflation. There have been brief periods in some countries when real wages have fallen, but the tendency for real wages to rise has become a well established norm for most people, most of the time. It would not be at all surprising, therefore, to find this experience built into expectations about the future growth of pay. A pay goal of this nature would not even need to be formulated in any coherent or sophisticated fashion. It could be based on simple perceptions, and in the nature of a decision rule.

If the structure of wages were not regarded as equitable, then we would expect some individuals or groups of workers to adjust their pay goals to take account of the inequities, as they perceived them. If, for example, $(\dot{P}^{e} + \alpha) < \dot{W}^{e}r1$, we could expect $\dot{W}i$ to increase. At the macro level, however, we are faced with the problem that there is no single reference group applicable to all employees. In Baxter (1988) I suggested a means by which this problem might be resolved. I introduced the notion of *relative deprivation* ($\dot{RD}$), which may be applied in circumstances in which employees' pay is perceived to be less than that to which they feel entitled – they must also feel that the level of pay to which they aspire is a *feasible* goal. Since $\dot{RD}$ is a subjective variable, and not directly measurable, a suitable proxy would have to be devised.

One possible means of constructing an indicator of $\dot{RD}$ would be to use self-rating scales which allowed individuals to show the extent of their dissatisfaction with their present pay. Such scales have been widely and successfully adopted in market research. A purist might object that the scales entail interpersonal comparisons, and that we cannot therefore be sure that the answers given are strictly comparable. Curtin (1977) has already demonstrated, however, that self-rating scales can be successfully used to measure feelings about equity and relative deprivation. The availability of such measures might have helped avoid some of the worst mistakes in experiments with incomes policies. One of the main reasons for the demise of such policies (in part, it seems, a consequence of the forms which they took and the ways in which they were introduced) in countries such as the United Kingdom and France, was almost certainly the inequities to which they gave rise, and the consequent build up in feelings of relative deprivation.

In the light of the above, our aggregate wage equation, showing the rate of change of money wages in any particular time period ($\dot{W}$), takes the following form:

$$\dot{W} = w(\dot{P}^e, \dot{W}^T, \dot{RD}) \quad (12.8)$$

where, $\dot{W}^T$ is the target rate of growth of real wages, and $\dot{RD}$ is the rate of change of relative deprivation.

I also demonstrated in Baxter (1988) that my analysis of the key behavioural factors underlying wage behaviour would lead us to expect both that wages would be 'sticky' in a downward direction, and that there would be constant upward pressure on wages. When individuals have strongly held perceptions of what constitutes equity in matters of pay (as evidence confirms) then any attempt by an employer or government unilaterally to reduce the pay of these individuals relative to that of others can be expected to meet firm resistance (unless pay was initially above the equitable level). If all pay were to be reduced proportionally, perhaps through taxation or (in real terms) through price increases, resistance would probably be less, but individuals still do not take kindly to having their standard of living reduced, and repercussions could therefore be expected, even if somewhat delayed.

Constant upward pressure on pay is likely to be a feature of any unsynchronised pay bargaining system. Most research on wage spillover has concentrated on trying to demonstrate the existence of pay rounds or pattern bargaining, or the influence of wage leaders, but as we showed in Baxter (1988), in a bargaining system in which wage relativities are closely bound up with strongly held perceptions of equity, *any* significant departure from the equitable norms could be expected to set off a chain reaction. The process seems to work most commonly when one group of employees gains an exceptionally large pay award, but, by exercising restraint, significant groups of workers might also help slow down the upward movement of pay.

The supply of labour[1]

There are strong grounds for questioning the standard neo-classical explanation of variations in labour supply, based principally on changes in real wages (see Baxter, 1988). When compared with labour market trends in practice there are too many anomalies and the theory leaves out of account too many important factors, including socioeconomic influences which bear on labour supply decisions. One crucial deficiency is that by concentrating on income, which denotes one's ability to command goods and services, and therefore the ability to satisfy wants, no account is taken of individuals' *unsatisfied* wants. If wants were static there would be more evidence to suggest that rising real incomes eventually enabled consumers to satisfy all their wants. There is on the contrary a good deal of evidence that unsatisfied wants remain appreciable at all but the highest levels of income – see, for example, Katona *et al.* (1971), Strumpel (1972) and Schmölders and Biervert (1972). Our hypothesis is that it is the continued growth of wants, and in particular the unsatisfied portion of these wants, which is the single most important factor underlying labour supply decisions – some evidence pointing in this direction can also be found in Katona *et al.* (1971). It is by no means the whole story, however, as we shall see below.

One difficulty with our hypothesis (as is so often the case in economics) is that there is no readily available, regularly published statistical measure of our key variable: unsatisfied wants. Since, however, we concern ourselves here with wants which can be translated into monetary values, the problem is not, in principle, insoluble – we should not forget, however, that work satisfies important needs of a non-pecuniary nature, such as the needs for belonging and, possibly also, self-actualisation. If, therefore, we represent an individual j's wants by Y^*_j, and the same individual's disposable income by Y_{dj}, then unsatisfied wants could be expressed as $(Y^*_j - Y_{dj})$. The implication is that so long as the value of $(Y^*_j - Y_{dj})$ is positive, there will be an incentive for j to increase his/her supply of labour.

A further refinement seems necessary to take account of the fact that a given 'wants gap' might be expected to have a greater effect on a person with a relatively low income – since the gap is likely to be perceived as larger by such a person than by one with a relatively high income. We therefore prefer to express our key variable in the form $(Y^*_j - Y_{dj})/Y_{dj}$. A further possible refinement could be introduced to allow for the fact that a person might only decide to react to a wants gap once it had reached a critical minimum level. There might, in other words, be a form of threshold effect, with labour supply only being affected when the critical value was reached. For some individuals it might be the case, too, that income exceeds wants, in which case labour supply could be expected to fall.

Since part of a person's disposable income may be saved, and not all devoted to consuming goods and services, one might argue that a more accurate statement of unsatisfied wants would be given by $(Y^*_j - C_j)/Y_{dj}$. To the extent, however, that saving is the result of a conscious decision, and found desirable in itself, a person's disposable income would seem to be the appropriate variable. I prefer the latter view, although it seems to be a matter worth investigating.

At the macro level, I have already shown that there is evidence that needs and their associated wants follow an inverted-U pattern over the lifetimes of individuals. In the case of families, the inverted-U pattern is likely to be even more marked, since children place heavier additional burdens on most families when parents are in their early and middle years. It would not be surprising, therefore, if unsatisfied wants were to be especially high during these years as well. The study by Schmölders and Biervert (1972) already referred to – which studied the 'level of aspiration' for 29 consumer durable goods in West Germany – suggests that unsatisfied wants are indeed especially high for families with young children (under six years of age in their classification) in comparison with other stages of the life cycle. The study also showed, however, that the highest level of unsatisfied wants was to be found among young people with no children – possibly because the survey covered only durable goods, and young people are still accumulating such goods. As one would expect, the level of aspiration was lowest among older people, although still positive, doubtless because income for this group was also lowest.

Schmölders and Biervert went on to analyse the levels of aspiration by age and found that it conformed closely with the family life cycle findings. The level of aspiration was again highest in the early years, then fell steadily and was least for those aged 55 or more. These findings appear compatible with our hypothesis. In the early years, most individuals not in full-time education join the labour force, and if there are no children both husband and wife are likely to be working. The labour supply for this group is, in effect, approaching 100 per cent, and there is little scope for increasing it, other than by working overtime.

In families with young children, on the other hand, parents are constrained in their ability to increase their labour supply during these years – a fuller discussion of the analysis which follows can be found in Baxter (1988). It is noticeable in the United Kingdom, for example, that the participation rate for married women in the labour force jumps sharply in the age range 35–49, when most children will be in school, some will already be in their teens, and others may even have left home. The effects of young children on female participation rates has been well demonstrated by Martin and Roberts (1984) in their study of the lifetime pattern of female employment. They were able to show that the presence of children and the age of the youngest child were much the most important determinants of labour force participation. It is the children rather than marital status as such which greatly influences labour force decisions. Age also plays a role, but a secondary one. Similar conclusions were reached by Joshi, Layard and Owen (1981) in an analysis based on age cohorts.

While children add greatly to family wants, yet also constrain the ability of mothers to participate in the labour force in order to raise family income, two developments since around the time of the Second World War have been instrumental in facilitating growing participation by women in the labour force of many countries, especially in the industrialised world. The first has been a drop in fertility rates, and the average size of families, and therefore in the length of the period during which very young children make it difficult for mothers to go out to work. Joshi *et al.* (1981) have estimated that one child less per family has the effect of raising the participation rate for females aged 20–59 in Great Britain by about 7 percentage points.

The second factor facilitating a rise in the female participation rate has been the enormous expansion of part-time employment. Martin and Roberts (1984) showed that the growth in female participation rates in Britain has been almost entirely associated with the growth of part-time employment – the full-time participation rate remained fairly level overall. Furthermore, part-time working has increased most noticeably among females over 30, and it has also risen sharply among women with young children.

The growing importance of part-time employment is in large measure explicable in terms of developments affecting the demand for such labour by employers – labour supply and labour demand are inextricably interlinked, a point not always given sufficient weight in labour market analysis. Robinson and Wallace (1984), in case studies of 21 organisations, found that in service industries part-time labour gave managers greater freedom in matching their labour requirements with changing patterns of operational and customer requirements. In manufacturing industry, the main benefits derived from maximising the use of capital equipment, for example by maintaining production during lunch breaks, or by maintaining production unbroken over a 15- or 16-hour day, without incurring premium payments for overtime or shift work. There was also a strong belief among employers that the productivity of part-time workers was greater than that of full-time labour.

When we move to the macro level, we once again face the difficult problem of trying to capture the effects of those variables which are important at the micro level. Finding a suitable proxy for the growth of wants and the existence of unsatisfied wants is, if anything, more problematic, although not, it would seem, impossible. Surveys could still be used to elicit information from individuals about the increase in income they feel would be necessary to reduce, or eliminate, their wants deficit. Since the information could be gathered in monetary terms, aggregation would not pose a problem. If our thesis is correct, most individuals – apart perhaps from those at the highest levels of income – could be expected consistently to express the view that they would like to have higher incomes, in order to be able to purchase additional goods and services (this would not preclude, say, the head of a family working less, if another family member were able to compensate, or more than compensate). Only the gathering of information over an appreciable period of time would enable us to see whether, and if so how, people's unsatisfied wants were changing.

There are, however, as I noted above, constraints on the supply of labour, especially in the more advanced industrial countries. Since a high proportion of males is usually already at work (and mainly full-time work) only females can provide a major source of additional labour. The life cycle, in particular the family life cycle, is also an important consideration. Since many females are mothers, it is females of a certain age who tend to be most readily available to join the labour force. Changes in the age-sex composition of a population could therefore have effects even at the macro level. Fertility rates and the average size of the family also affect the labour supply, since the smaller the family, generally the less time is spent on looking after very young children (who are the greatest deterrent to mothers going out to work).

One further point on the labour supply side – usually ignored – is that labour supply is unlikely to be infinitely elastic. The reason why married women have made up the greater part of the growth of the labour supply is because they have constituted the greatest untapped reservoir of labour. Eventually, however, unless other sources are found – there is now talk of making greater use of retired, elderly persons – the supply of labour must eventually taper off, even if wants remain unsatisfied. We will then have to rely almost entirely on productivity growth to generate greater wealth – which could then be used to pay for more imports, or, alternatively, immigration might be seen as the answer.

Finally, on the labour demand side, some indicator or changes in employers' demand for part-time workers would be likely to help explain changes in the supply of part-time female labour.

In the light of the above comments, we would expect an aggregate labour supply schedule to include the following variables:

$$N_s = n\,[(Y^* - Y_d)/Y_d, AGE, SIZ, PT] \tag{12.9}$$

where, Y^* and Y_d represent aggregate wants (expressed in monetary terms) and aggregate disposable income, respectively, *AGE* is the total number of females aged 20–35 (to represent the ages when mothers are most likely to be kept out of the labour force by a young child), *SIZ* is the average size of a family and *PT* is firms' demand for part-time labour. I am not, of course, implying that all other factors are unimportant; only that these variables are the ones suggested by our study.

MONEY MARKETS

Despite its central importance to economists, the workings of the monetary system have attracted relatively little attention from psychologists and other social scientists. The area of saving is to some extent an exception, although even here much work remains to be done. As we shall see, many aspects of personal saving link closely with the concepts and ideas I have highlighted elsewhere in the present study.

Personal saving

Keynes (1936), drawing on the work of Fisher (1930), identified 'eight main motives or objects of a subjective character' which led individuals to save:[2]

(i) to provide for unseen contingencies;
(ii) to provide for future divergence between individual, or family, income and needs; e.g., in relation to old age, education or the maintenance of dependents;
(iii) to enjoy interest and appreciation, i.e., a larger real consumption at a later date in preference to a smaller immediate consumption;
(iv) to enjoy a gradually improving standard of life;
(v) to enjoy a sense of independence and the power to do things;
(vi) to provide funds for speculative and business projects;
(vii) to bequeath a fortune;
(viii) to satisfy pure miserliness.

Keynes (and most early writers) clearly understood the important psychological basis of saving. Unfortunately, his emphasis has not been adequately reflected in the work of later economists. The individual and family life cycles lie at the heart of Keynes's savings motives, even if not explicitly spelled out. Yet the life cycle concept as it later developed in economics is almost wholly devoid of psychological content, as Wärneryd (1989) has rightly pointed out – nor is a distinction made between the individual and *family* life cycles.

Representative surveys conducted by the Survey Research Center at the University of Michigan (see Katona, 1975) have confirmed the validity of at least some of Keynes's motives for saving, and have provided an indication of their relative importance. Much the most important reason given by individuals for saving is to provide for rainy days (emergencies, illness, unemployment), with approaching one-half of all respondents citing this reason. Around 30 per cent cited the need to provide for retirement and old age. Children's needs (primarily education – seen as a need) were mentioned by about one-quarter. Thereafter, buying a house (8 per cent) and the purchase of durable goods (6–7 per cent) were the only other two motives referred to with any great frequency. Hardly any consumers mentioned saving for the purpose of earning additional income, or to bequeath money to their heirs (with the exception of a few very wealthy people).

The question of who does most saving was found to depend in some measure on the definition of saving used. Katona (1975) distinguished between: *contractual saving* (arising from contractual obligations, such as mortgage payments and instalment debt repayments), fulfilled as a matter of routine, requiring no new decisions; *discretionary saving* (such as additions to deposits in banks or savings and loan associations, and the purchase of bonds, etc.) generally arising from definite decisions to save, although Katona also distinguished a third category, *residual saving*, to denote funds that individuals simply failed to spend, and which increased savings balances without a deliberate decision being taken.

When discretionary saving was taken into account, it was found that most saving was done by middle-aged people (those between approximately 35–40 and 60 years of age) with relatively high income (those with an annual income of more than $12,500, at the levels of income prevailing in the early 1970s). These findings tally with studies of individual and household income and consumption by, for example, Thurow (1969), Ghez and Becker (1975) and Kotlikoff and Summers (1981), showing that the gap between income and consumption is greatest in the age range of around 35–60. Only when the broadest possible definition of saving was used did the frequent savers include younger married people in the middle income groups who were accumulating assets by buying houses, automobiles and appliances on credit, and repaying their debts.

The principal economic theories of consumption, and therefore saving (the life cycle and permanent income hypotheses) lay great stress on the life cycle, with individuals taking a lifetime view of their likely future earnings, and deciding their consumption accordingly. The life cycle portrayed, however, is little more than a mathematical device, with no attempt to go into the fuller implications of the concept – nor, as we noted above, is any distinction made between the *individual* life cycle and the *family* life cycle, both of which are important. The psychological literature on saving – useful surveys can be found in Furnham and Lewis (1986) and Lea *et al.* (1987) – also highlights the life cycle, but it is only one among quite a diversity of theories. It is my contention that the individual life cycle and the family life cycle, founded as they are on needs, together provide a unifying structure which greatly assists us in understanding saving, even if it is not the whole story – it is rather strange, after all, that economics accords such importance to the role of the life cycle in consumption, yet generally neglects its role in discussions of saving.

If we look again at the motives for saving identified by Keynes and Katona, we find that a number of them fit into the life cycle framework set out in the earlier sections of the present study: the likelihood of divergence between future individual (or family) income and needs; the desire to enjoy a gradually improving standard of life, rather than one which fluctuates; the desire to provide for retirement; the wish to provide for children's future needs, such as education; the buying of a house. All of these may be said to be closely linked with the individual and family life cycles of needs and their associated wants. The patterns of consumption and saving are also, as we noted, strongly linked to age. Saving through pension plans is yet further evidence of a desire to provide for future needs; and even the wish of a minority of, generally wealthy, people to bequeath their wealth, usually to their children, can be viewed as a life cycle want (even if probably not a *need*) – see Lea *et al.* (1987).

A second major reason for saving, although it is not always specifically identified as such, is uncertainty. Moreover, much of this uncertainty is closely associated with the life cycle, in that one of the greatest uncertainties of all is a particular individual's life span. If that were known with certainty, individual and family decision-making would be greatly facilitated. Individuals may, of course, be guided by the information available about average life expectancy, but if they are prudent they will also anticipate the possibility of living longer. The savings set aside to compensate for loss of earnings in old age may, however, be too little or too large, depending upon whether an individual is optimistic or pessimistic about his/her own life expectancy. Virtually all the life cycle-related reasons for saving will be affected by the views people take of their life expectancy. Means of mitigating the consequences of uncertainty, such as life insurance, are available, but they do not remove uncertainty altogether.

The possibility of ill-health is a further major source of uncertainty. Yet again there is an association with the life cycle, since medical needs tend to be greatest for children and the elderly. Insurance against ill-health is possible, of course, but, as with death, coverage is frequently incomplete in some respects; and the fuller the coverage, the greater the expense. It is not surprising that national health provision is popular where it works effectively, as in countries like Britain and France; but even comprehensive provision is unlikely to compensate fully for the consequences of ill-health on an individual's, or a family's, finances, and saving for this purpose will therefore remain a priority for many.

A third major cause of uncertainty which leads people to save is the possibility of unemployment. This was well demonstrated in some industrial countries as unemployment rose to exceptionally high levels during the 1970s and 1980s. In the United Kingdom, for example, high unemployment in the period 1980–2, and again in 1990–2, was associated with high levels of saving. The association may depend, however, not just on the *level* of unemployment, but also on its rate of change, and individuals' perceptions of the threat it poses to their own jobs. The threat of unemployment may even be said to give rise to *true* uncertainty for most people, since no two economic recessions are ever the same, and the incidence of unemployment varies appreciably.

While we lay particular stress on the individual and family life cycles, and on uncertainty, as explanations of the desire to save, the phenomenon of saving is complex, and other factors are also at work. Duesenberry's (1949) relative income hypothesis emphasised the importance of *relative* income to consumption, and therefore to saving. His theory also stressed the idea that a consumer's spending was influenced not just by other consumers in the same income bracket but by the highest income previously experienced – it is this last aspect which has featured in empirical tests of the hypothesis at the aggregate level. In other words, once consumers had experienced the lifestyle associated with a particular level of income, their spending habits did not immediately, and fully, adjust to a sudden change in income (especially a drop in income) such as might occur during a business cycle. Duesenberry's theory is now somewhat neglected, but his emphasis on the importance of relative income is, in my view, undoubtedly correct. There is a good deal of evidence that relative income matters greatly to individuals, whether as consumers or income earners (see Baxter, 1988), and it is therefore a matter which I have also stressed in other sections of the present study.

Wärneryd (1989) has stressed yet another factor in saving decisions: an individual's self-control, which can be conceptualised as degree of time preference. Persons with low self-control are assumed to have a strong preference for the present. They can be said to require a high interest rate in their discount functions. Remoteness in time may even lead to a change in personal preferences. An individual may prefer A to B, but nevertheless choose B if A is not going to be available for a considerable time – many consumers must have experienced such a situation, for example in trying to purchase a consumer durable, or an item of clothing unavailable at the time in a particular size or colour. As Ainslie (1975) has pointed out, the implication is that the discount functions for the two goods cross somewhere, and that a change of taste has taken place. It is worth noting, finally, that even the degree of self-control can be represented, in part at least, as the product of uncertainty. The old proverb, 'a bird in the hand is worth two in the bush' aptly expresses the situation.

When it comes to explaining variations in saving at the aggregate level of the total economy, we are again faced with the problem that not all variables which are important at the micro level may be revealed as significant in empirical tests at the macro level. Nevertheless, we can certainly hope to catch the influence of the individual and family life cycles. In cross-section studies we could expect saving to be closely associated with age, especially in the 35–60 age range. Changes in the age distribution of the population may even prove to be significant in time series studies. Sex does not appear, however, to be a factor determining attitudes to saving (Furnham, 1985). Since the presence of children is so important in determining the financial burdens falling on families, the average number of children per family, and long-term variations in the average, could also be expected to have a bearing on variations in saving. So, too, could long-term changes in average life expectancy.

True uncertainty is not a factor easily represented in empirical work, but we did note above how high, and perhaps especially rapidly increasing, unemployment does appear to give rise to concerns about job prospects, and a desire to save to cover a possible shortfall in income. Such increased saving could only give temporary respite, however, and eventually consumption would have to fall. There seems, on the face of it, to be a possible link here with Duesenberry's relative income hypothesis. One reason consumers could resist reducing their consumption following a drop in income would be if they had anticipated the drop in income by increasing their saving beforehand.

Our view of personal saving seems, then, to integrate quite closely with our view of personal consumption. Right at the centre are the individual and family life cycles, and linked to these are the consequences for saving of uncertainty and the importance of relative incomes. We might therefore represent our saving function at the aggregate level in the following form:

$$S = s(AGE, CHL, LIF, U) \tag{12.10}$$

where, *AGE* is the age *distribution* of the population, *CHL* is the average number of children per family, *LIF* is the average life expectancy, and *U* the unemployment rate (with the possibility of a rate of change variable also being introduced).

The demand for, and the supply of, money

The study of the behavioural influences on the demand for, and the supply of, money is not well developed, and I will therefore spend very little time on these topics, despite their importance. So far as the demand for the cash component of money is concerned, institutional developments appear to have greatly reduced the need to hold money for transactions and precautionary purposes. The growth in the importance of cheque accounts and the advent of charge cards means that there is no longer such a large requirement for ready cash, despite the growth in incomes. Likewise, unanticipated payments can now be made by cheque or charge card. New developments continue apace which seem likely to reduce the demand for cash still further. Greater facility in switching money between interest bearing and non-interest bearing (or between high interest bearing and lower interest bearing) deposits may also reduce the demand for the other components of money narrowly defined.

Money supply is usually treated as exogenous (set by the government) in economics, but some economists have argued that policy instruments respond to political pressures, and that there is in fact a *political business cycle*. The existence of the latter is still in doubt (see Nordhaus, 1989, for a survey of the evidence) but on the monetary side there is evidence that, at least during certain periods, the central authorities have bowed to political pressures. Studies of the role of the Federal Reserve in the United States suggest, for example, that in at least one year (1972) the Federal Reserve succumbed to political pressures for an easy money policy, although in others (1956, 1980) it resisted pressures and incurred the displeasure of incumbent Presidents (Kettle, 1986). Beck (1984) and Chappell and Keech (1988) found substantial evidence of the Federal Reserve 'bending with the political winds', while Grier (1987) has claimed that there is evidence of a four-year electoral cycle influencing monetary policy. On the other hand, changes in the Federal Reserve discount rate do not appear to show an *active* election bias.

Evidence from elsewhere seems to be sparse. In the United Kingdom, it might be possible to make out a case for political influence behind the rapid increase in money supply in 1972 and 1973, prior to a General Election, and again from around mid-1985, prior to the General Election of 1987. It is another matter, however, to demonstrate a *consistent tendency* for money supply changes to vary according to the election cycle. There is a need for a good deal more research in this area.

13 Conclusions and Implications

In order to place the behavioural approach to economics in context, it is helpful, it seems, to contrast it in methodological terms with the now standard neo-classical approach. The latter is founded on what Dow (1985) has called the 'Cartesian/Euclidean' mode of thought. That is, it is founded on a system of axiomatic logic. Key axioms which are either true by definition or 'self-evident' are adopted and by a process of deduction used to formulate precise predictions, which are then tested against the facts, so far as these can be ascertained. The key axiom is usually identified as the assumption that individuals behave 'rationally'. As Arrow (1987) has pointed out, among classical economists the idea of rationality had the limited meaning of preferring more to less, and, although that might be interpreted as the maximisation of profits, it was not until the 1880s that the assumption of profit maximisation was explicitly formulated. Nor did the classicists advance a hypothesis of rationality on the part of consumers. Not until the marginalist revolution brought about by Jevons, Walras, Menger and others were rational consumers assumed to maximise utility, subject to a budget constraint.

As I noted in my Introduction, Arrow (1987) and Simon (1987) have very forcefully drawn attention to the severe limitations of the rationality hypothesis. The practice in economics has frequently been to start with the rationality assumption, defined as utility and profit maximisation, but then to add supplementary hypotheses, such as homogeneity across individual agents, additivity and separability, as the original hypotheses have been shown to be inadequate. The process continues until the theoretician obtains the desired end result. Such procedures serve to emphasise just how weak the rationality hypothesis is on its own. They also raise serious questions about where economics is heading. Some of the supplementary hypotheses, such as homogeneity, are designed to shut out the real world – Arrow (1987) regards the homogeneity assumption as particularly dangerous, since it denies the fundamental assumption underlying an economy: that gains from trade arising from individual differences are there to be exploited. In other cases resort to supplementary hypotheses is designed to admit some, but only some, features of the world as we find it, and then only grudgingly and often partially – the existence of the life cycle, for example, is acknowledged in the analysis of the consumption function, but it does not feature among the central micro-foundations of economics, applicable to all other parts of the subject (it is only recently, to take one example, that attempts have been made to incorporate the life cycle in labour supply analysis).

In contrast to the neo-classical deductive approach, behavioural economics, drawing heavily as it does on psychology, sociology and the other social sciences, is by nature more inductive. That is, rather than use a linear system of logical deduction from basic axioms (which it is difficult to render watertight) it employs several strands of argument from different starting points, each strand ideally reinforcing the other and helping weld together a stronger, more coherent whole (see Dow, 1985, again for a useful discussion). Behavioural economics cannot therefore claim the mathematical, predictive certainty of some neo-classical economics, but it benefits, on the other hand, from being much more broadly based. Rather than being reductionist or atomistic, it may be described as 'holistic', in the sense that it focuses on the nature of the economic system as a whole, including its social, political, physical and other relevant aspects. Such a system is better suited to explanation rather than prediction, since the actors in the drama have a full range of options open to them, rather than being constrained to act in one particular fashion. This does not mean, of course, that hypothesis testing is unimportant to inductive methods, but rather that the hypotheses to be tested emerge from observations of particular conjuctions of events, rather than from the application of axiomatic deduction.

An economist who takes the trouble to read some of the psychological and other social science literature cannot help but be struck by the wealth of empirical research findings already available. Many of these findings, upon reflection, point in certain directions, often of direct relevance to economic problems, and have common links uniting them. The principal purpose of the present study has been to try and bring out these links, using them in the process to formulate testable hypotheses. A great deal of work, however, remains to be done. At almost every stage of the present study there is a need for further research – and in some instances a need, too, to develop new statistical series, often relating to subjective variables, which would facilitate that research. Additional work should enable the links between variables to be specified more precisely, or in alternative forms, but the way ahead seems to point to a sort of iterative procedure by which hypotheses are tested, modified and developed in the light of the empirical findings, rather as has occurred in certain fields of economics, notably that of the consumption function.

On the basis of the evidence examined in the present study, certain key features of the behavioural approach emerge – it must be stressed once again, however, that there is no attempt here to claim that the list is in any way exclusive, or comprehensive. First, personal characteristics vary appreciably between some individuals; moreover, these characteristics vary over time. It is, therefore, in many instances an unwarranted simplification to make use of 'homogeneous' or 'representative' individuals for the purposes of analysis. It has been shown that even at the macro level the so-called 'demographic' variables, which are a reflection of inter-personal differences, have significant effects. The basis of these differences, I have argued, is differences in personal needs, and in the personal wants associated with these needs. The concept of needs, especially in its rigid hierarchical form, as outlined by Maslow, is not looked upon favourably by many psychologists, but it is hoped that the evidence in the present study will go some way towards persuading them that the idea of personal needs has some content.

Not only do individuals have personal needs, there is also evidence to show that these needs follow a particular pattern: a life cycle. Where individuals group together in families, there is further evidence of a family life cycle. In a skeletal, partial manner economics has admitted the importance of the life cycle, but, as we noted earlier, has yet to incorporate it in its micro-foundations. Changes in personal and family consumption simply cannot be fully understood or explained unless the life cycle is given its proper place in the core of microeconomic theory.

Nor can one hope fully to understand individual behaviour if it is divorced from its social and physical environments. Not only is the economic behaviour of individuals influenced by the general environment in which they live and work, they also join socioeconomic groups of various sorts, and these groups may develop goals which are not identical with the goals of individual members, even if strongly influenced by the latter. Once again, the evidence that the social and physical environments influence individual and socioeconomic group behaviour is simply too strong to be ignored. Economics can attempt to extend its explanatory power into these areas, as Becker and others have done, but this can only be achieved by the introduction of supplementary, or auxiliary, hypotheses, in order to broaden the narrow theoretical base of economics. The question arises, however, of whether it is better to continue introducing supplementary hypotheses on an ad hoc basis or to seek more comprehensive (one might also say more rational) foundations which can cope better with the world as we find it.

Decision-making in neo-classical economics is undertaken by individuals with superhuman attributes, and in a highly mechanistic fashion, reminiscent of robots rather than human beings. The evidence that, in practice, individuals do not behave as assumed in the neo-classical model is too solid to ignore. Two types of decision-making seem to stand out from the evidence. First, despite – or perhaps because of – a rapidly changing environment and the uncertainty to which it gives rise, there is a strong element of stability in economic behaviour. Much decision-making is routine, or habitual, continuing largely unchanged from one time period to the next. Quite how important this habitual element is, is not clear from the evidence at present available, but it does appear sufficiently important to impart a large measure of stability to most economies.

In stark contrast to habitual decision-making, complex decision-making attempts to cope with circumstances in which information is often incomplete, and the future full of uncertainties. Some decisions can be taken on the basis of calculations of probabilities, but in many instances the information on which to base such calculations is simply not available. In the latter cases, there is again a good deal of evidence that individuals (whether acting on their own behalf or on behalf of socioeconomic organisations) resort to a variety of simplifying decision rules. These decision rules appear at all levels of social aggregation, right up to that of national governments. In the face of such evidence, it is impossible to maintain that behaviour must always be maximising behaviour. Even if, in choosing the rules, decision makers are guided by neo-classical economics, the rules, by their nature, represent a departure from the tenets of neo-classical economics, and cannot therefore result in maximising outcomes (other than by the accident of events). A look at the world around us, with its high and persistent unemployment, and imperfectly functioning markets, surely serves to confirm this conclusion.

The transition from micro- to macro-economics poses many problems, which in neo-classical economics are overcome in part by such expedients as assuming away differences between individuals (and therefore also between firms, which are largely assumed to be run by individual entrepreneurs). Not even the sex divide is admitted. A behavioural approach, on the other hand, accepts from the outset that individuals differ, and that individuals acting as a group may behave differently from the same individuals acting independently. Aggregation entails summing the actions of each individual (as a decision-making unit) and those of each socioeconomic decision-making centre (or, more accurately, of each decision-making unit within these centres). Given a common unit of measurement, such as money, we can obtain an indication of aggregate behaviour in an economy.

Our study shows that, even at the macro level, a behavioural approach yields significant insights, and offers the prospect of improving our understanding and explanation of economic changes. In the consumer field, routine/habitual behaviour appears much more important than economists have recognised. Rather than trying to explain variations of consumer spending in total, there is a strong case for breaking it down into at least two major segments: routine/habitual and complex. To some degree, this divide may mirror the non-durable-durable goods distinction, but it goes well beyond that. In analysing consumer behaviour it is also important to reflect the changing needs of a population by means of variables representing the individual and family life cycles. Such variables have been shown to be important. They are often simply referred to as 'demographic' variables, and introduced on an ad hoc basis. The needs-based approach I have adopted provides a theoretical rationale for their use.

The routine/habitual-complex dichotomy is also, as I noted above, reflected in decision-making by socioeconomic groups. The evidence shows that a majority of even the largest firms still employs very simple decision rules when choosing between investment projects. The finding is not all that surprising, since, in terms of results, there seems to be little to choose between the simple and complex approaches. The relatively short, fixed time horizons used in order to cope with manifold uncertainties suggest that much investment by firms will be closely related to output, along the familiar lines of the accelerator model. Simple decision rules adopted by many firms in setting their prices also suggest that, although by no means the whole story, the prices of firms' output will to some degree be related to changes in their costs, in particular to changes in their unit wage costs, the prices of raw materials and the prices of imports.

At the level of national government, we see one of the clearest demonstrations of the importance of routine/habitual spending. Government expenditure is very largely endogenous. It reflects the wishes of the governed that the State should ensure that the most basic needs of the populace, such as that for security, are satisfied. To this end, the State generally acts as provider of last resort, and undertakes the functions of defence and maintenance of law and order. In the case of merit goods, the State is often felt to be the most satisfactory general provider. The nature of the obligations placed on governments is such that the former continue very largely uninterrupted over time, despite occasional attempts to 'roll back the State'. A major change in the role of the State in modern societies is only likely if people's perceptions alter in such a manner that they feel better able to satisfy their needs via their own efforts.

Some behavioural features of the labour market also make an impact at the macro level. Social comparisons and notions of equity are sufficient to ensure that wages are inflexible in a downward direction, and, together with the desire to satisfy growing wants, also provide constant upward pressure on wages. It is for these reasons that governments (but less so employers, it seems) often seek to discourage the use of wage comparisons and equity arguments in pay negotiations. Only if there is a reasonable national consensus about pay relativities, however, can countries hope to avoid the harmful side effects of pay negotiations.

I have also argued in the present study that the pressure of rising wants, and in particular the extent to which these wants are unsatisfied, has underpinned the expanding supply of labour, especially female labour, which has characterised the labour markets of many countries in recent years. Considerations of whether or not to work, or how much to work, concern a great deal more than the balance between work and leisure. In addition to wants (and linked through them with changing needs) the family life cycle is central to any analysis. Nor can changes in the nature of employers' labour demands be left out of account.

It will be apparent from our study, it is hoped, that although there is a strong element of underlying stability in the system of which the economy is part, the system is nevertheless dynamic and changing. Talk of such a system, or even part of the system, being in equilibrium at any given point in time is simply not sustainable – Arrow (1987) makes the point succinctly. I have not attempted to formally set out a theory of the business cycle, but the elements of such a theory are clearly there. A multiplier-accelerator effect would be present, augmented by changes in consumer and business expectations. Pent-up frustrations over wages – both with regard to their real value and in respect of relativities – also seem likely to have a role, even if not necessarily in an entirely regular manner. Over the longer term, changing needs and wants, together with all forms of environmental changes (social and physical as well as economic) will have economic consequences. The economy and the actors within it are part of a much larger whole from which they cannot be divorced, convenient though such an assumption might be.

We turn, finally, to the question of how, in the light of our study, we now view the behavioural approach to economics in relation to standard neoclassical economics. Economists face a difficult dilemma. They are heirs to an academic discipline which has greatly improved our knowledge of how economies function. We now know a great deal more about such matters as the workings of markets, and the implications of imperfections in these markets. We are also now able, because of improvements in our knowledge, to avoid the worst excesses of the business cycle. These, and of course many others, are no mean achievements. There seems to be a growing appreciation, however, that despite the successes of the past, the economist's present tool kit will somehow or other have to be augmented if the subject is to extend its coverage to other areas of interest to economists. As was noted above, until now this has been accomplished by the practice of introducing supplementary hypotheses into economic analysis. Without the broader theoretical base to underpin such a practice, however, economics will end up largely as a collection of ad hoceries.

The central core of neo-classical economics, as set out in the Arrow-Debreu model of maximising behaviour, offers a yardstick against which economic behaviour may be judged. While not of the world as we find it, there is a good deal to be gained by constant comparisons between markets as they exist and markets as they might be in ideal circumstances. Such comparisons can help make the costs and benefits of new (and old) policy measures more 'transparent'. It would be foolish, therefore, to jettison entirely the neo-classical heritage, as some of those disenchanted with the old economics have advocated. It would be much more productive, it seems, to retain the old core, and those extensions of it which seem fruitful, but to turn our attention increasingly to developing a much more broadly based economics which integrates more closely with the advances made in the other social sciences.

There does not to the present writer seem to be any inherent contradiction in simultaneously retaining and developing both paradigms, so long as we are clear about the essential differences between the two. One represents a restricted, axiomatic, deductive, and necessarily partial, approach, offering an integrated structure capable of yielding a number of precise predictions. The other recognises no artificial subject boundaries, and is therefore by nature more holistic, using an inductive approach to guide researchers in their work. On the surface these research traditions may appear very distinctive, and even irreconcilable, but in practice the two seem likely increasingly to overlap with the passage of time. If only a small fraction of the time and effort at present devoted to devising still more variations on old neo-classical themes could be turned to developing the behavioural aspects of economics, progress could be very rapid indeed. We might even hope to offer greater inspiration to the younger generation of economists, many of whom, it seems, regard their present efforts in economics as little more than a game (Colander and Klamer, 1987) in which they must engage if they are to further their careers in the profession.

Notes

Chapter 4

1. Bureau of the Census, *Statistical Abstracts of the United States*.
2. *Social Trends* (London, HMSO).

Chapter 7

1. Lancaster also noted that goods in combination may possess characteristics different from those pertaining to the goods separately, and the same is true of goods and satisfiers.
2. Risk and uncertainty are here defined in the manner suggested by Keynes and others. Risk refers to decisions involving chance in the form of probabilities, whereas uncertainty characterises decision-making situations in which the probabilities of outcomes are, for whatever reason, unquantifiable. In the text we often refer to this definition of uncertainty as 'true uncertainty', since in economics 'uncertainty' is still often associated with analysis assuming probabilities.

Chapter 12

1. Some of the discussion in this section is more appropriate to those chapters concerned with individual decision-making, but it seemed helpful to consider micro and macro together at this point.
2. Keynes (1936) also listed four reasons why government, business and other institutions might save (a very neglected field, considering its importance): the motive of enterprise – to secure resources for capital investment; the motive of liquidity; the motive of improvement – to secure a gradually increasing income; the motive of financial prudence.

Bibliography

[illegible]

Bibliography

Adams, F.G. and Klein, L.R. (1972) 'Anticipations Variables in Macro-Econometric Models', in Strumpel, B., Morgan, J.N., and Zahn, E. (eds.) *Human Behavior in Economic Affairs*. Amsterdam: Elsevier.

Adams, J.S. (1963) 'Toward an Understanding of Inequity', *Journal of Abnormal and Social Psychology* **67**, pp. 422–36.

Adams, J.S. (1965) 'Inequity in Social Exchange', in Berkowitz, L. (ed.) (1965) *Advances in Experimental Social Psychology* **2**. New York and London: Academic Press.

After, D.E. (1972) 'Government', in *International Encyclopaedia of the Social Sciences*. London: Collier and Macmillan, pp. 214–30.

Ainslie, G. (1975) 'Specious Reward: A Behavioral Theory of Impulsiveness and Impulse Control', *Psychological Bulletin* **82**, pp. 463–96.

Ajzen, I. and Fishbein, M. (1977) 'Attitude-Behavior Relations: A Theoretical Analysis and Review of Empirical Research', *Psychological Bulletin* **84**, pp. 888–918.

Alchian, A.A. and Demsetz, H. (1972) 'Production, Information Costs and Economic Organization', *American Economic Review* **62**, pp. 777–95.

Alderfer, C.P. (1972) *Existence, Relatedness and Growth: Human Needs in Organisational Settings*. New York: Free Press.

Allais, M. (1953) 'Le Comportement de l'Homme Rationnel devant le Risque: Critique des Postulats et Axiomes de l'Ecole Americaine', *Econometrica* **24**, pp. 503–46.

Aoki, M. (1984) *The Co-operative Game Theory of the Firm*. Oxford: Clarendon Press.

Arkes, H.R. and Garske, J.P. (1982) *Psychological Theories of Motivation*. Monterey, California: Brookes/Cole Publishing Company.

Arndt, J. (1967) *Word of Mouth Advertising: a Review of the Literature*. New York: Advertising Research Foundation.

Arndt, J. (1968) 'Selective Processes in Word-of-Mouth', *Journal of Advertising Research* **8**, pp. 19–22.

Arrow, K.J. (1951) *Social Choice and Individual Values*. New Haven: Yale University Press.

Arrow, K.J. (1967) 'Values and Collective Decision-Making', in Hook, S. (ed.) *Human Values and Economic Policy*. New York: New York University Press.

Arrow, K.J. (1987) 'Rationality of Self and Others in an Economic System', in Hogarth, R.M. and Reder, M.W. (eds.), *Rational Choice: the Contrast between Economics and Psychology*. Chicago: University of Chicago Press.

Atkin, C.K. (1978) 'Observation of Parent-Child Interaction in Supermarket Decision-Making', *Journal of Marketing* **42**, pp. 41–5.

Atkinson, A.B. (1972) *Unequal Shares: Wealth in Britain*. London: Allen Lane The Penguin Press.

Balkin, M. (1956) 'Prices in the Clothing Industry', *Journal of Industrial Economics* **5**, pp. 1–15.

Bar-Hillel, M. (1973) 'On the Subjective Probability of Compound Events', *Organizational Behavior and Human Performance* **9**, pp. 396–406.

Barback, R.H. (1964) *The Pricing of Manufactures*. London: Macmillan.

Baumol, W.J. (1967) *Business Behavior, Value and Growth*. New York: Harcourt, Brace and World.

Baumol, W.J. and Oates, W.E. (1971) 'The Use of Standards and Prices for Protection of the Environment', in Bohm, P. and Kneese, A.V. (eds.) *The Economics of Environment*. London: Macmillan.

Baumol, W.J. and Oates, W.E. (1975) *The Theory of Environmental Policy*. Englewood Cliffs, N.J.: Prentice-Hall.

Baumol, W.J. and Oates, W.E. (1979) *Economics, Environmental Policy and the Quality of Life*. Englewood Cliffs: N.J., Prentice-Hall.

Baumol, W.J. and Stewart, M. (1971) 'On the Behavioral Theory of the Firm', in Marris, R. and Wood, A. (eds.) *The Corporate Economy*. London: Macmillan.

Baxter, J.L. (1973) 'Inflation in the Context of Relative Deprivation and Social Justice', *Scottish Journal of Political Economy* **20**, pp. 263–82.

Baxter, J.L. (1988) *Social and Psychological Foundations of Economic Analysis*. London: Harvester-Wheatsheaf.

Beck, N. (1984) 'Domestic Political Sources of American Monetary Policy: 1955–82', *Journal of Politics* **46**, pp. 786–817.

Beckerman, W. (1972) 'Environmental Policy Issues: Real and Fictitious', in Organisation for Economic Co-operation and Development, *Problems of Environmental Economics*. Paris: OECD.

Bell, D. (1982) 'Regret in Decision-Making under Uncertainty', *Operations Research* **30**, pp. 961–81.

Bernanke, B.S. (1983) 'The Determinants of Investment: Another Look', *American Economic Review, Papers and Proceedings* **73**, pp. 71–5.

Bernoulli, D. (1954) 'Expositions of a New Theory on the Measurement of Risk', *Econometrica* **22**, pp. 23–6.

Bettman, J.R. (1979) *An Information Processing Theory of Consumer Choice*. Reading, Mass.: Addison-Wesley.

Bishop, D.W. and Ikeda, M. (1970) 'Status and Role Factors in the Leisure Behavior of Different Occupations', *Sociology and Social Research* **54**, pp. 190–208.

Bither, S.W. and Miller, S. (1969) 'A Cognitive Theory of Brand Preference', in MacDonald, P.R. (ed.) *Marketing Involvement in Society and the Economy*. Chicago: American Marketing Association.

Blaug, M. (1985) *Economic Theory in Retrospect*. Cambridge: Cambridge University Press.

Bonfield, E.H. (1978) 'Perception of Marital Roles in Decision Processes: Replication and Extension', in Hunt, J.K. (ed.) *Proceedings of the Association for Consumer Research*. Ann Arbor: Mich., Association for Consumer Research.

Brown, J.N. and Ashenfelter, O. (1986) 'Testing the Efficiency of Employment Contracts', *Journal of Political Economy* **94**, pp. 540–87.

Buchanan, J.M. (1986) *Liberty, Market and State: Political Economy in the 1980s*. Brighton: Wheatsheaf.

Buchanan, J.M. and Tullock, G. (1962) *The Calculus of Consent*. Ann Arbor: University of Michigan Press.

Caldwell, B.C. (1982) *Beyond Positivism: Economic Methodology in the Twentieth Century*. London: George Allen and Unwin.

Calvo, G. (1978) 'Urban Unemployment and Wage Determination in LDC's: Trade Unions in the Harris-Todaro Model', *International Economic Review* **19**, pp. 65–81.

Carruth, A.A. and Oswald, A.J. (1983) 'Miners' Wages in Post-war Britain: An Application of a Model of Trade Union Behaviour', *mimeo*, University of Kent.

Carter, C.F. (1953) 'A revised Theory of Expectations', *Economic Journal* **63**, pp. 811–20.

Chappell, H.W. and Keech, W.R. (1988) 'The Unemployment Rate Consequences of Partisan Monetary Policies', *Southern Economic Journal* **55**, pp. 107–22.

Clark, A. and Oswald, A. (1989) 'An Empirical Study of Union Preferences', *Discussion Paper* No. 352. London: Centre for Labour Economics, London School of Economics.

Clark, P.K. (1979) 'Investment in the 1970s: Theory, Performance and Prediction', *Brookings Papers* **1**, pp. 73–113. Washington, D.C.: The Brookings Institution.

Coase, R.H. (1937) 'The Nature of the Firm', *Economica* **4**, pp. 386–405.

Coca Cola Company (1981) 'Measuring the Grapevine: Consumer Response and Word-of-Mouth'.

Colander, D.C. and Klamer, A. (1987) 'The Making of an Economist', *Journal of Economic Perspectives* **1**, pp. 95–111.

Coleman, J. (1959) 'Social Processes in Physicians' Adoption of a Drug', *Journal of Chronic Diseases* **9**, pp. 1–19.

Coleman, R.P. (1960) 'The Significance of Social Stratification in Selling', in Bell, M.L. (ed.) *Marketing: A Maturing Discipline*. Chicago: American Marketing Association, pp. 171–84.

Coleman, R.P. (1983) 'The Continuing Significance of Social Class to Marketing', *Journal of Consumer Research* **10**, pp. 265–80.

Coleman, R.P. and Rainwater, L. (1978) *Social Standing in America: New Dimensions of Class*. New York: Basic Books.

Comanor, W.S. and Leibenstein, H. (1969) 'Allocative Efficiency, X-Efficiency and the Measurement of Welfare Losses', *Economica* **36**, pp. 304–9.

Coombs, C.H. (1975) 'Portfolio Theory and the Measurement of Risk', in Kaplan, M.F. and Schwartz, S. (eds.), *Human Judgement and Decision Processes*. New York: Academic Press.

Coombs, C.H. (1980) 'Risk Preference and the Theory of Risk', in Lantermann, E. and Feger, H. (eds.) *Similarity and Choice*. Bern: Hans Huber.

Cotton, W.R. (1972) 'Leisure and Social Stratification', in Thielbar, G.W. and Feldman, S.D. (eds.) *Issues in Social Inequality*. Boston: Little, Brown, pp. 520–38.

Cunningham, I.C.M. and Green, R.T. (1974) 'Purchasing Roles in the U.S. Family, 1955–1973', *Journal of Marketing* **38**, pp. 61–4.

Curtin, R.T. (1977) *Income Equity among U.S. Workers: The Bases and Consequences of Deprivation*. New York: Praeger.

Cyert, R.M. and March, J.G. (1963) *A Behavioral Theory of the Firm*. Englewood Cliffs, N.J.: Prentice-Hall.

Cyert, R.M., Simon, H.A. and Trow, D.B. (1956) 'Observation of a Business Decision', *Journal of Business* **29**, pp. 237–48.

Dagnoli, J. (1987) 'Impulse Governs Shoppers', *Advertising Age* **93**.

Daly, H. (1972) *Toward a Steady State Economy*. San Francisco: W.H. Freeman.

Dasgupta, P.S. and Heal, G.M. (1979) *Economic Theory and Exhaustible Resources*. Cambridge: Cambridge University Press.

Davis, H.L. (1976) 'Decision-Making within the Household', *Journal of Consumer Research* **2**, pp. 241–60.

Davis, H.L. and Rigaux, B.P. (1974) 'Perception of Marital Roles in Decision Processes', *Journal of Consumer Research* **1**, pp. 51–62.

De Finetti, B. (1937) 'La Prevision: Ses Lois Logiques, Ses Sources Subjectives', *Annales de l'Institut Poincare* **7**, pp. 1–68.

De Menil, G. (1971) *Bargaining: Monopoly Power Theory Versus Union Power*. Cambridge: Ma., Massachusetts Institute of Technology Press.

Dertouzos, J.N. and Pencavel, J.H. (1981) 'Wage and Employment Determination under Trade Unionism: The International Typographical Union', *Journal of Political Economy* **89**, pp. 1162–81.

Dichter, E. (1983) 'The Shifting Power of Influentials in Purchase Decisions', *Ad Forum* (July) p. 55.

Donne, J. (1987) *Devotions upon Emergent Occasions*, Raspa, A. (ed.) New York: Oxford University Press.

Dow, S.C. (1985) *Macroeconomic Thought: A Methodological Approach*. Oxford: Basil Blackwell.

Downs, A. (1957) *An Economic Theory of Democracy*. New York: Harper and Row.

Duesenberry, J.S. (1949) *Income, Saving and the Theory of Consumer Behavior*. Cambridge, Mass.: Harvard University Press.

Dunlop, J.T. (1944) *Wage Determination under Trade Unions*. New York: Macmillan.

Dunlop, J.T. (1950) *Wage Determination under Trade Unions*, 2nd ed.. Fairfield, N.J.: Augustus M. Kelly.

Earl, P.E. (1980) 'Characteristic Filtering: Towards a Behavioural Theory of Individual Choice', *University of Stirling Discussion Papers in Economics, Finance and Investment*, No. 84.

Earl, P.E. (1983) *The Economic Imagination: Towards a Behavioural Analysis of Choice*. Brighton: Wheatsheaf Books, and New York, M.W. Sharpe.

Edwards, W. (1954) 'The Theory of Decision-Making', *Psychological Bulletin* **51**, pp. 380–417.

Edwards. W. (1955) 'The Prediction of Decisions Among Bets', *Journal of Experimental Psychology* **51**, pp. 201–14.

Engel, J.F., Blackwell, R.D. and Miniard, P.W. (1990) *Consumer Behaviour*. London: Dryden Press.

Fair, R.C. and Dominguez, K.M. (1991) 'Effects of the Changing US Age Distribution on Macroeconomic Equations', *American Economic Review*, pp. 1276–94.

Farber, H.S. (1978) 'Individual Preferences and Union Wage Determination: The Case of the United Mine Workers', *Journal of Political Economy* **86**, pp. 923–42.

Farber, H.S. (1986) 'The Analysis of Union Behavior', in Ashenfelter, O. and Layard, R. (eds.), *Handbook of Labor Economics*, Vol. II, Amsterdam, North-Holland.

Farley, J.U., Howard, J.A. and Ring, L.W. (1974) *Consumer Behavior: Theory and Application*. Boston: Allyn and Bacon.

Farley, J.U. and Lehmann, D.R. (1977) 'An Overview of Empirical Applications of Buyer Behavior System Models', in Perreault, W.D. (ed.) *Advances in Consumer Research*. Atlanta: Association for Consumer Research.

Ferber, R. (1973) 'Family Decision-Making and Economic Behavior: A Review', in Sheldon, E.B. (ed.) *Family Economic Behavior: Problems and Prospects*. Philadelphia: Lippincott.

Ferber, R. and Nicosia, F. (1972) 'Newly Married Couples and their Asset Accumulation Decisions', in Strumpel, B., Morgan, J.H. and Zahn, E. (eds) *Human Behavior in Economic Affairs: Essays in Honor of George Katona*. San Francisco: Jossey-Bass; Amsterdam: Elsevier, pp. 161–87.

Festinger, L. (1954) 'A Theory of Social Comparison Processes', *Human Relations* **7**, pp. 117–140.

Financial Statement and Budget Report (1989). London: Her Majesty's Stationery Office (HMSO).

Fishbein, M.A. (1963) 'An Investigation of the Relationships between Beliefs about an Object and the Attitude toward that Object', *Human Relations* **16**, pp. 233–9.

Fishbein, M.A. and Ajzen, I. (1975) *Belief, Attitude, Intention and Behavior: An Introduction to Theory and Research*. Reading: Mass., Addison-Wesley.

Fisher, A. (1981) *Resource and Environmental Economics*. Cambridge: Cambridge University Press.

Fisher, I. (1930) *The Theory of Interest*. New York: Macmillan.

Fisher, I.W. and Hall, G.R. (1969) 'Risk and Corporate Rates of Return', *Quarterly Journal of Economics* **83**, pp. 403–19.

Ford, J.L. (1983) *Choice, Expectation and Uncertainty*. Oxford: Martin Robertson (Basil Blackwell).

Ford, J.L. (1987) *Economic Choice under Uncertainty: A Perspective Theory Approach*. Aldershot: Edward Elgar (Gower Publishing).

Ford, J.L. (1991) 'Perspective Theory, Preference Reversal, the Allais Paradox and Other Phenomena: An Exposition and a Defence', University of Birmingham, Department of Economics Discussion Paper, No. 91–13.

Foster, J. (1987) 'Class', in Eatwell, J., Milgate, M. and Newman, P. (eds.), *The New Palgrave: A Dictionary of Economics*. London: Macmillan, pp. 432–4.

French, J.R. and Raven, B. (1968) 'The Bases of Social Power', pp. 259–69 in Cartwright, D. and Zander, A. (eds.) *Group Dynamics: Research and Theory*. New York: Harper and Row.

Friedman, M. (1953) 'The Methodology of Positive Economics' in Friedman, M., Essays in *Positive Economics*. Chicago, Ill.: University of Chicago Press.

Friedman, M. (1968) 'The Role of Monetary Policy', *American Economic Review* **58**, pp. 1–17.

Fritzsche, D.J. (1981) 'An Analysis of the Energy Consumption Patterns by Stage of Family Life Cycle', *Journal of Marketing Research* **18** (May), pp. 227–32.

Furnham, A. (1985) 'Why do People Save? Attitudes to, and Habits of, Saving Money in Britain', *Journal of Applied Psychology* **15**, pp. 354–73.

Furnham, A. and Lewis, A. (1986) *The Economic Mind: The Social Psychology of Economic Behaviour*. Brighton: Wheatsheaf.

Galbraith, J.K. (1969) *The Affluent Society*, 2nd ed., revised. London: Hamish Hamilton.

Ghez, G.R. and Becker, G.S. (1975) *The Allocation of Time and Goods over the Life Cycle*. New York: National Bureau of Economic Research.

Gilbert, D. and Kahl, J.A. (1982) *The American Class Structure: A New Synthesis*. Homewood: Ill., Dorsey Press.

Gordon, B.F. (1966) 'Influence and Social Comparison as Motives for Affiliation', *Journal of Experimental Social Psychology*, Supplement **1**, pp. 55–65.

Gordon, R.A. (1961) *Business Leadership in the Large Corporation*. Berkeley: University of California.

Granbois, D.H. (1977) 'Shopping Behavior and Preferences', in *Selected Aspects of Consumer Behavior: A Summary from the Perspective of Different Disciplines.* Washington, D.C.: U.S. Government Printing Office, pp. 259–98.

Green, R.T., Leonardi, J.P., Chandon, J.L., Cunningham, I., Verhage, B. and Strazzieri, A. (1983) 'Societal Development and Family Purchasing Roles: A Cross-National Study', *Journal of Consumer Research* **9**, pp. 436–42.

Grier, K.B. (1987) 'Presidential Elections and Federal Reserve Policy: An Empirical Test', *Southern Economic Journal* **54**, pp. 475–86.

Grossman, G. (1983) 'Union Wages, Seniority and Unemployment', *American Economic Review* **73**, pp. 277–90.

Hague, D.C. (1949) 'Economic Theory and Business Behaviour', *Review of Economic Studies* **16**, pp. 144–57.

Haines, W.W. (1982) 'The Psychoeconomics of Human Needs: Maslow's Hierarchy and Marshall's Organic Growth', *Journal of Behavioral Economics* **11** (Winter), pp. 97–121.

Haka, S.F., Gordon, L.A. and Pinches, G.E. (1985) 'Sophisticated Capital Budgeting Selection Techniques and Firm Performance', *The Accounting Review* **50**, pp. 651–68.

Hall, R.L. and Hitch, C.J. (1939) 'Price Theory and Business Behaviour', *Oxford Economic Papers* **2**, pp. 12–45, reprinted in Wilson, T. and Andrews, P.W.S. (eds.), *Oxford Studies in the Price Mechanism.* Oxford: Clarendon Press.

Hansen, F. (1969) 'Consumer Choice Behavior: An Experimental Approach', *Journal of Marketing Research* **4**, pp. 436–43.

Harting, A. (1980) 'Cultural Differences Offer Rewards', *Advertising Age* (April), pp. S–21.

Hill, R. (1963) 'Judgement and Consumership in the Management of Family Resources', *Sociology and Social Research* **47**, pp. 460–6.

Hill, R.W. and Hillier, T.J. (1977) *Organisational Buying Behaviour: The Key to More Effective Selling to Industrial Markets.* London: Macmillan.

Hirsch, F. (1977) *Social Limits to Growth.* London: Routledge and Kegan Paul.

Hirschman, E.C. (1981) 'American Jewish Ethnicity: Its Relationship to Some Selected Aspects of Consumer Behavior', *Journal of Marketing* **45**, pp. 102–10.

Hisrich, R.D. and Peters, M.P. (1974) 'Selecting the Superior Segmentation Correlate', *Journal of Marketing* **38**, pp. 60–3.

Hogarth, R.M. and Reder, M.W. (eds.) (1987) *Rational Choice: The Contrast between Economics and Psychology.* Chicago and London: University of Chicago Press.

Hotelling, H. (1929) 'Stability in Competition', *Economic Journal* **39**, pp. 41–57.

Howard, J.A. and Sheth, J.N. (1969) *The Theory of Buyer Behavior.* New York: Wiley.

Howard, J.A. (1974) 'The Structure of Buyer Behavior', in Farley, J.U., Howard, J.A. and Ring, L.W., *Consumer Behavior: Theory and Application.* Boston: Allyn and Bacon.

Howe, M. (1962) 'Marginal Analysis in Accounting', *Yorkshire Bulletin of Economic and Social Research* **14**, pp. 81–9.

Hyman, H.H. (1942) 'The Psychology of Status', *Archives of Psychology*, No. 269, pp. 5–38, 80–6.

Johnson, G.E. (1975) 'Economic Analysis of Trade Unionism', *American Economic Review, Papers and Proceedings* **65**, pp. 23–9.

Johnston, W.J. and Spekman, R.E. (1987) 'Industrial Buying Behavior: Where we are and Where we need to Go', in Sheth, J.N. (ed.) *Research in Consumer Behavior*, Vol. II. Greenwich: Connecticut, JAI Press, pp. 83–111.

Joshi, H. Layard, R. and Owen, S. (1981) *Female Labour Supply in Post-war Britain: A Cohort Approach*, Discussion Paper No. 79. Centre for Labour Economics: London School of Economics.

Junankar, P.N. (1972) *Investment: Theories and Evidence*. London: Macmillan.

Kahneman, D. and Tversky, A. (1979) 'Prospect Theory: An Analysis of Decision Under Risk', *Econometrica* **47**, pp. 263–91.

Kahneman, D., Slovic, P. and Tversky, A. (1982) *Judgement under Uncertainty: Heuristics and Biases*. New York: Cambridge University Press.

Kaplan, A.D.H., Dirlam, J.B. and Lanzillotti, R.F. (1958) *Pricing in Big Business*. Washington, D.C.: The Brookings Institution.

Katona, G. (1951) *Psychological Analysis of Economic Behavior*. New York: McGraw-Hill.

Katona, G. (1960) *The Powerful Consumer*. New York: McGraw-Hill.

Katona, G. (1975) *Psychological Economics*. New York: Elsevier.

Katona, G. and Mueller, E. (1955) 'A Study of Purchasing Decisions', in Clark, L.H. (ed.), *Consumer Behavior: The Dynamics of Consumer Reaction*. New York: New York University Press, pp. 30–87.

Katona, G., Strumpel, B. and Zahn, E. (1971) *Aspirations and Affluence: Comparative Studies in the United States and Western Europe*. New York: McGraw-Hill.

Kettle, D.F. (1986) *Leadership at the Fed*. New Haven: Yale University Press.

Keynes, J.M. (1936) *The General Theory of Employment, Interest and Money*. London: Macmillan.

Kidd, D.P. and Oswald, A.J. (1983) 'A Dynamic Model of Trade Union Behaviour', *mimeo*, University of Oxford.

Kotlikoff, L.J. and Summers, L.H. (1981) 'The Role of Intergenerational Transfers in Aggregate Capital Accumulation', *Journal of Political Economy* **89**, pp. 706–32.

Krugman, H.E. (1965) 'The Impact of Television Advertising: Learning Without Involvement', *Public Opinion Quarterly* **29**, pp. 349–56.

Kunreuther, H. *et al*. (1978) *Disaster Insurance Protection: Public Policy Lessons*. New York: Wiley.

Lancaster, K.J. (1966) 'A New Approach to Consumer Theory', *Journal of Political Economy* **74**, pp. 132–157.

Lancaster, K.J. (1971) *Consumer Demand: A New Approach*. New York: Columbia University Press.

Latané, B. (1966) 'Studies in Social Comparison: Introduction and Overview', *Journal of Experimental Social Psychology*. Supplement 1: pp. 1–5.

Laumann, E.O. and House, J.S. (1970) 'Living Room Styles and Social Attributes: The Patterning of Material Artifacts in a Modern Urban Community', *Sociology and Social Research* **54**, pp. 324–7.

Lazarsfeld, P.F., Berelson, B. and Gaudet, H. (1948) *The People's Choice*. New York: Columbia University Press.

Lea, S.E.G., Tarpy, R.M. and Webley, P. (1987) *The Individual in the Economy: A Survey of Economic Psychology*. Cambridge: Cambridge University Press.

Lederer, K. (ed.) (1980) *Human Needs: A Contribution to the Current Debate*. Cambridge, Mass.: Oelgeschlager, Gunn and Hain.

Leibenstein, H. (1966) 'Allocative Efficiency vs X-Efficiency', *American Economic Review* **56**, pp. 392–415.

Leibenstein, H. (1976) *Beyond Economic Man: A New Foundation for Microeconomics*. Cambridge, Mass.: Harvard University Press.

Levy, S.J. (1966) 'Social Class and Consumer Behavior', in Newman, J.W. (ed.) *On Knowing the Consumer*. New York: John Wiley, pp. 146–60.

Locke, E.A. and Henne, D. (1986) 'Work Motivation Theories', in Cooper, C.L. and Robertson, I. (eds.) *International Review of Industrial and Organizational Psychology*, pp. 1–35. New York: John Wiley.

Loomes, G. and Sugden, R. (1982) 'Regret Theory: An Alternative Theory of Rational Choice under Uncertainty', *Economic Journal* **92**, pp. 805–24.

Loudon, D.L. and Bitta, J.D. (1984) *Consumer Behavior*. New York: McGraw-Hill.

McCormick, B.J. (1969) *Wages*. Harmondsworth, Middlesex: Penguin Books.

McGrath, J.E. (1984) *Groups: Interaction and Performance*. Englewood Cliffs, N.J.: Prentice-Hall.

McLelland, D.C. (1961) *The Achieving Society*. Princeton, N.J.: D. Van Nostrand.

McLelland, D.C. (1987) *Human Motivation*. Cambridge: Cambridge University Press.

Machina, M.J. (1987) 'Choice under Uncertainty: Problems Solved and Unsolved', *Journal of Economic Perspectives* **1**, pp. 121–54.

MaCurdy, T.E. and Pencavel, J.H. (1986) 'Testing between Competing Models of Wage and Employment Determination in Unionized Labor Markets', *Journal of Political Economy* **94**, pp. S3–S39.

Maloney, J.C. and Silverman, B. (eds.) (1979) *Attitude Research Plays for High Stakes*. Chicago: American Marketing Association.

Marris, R. (1964) *The Economic Theory of "Managerial" Capitalism*. London: Macmillan.

Marshall, A. (1961) *Principles of Economics* (9th ed.). London: Macmillan.

Martin, J. and Roberts, C. (1984) *Women and Employment: A Lifetime Perspective*. London: Her Majesty's Stationery Office.

Martineau, P. (1958) 'Social Classes and Spending Behaviour', *Journal of Marketing* **23**, pp. 121–30.

Maslow, A.H. (1970) *Motivation and Personality*. New York: Harper and Row.

Maxcy, G. and Silberston, A. (1959) *The Motor Industry*, Cambridge Studies in Industry. London: Allen and Unwin.

Mayhew, K. and Turnbull, P. (1989) 'Models of Union Behaviour: A Critique of Recent Literature', in Drago, R. and Perlman, R. (eds.), *Microeconomic Issues in Labour Economics*. London and New York: Harvester-Wheatsheaf.

Michael, R.T. and Becker, G.S. (1973) 'On the New Theory of Consumer Behavior', *Swedish Journal of Economics* **75**, pp. 378–405.

Miniard, P.W. and Cohen, J.B. (1983) 'Modeling Personal and Normative Influences on Behavior', *Journal of Consumer Research* **10**, pp. 169–80.

Mishan, E.J. (1971) *Cost-Benefit Analysis*. New York: Praeger.

Moore, J.S. and Reichert, A.K. (1983) 'An Analysis of the Financial Market Techniques Currently Employed by Large U.S. Corporations', *Journal of Business Finance and Accounting* **10**, pp. 623–45.

Moschis, G.P. (1985) 'The Role of Family Communication in Consumer Socialization of Children and Adolescents', *Journal of Consumer Research* **11**, pp. 898–913.

Moschis, G.P. and Moore R.L. (1980) 'Purchasing Behavior of Adolescent Consumers', in Bagozzi, R.P. *et al.*, *Marketing in the 80s*, Chicago, 1980, Educators' Conference Proceedings, pp. 89–92.

Mosteller, F. and Nogee, P. (1951) 'An Experimental Measurement of Utility', *Journal of Political Economy* **59**, pp. 371–404.

Mueller, D.C. (1989) *Public Choice II*. Cambridge: Cambridge University Press.

Murphy, P.E. and Staples, W.A. (1979) 'A Modernized Family Life Cycle', *Journal of Consumer Research* **6**, (June), pp. 12–22.

Myers, J.H. and Mount, J.F. (1973) 'More on Social Class vs. Income as Correlates of Buying Behavior', *Journal of Marketing* **37**, pp. 71–3.

Myers, J.H. and Robertson, T.S. (1972) 'Dimensions of Opinion Leadership', *Journal of Marketing Research* **9**, pp. 41–6.

Myers, J.H., Stanton, R.R. and Haug, A.F. (1971) 'Correlates of Buying Behavior: Social Class vs. Income', *Journal of Marketing* **35**, pp. 8–15.

Newcomb, T.M. (1943) *Personality and Social Change*. New York: Dryden Press.

Newcomb, T.M. (1972) 'Expectations as a Social-Psychological Concept', in Strumpel, B., Morgan, J.M. and Zahn, E. (eds.) *Human Behavior in Economic Affairs*. Amsterdam: Elsevier.

Nicosia, F.M. (1966) *Consumer Decision Processes*. Englewood Cliffs, N.J.: Prentice-Hall.

Niskanen, W.A. (1971) *Bureaucracy and Representative Government*. Chicago: Aldine-Atherton.

Nordhaus, W.D. (1989) 'Alternative Approaches to the Political Business Cycle', in Brainard, W.C. and Perry, G.L. (eds.), *Brookings Papers on Economic Activity* **1**, pp. 1–68. Washington: Brookings Institution.

O'Brien, D.P. (1976) 'The Longevity of Adam Smith's Vision: Paradigms, Research Programmes and Falsifiability in the History of Economic Thought, *Scottish Journal of Political Economy* **23**, pp. 133–51.

Ofshe, R. (1972) 'Reference Conflict and Behavior', pp. 88–116 in Berger, J., Zelditch, M. and Anderson, B., *Sociological Theories in Progress*. Boston: Houghton Mifflin.

Olander, F. and Seipel, C.M. (1970) *Psychological Approaches to the Study of Saving*. Urbana, Ill.: Bureau of Economics and Business Research, University of Illinois.

Olshavsky, R.W. and Granbois, D.H. (1979) 'Consumer Decision-Making: Fact or Fiction?', *Journal of Consumer Research* **6**, pp. 93–100.

Oswald, A.J. (1985) 'The Economic Theory of Trade Unions: An Introductory Survey', *Scandinavian Journal of Economics* **87**, pp. 160–93.

Oswald, A. (1987) 'Efficient Contracts on the Labour Demand Curve: Theory and Facts', *Discussion paper No. 284*. London: Centre for Labour Economics, London School of Economics.

Pearce, D.W. (1976) *Environmental Economics*. London: Longman.

Pencavel, J.H. (1984) 'The Trade-off between Wages and Employment in Trade Union Objectives', *Quarterly Journal of Economics* **99**, pp. 215–32.

Peters, W.H. (1970) 'Relative Occupational Class Income: A Significant Variable in the Marketing of Automobiles', *Journal of Marketing* **34**, pp. 74–7.

Pollis, N.P. (1968) 'Reference Group Re-examined', *British Journal of Sociology* **19**, pp. 300–7.

Price, L.L. and Feick, L.F. (1984) 'The Role of Interpersonal Sources in External Search: An Informational Perspective', in Kinnear, T.C. (ed.) *Advances in Con-*

sumer Research IX, pp. 250–5. Ann Arbor, Mich.: Association for Consumer Research.

Qualls, W.J. (1982) 'Changing Sex Roles: Its Impact upon Family Decision-Making', in Mitchell, A. (ed.) *Advances in Consumer Research*, vol. 9, pp. 267–70. Ann Arbor: Mich.: Association for Consumer Research.

Qualls, W.J. (1987) 'Household Decision Behavior: The Impact of Husbands' and Wives' Sex Role Orientation', *Journal of Consumer Research* **14**, pp. 264–79.

Ramsey, F. (1931), 'Truth and Probability', in Braithwaite, R. (ed.) *The Foundations of Mathematics and Other Logical Essays*. New York: Harcourt Brace.

Rawls, J. (1971) *A Theory of Justice*. Cambridge, Mass.: Harvard University Press.

Ray, M. (1973) 'Marketing Communication and the Hierarchy of Effects', in Kline, F.G. and Clark, P. (eds.), *Sage Annual Reviews in Communication Research*. Beverley Hills: Sage Publications.

Ray, M.L. (1974) 'Consumer Initial Processing: Definitions, Issues and Applications' in Hughes, G.D. and Ray, M.L. (eds.), *Buyer/Consumer Information Processing*. Chapel Hill: University of North Carolina Press, pp. 145–56.

Reynolds, F.D. and Wells, W.D. (1977) *Consumer Behavior*. New York: McGraw-Hill.

Robbins, J.E. and Robbins, S.S. (1979) 'Segmentation for Fine Arts Marketing: Is King Tut Classless as Well as Ageless?' in Beckwith, M. *et al.* (eds.), *1979 Educators' Conference Proceedings*. Chicago: American Marketing Association, pp. 479–84.

Robertson, R.S. (1971) *Innovative Behavior and Communication*. New York: Holt.

Robinson, O. and Wallace, J. (1984) 'Growth and Utilisation of Part-time Labour in Great Britain', *Employment Gazette*, pp. 391–7. London: Her Majesty's Stationery Office.

Robinson, P.J., Faris, C.W. and Wind, Y. (1967) *Industrial Buying and Creative Marketing*. Boston: Allyn and Bacon.

Rogers, E.M. and Shoemaker, F.F. (1971) *Communication of Innovations*. New York: Free Press.

Rokeach, M. (1973) *The Nature of Human Values*. New York: Free Press.

Rosen, S. (1970) 'Unionism and the Occupational Wage Structure in the United States', *International Economic Review* **11**, pp. 269–86.

Rosenberg, M.J. (1956) 'Cognitive Structure and Attitudinal Effect', *Journal of Abnormal and Social Psychology* **53**, pp. 367–72.

Ross, A.M. (1948) *Trade Union Wage Policy*. Berkeley and Los Angeles: University of California Press.

Ryan, M.J. and Bonfield, E.H. (1975) 'The Fishbein Extended Model and Consumer Behavior', *Journal of Consumer Research* **2**, pp. 118–36.

Saunders, P. and Klau, F. (1985) *The Role of the Public Sector: Causes and Consequences of the Growth of Government*. Paris: Organisation for Economic Co-operation and Development (OECD).

Savage, L.J. (1954) *The Foundations of Statistics*. New York: John Wiley.

Sawyer, M.C. (1979) *Theories of the Firm*. London: Weidenfeld and Nicolson.

Sawyer, M.C. (1989) *The Challenge of Radical Political Economy: An Introduction to the Alternatives to Neo-Classical Economics*. Hemel Hempstead: Harvester Wheatsheaf.

Schaninger, C.M. (1981) 'Social Class versus Income Revisited: An Empirical Investigation', *Journal of Marketing Research* **18**, pp. 192–208.

Schiffman, L.G. and Kanuk, L.L. (1987) *Consumer Behavior*. Englewood Cliffs, N.J.: Prentice-Hall.

Schmölders, G. and Biervert, B. (1972) 'Level of Aspiration and Consumption Standard: Some General Findings', in Strumpel, B., Morgan, J.N. and Zahn, E. (eds.), *Human Behavior in Economic Affairs: Essays in Honor of George Katona*. Amsterdam: Elsevier.

Schoemaker, P.J.H. (1982) 'The Expected Utility Model: Its Variants, Purposes, Evidence and Limitations', *Journal of Economic Literature* **20**, pp. 529–63.

Scitovsky, T. (1976) *The Joyless Economy*. New York: Oxford University Press.

Sexton, D.E. (1972) 'Black Buyer Behavior', *Journal of Marketing*, pp. 36–8.

Shackle, G.L.S. (1952) *Expectations in Economics*. Cambridge: Cambridge University Press.

Shackle, G.S. (1972) *Epistemics and Economics*. Cambridge: Cambridge University Press.

Sherif, M. (1953) 'The Concept of Reference Groups in Human Relations', pp. 203–31 in Sherif, M. and Wilson, M.O. (eds.) *Group Relations at the Crossroads*. New York: Harper.

Sheth, J.N. (1973) 'A Model of Industrial Buyer Behavior', *Journal of Marketing* **37**, pp. 50–6.

Sheth, J.N. (1974) *Models of Buyer Behavior: Conceptual, Quantitative and Empirical*. New York: Harper and Row.

Silberston, A. (1970) 'Price Behaviour of Firms', *The Economic Journal* **80**, pp. 511–82.

Simon, H.A. (1955) 'A Behavioral Model of Rational Choice', *Quarterly Journal of Economics* **69** (February), pp. 99–118.

Simon, H.A. (1957) *Models of Man, Social and Rational: Mathematical Essays on Rational Human Behavior in a Social Setting*. New York: Wiley.

Simon, H.A. (1976) *Administrative Behavior*. New York: The Free Press.

Simon, H.A. (1987) 'Rationality in Psychology and Economics', in Hogarth, R.M. and Reder, M.W. (eds.), *Rational Choice: The Contrast between Economics and Psychology*. Chicago: University of Chicago Press.

Slocum, J.W. and Mathews, H.L. (1970) 'Social Class as Indicators of Consumer Credit Behavior', *Journal of Marketing* **34**, pp. 69–74.

Slovic, P. and Lichtenstein, S. (1971) 'Comparison of Bayesian and Regression Approaches to the Study of Information Processing in Judgement', *Organizational Behavior and Human Performance* **6**, pp. 649–744.

Slovic, P., Lichtenstein, S. and Fischoff, B. (1988) 'Decision-Making', in Atkinson, R.C. *et al.* (eds.), *Stevens' Handbook of Experimental Psychology*, vol.2. New York: Wiley.

Stafford, J.E. and Cocanougher, A.B. (1977) 'Reference Group Theory', ch. 16 in Ferber, R. (ed.) *Selected Aspects of Consumer Behavior*. Washington, D.C.: Government Printing Office.

Stewart, F. (1985) *Planning to Meet Basic Needs*. London: Macmillan.

Stoner, J.A.F. and Wankel, C. (1986) *Management*. Englewood Cliffs: N.J., Prentice-Hall.

Strumpel, B. (1972) 'Economic Behavior and Economic Welfare – Models and Interdisciplinary Approaches' in Strumpel, B. *et al.* (eds.) *Human Behavior in Economic Affairs*. Amsterdam: Elsevier.

Suls, J.M. and Miller, R.L. (1977) *Social Comparison Processes: Theoretical and Empirical Perspectives*. Washington: Hemisphere Publishing.

Summers, J.O. (1971) 'New Product Interpersonal Communications', in Allvine, F.C. (ed.) *Combined Proceedings of the American Marketing Association*, Series No. 33.

Thomas, K. (1976) 'Conflict and Conflict Management', in Dunnette, M.D. (ed.) *Handbook of Industrial and Organizational Psychology*. Chicago: Rand McNally.

Thompson, J.D. and Tuden, A. (1959) 'Strategies, Structures and Processes of Organizational Decision', in Thompson, P.B. *et al.* (eds.) *Comparative Studies in Administration*. Pittsburgh: University of Pittsburgh Press, pp. 195–216.

Thurow, L.C. (1969) 'The Optimum Lifetime Distribution of Consumption Expenditures', *American Economic Review* **59**, pp. 324–30.

Treiman, D.J. (1977) *Occupational Prestige in Comparative Perspective*. New York: Academic Press.

Turner, H.A. (1959) *Trade Union Growth, Structure and Policy*. London: Allen and Unwin.

Turner, R.H. (1955) 'Reference Groups of Future-Oriented Men', *Social Forces* **34**, pp. 130–6.

Tversky, A. (1969) 'Intransitivity of Preferences', *Psychological Review* **76**, pp. 31–48.

Tversky, A. (1972) 'Elimination by Aspects: A Theory of Choice', *Psychological Review* **79**, pp. 281–99.

Tversky, A. and Kahneman, D. (1974) 'Judgement under Uncertainty: Heuristics and Biases, *Science* **185**, pp. 1124–31.

Von Neumann, J. and Morgenstern, O. (1947) *Theory of Games and Economic Behavior*. Princeton, N.J.: Princeton University Press.

Wagner, J. and Hanna, S. (1983) 'The Effectiveness of Family Life Cycle Variables in Consumer Expenditure Research', *Journal of Consumer Research* **10**, pp. 281–91.

Ward, S. and Wackman, D.B. (1972) 'Children's Purchase Influence Attempts and Parental Yielding', *Journal of Marketing Research* **9**, pp. 316–9.

Ward, S., Wackman, D.B. and Wartella, E. (1977) *How Children Learn to Buy*. Beverly Hills: Sage Publications.

Wärneryd, K.-E. (1989) 'Improving Psychological Theory through Studies of Economic Behaviour: The Case of Saving', *Applied Psychology: An International Review* **38**, pp. 213–6.

Warshaw, P.R. (1980) 'A New Model for Predicting Behavioral Intentions: An Alternative to Fishbein', *Journal of Marketing* **17**, pp. 153–72.

Webster, F.E. and Wind, Y. (1972) *Organizational Buying Behavior*. Englewood Cliffs, N.J.: Prentice-Hall.

Wellington, A. (1981) 'Traditional Brand Loyalties', *Advertising Age* (May), p. S–2.

Williamson, O.E. (1964) *The Economics of Discretionary Behavior: Managerial Objectives in a Theory of the Firm*. Englewood Cliffs, N.J.: Prentice-Hall.

Williamson, O.E. (1975) *Markets and Hierarchies: Analysis and Anti-Trust Implications*. New York: Free Press.

Winter, D.G. (1973) *The Power Motive*. New York: Free Press.

Woodside, A.G. and Motes, W.H. (1979) 'Husband and Wife Perceptions of Marital Roles in Consumer Decision Processes for Six Products', in Beckwith, N. *et al.* (eds.) *1979 Educators' Conference Proceedings*. Chicago: American Marketing Association, pp. 214–19.

Author Index

Subject Index